BRAND
HIJACK

BRAND
HIJACK

marketing without marketing

ALEX WIPPERFÜRTH

PORTFOLIO

PORTFOLIO
Published by the Penguin Group
Penguin Group (USA) Inc., 375 Hudson Street, New York, New York 10014, U.S.A.
Penguin Group (Canada), 10 Alcorn Avenue, Toronto, Ontario Canada, M4V 3B2
(a division of Pearson Penguin Canada Inc.)
Penguin Books Ltd, 80 Strand, London WC2R 0RL, England
Penguin Ireland, 25 St. Stephen's Green, Dublin 2, Ireland (a division of Penguin Books Ltd)
Penguin Books Australia Ltd, 250 Camberwell Road, Camberwell, Victoria 3124, Australia
(a division of Pearson Australia Group Pty Ltd)
Penguin Books India Pvt. Ltd, 11 Community Centre, Panchsheel Park, New Delhi-110 017, India
Penguin Group (NZ), Cnr Airborne and Rosedale Roads, Albany, Auckland 1310,
New Zealand (a division of Pearson New Zealand Ltd)
Penguin Books (South Africa) (Pty) Ltd, 24 Sturdee Avenue, Rosebank, Johannesburg 2196,
South Africa

Penguin Books Ltd, Registered Offices: 80 Strand, London WC2R 0RL, England

First Published in 2005 by Portfolio, a member of Penguin Group (USA) Inc.

1 3 5 7 9 10 8 6 4 2

Advertisement for Dr. Martens used by permission of Cole & Weber/Red Cell.
Advertisement for Puma used by permission of Puma AG.

PUBLISHER'S NOTE: This publication is designed to provide accurate and authoritative information in regard to the subject matter covered. It is sold with the understanding that the publisher is not engaged in rendering legal, accounting or other professional services. If you require legal advice or other expert assistance, you should seek the services of a competent professional.

LIBRARY OF CONGRESS CATALOGING IN PUBLICATION DATA
Wipperfürth, Alex,
Brand hijack : marketing without marketing / Alex Wipperfürth.
p. cm.
Includes bibliographical references and index.
ISBN 1-59184-078-3
1. Brand name products—Marketing.   2. Consumer behavior.   3. Brand choice.
4. Brand loyalty.   I. Title.
HD69.B7W553   2005
658.8'27—dc22   2004057391

This book is printed on acid-free paper. ∞

Printed in the United States of America

Contents

PART III: THE HIJACK, CORPORATE STYLE

PART IV: THE HIJACKER

PART V: THE BRAND HIJACK ROADMAP

PART I

MARKETING WITHOUT MARKETING

CHAPTER 1

The "No Marketing" Myth

We have a message for the movers and shakers on Madison Avenue: "Tone down the relentless yammering; you're talking too loud for us to listen."

—Letter to the Editor, *The New York Times*

Corporate America is confused. How else could you explain some pretty weird behavior from the Fortune 500: Nestlé invading blog sites, Sony creating fictitious reviews to promote feature film duds. The past decade's most successful brand launches—most of which eschewed traditional marketing templates—have the big guns taking some rather embarrassing stabs in the dark.

In our own search for answers, we—the professional marketers— had always found comfort in our ability to revert back to the *immutable laws of marketing:* Branding is the most critical element of commercial success; Find a relevant and compelling connection between your product performance and your target audience; Create advertising around an aspirational image associated with the brand. These and other fundamentals had always kept us on track.

But a string of recent success stories should be forcing us to ask the question: Are those laws becoming obsolete?

How did Starbucks and eBay build billion dollar valuations without leading with a quintessential advertising campaign?

How did Palm and Red Bull ignore what consumers said they wanted, yet create new markets?

How did Pabst Blue Ribbon become the fastest-growing domestic beer in 2002 when it tastes like backwash and hardly can be said to offer aspirational benefits?

Are these examples outliers—mere lucky accidents—or do they signal the emergence of new marketing fundamentals?

The New York Times called the success of these brands, "The Marketing of No Marketing." But don't believe the headline. Behind each of these successes is a complex orchestration of activities that only *appears* inconsequential.

Brands like Starbucks and Red Bull—the leaders of the "no-marketing" school of thought—are spending hundreds of millions of dollars in non-advertising each year, creating the illusion for their passionate user base that success happened serendipitously. In a rare moment of weakness, a Red Bull PR manager confessed to journalist Rob Walker:

> The perception that these events don't cost much to produce is good for us. We don't want to be seen as having lots of money to spend. But it's not as easy and inexpensive as people think.

The ultimate irony of this phenomenon is that consumers are in on the joke. Meanwhile, corporate America is desperately trying to copy the new marketing template, and in the process proving over and over again that it just cannot get it right.

Why haven't Coke, Pepsi, and Anheuser-Busch been able to make a dent in Red Bull's business, despite their respective distribution omnipresence and deep, deep pockets? Why hasn't a single Hollywood studio been able to reproduce the go-to-market template and resulting runaway success of *The Blair Witch Project,* despite numerous high-profile attempts?

Let's face it: When it comes to twenty-first-century marketing, consumers are more clued in than the professionals.

THE NEXT CHALLENGE

How do you market to an audience that rejects marketing? Don't laugh. As schizophrenic as this question may sound, its time has come.

Increasingly, consumers are ignoring corporate America's overt advances. They rejected Coke's omnipresence at the Atlanta Olympics, calling it the "Red Rash." Levi Strauss provoked a backlash when its "Queen Street Takeover" campaign smothered a strip in bohemian Toronto with advertising for SILVERTAB jeans.

Of course, this is hardly a new trend. Urban subcultures have for years worn their anti-corporate attitudes as badges of honor. Ironically, in today's climate these anti-brand communities are some of corporate America's most logo-loyal consumers. Cases in point: anti-corporate bike messengers like Kyle Hanson swear by their Timbuk2 bags. Burning Man free spirits like "Ginger" think old-school VW bugs are the only way to travel. Kyle and Ginger may bring a cocky smile to the faces in the corporate ivory towers, where they serve as much-needed reassurances that branding remains powerful.

However, winning the loyalty of the disaffected and disenfranchised is not the most pressing concern of the marketing industry. The real challenge we face is that even mainstream brand enthusiasts are now rejecting the obvious and the loud. Today's marketers are struggling with a populace that appears immune to their advances.

Take Signe Nordli, the cover girl for *Playboy*'s "Women of Starbucks" issue: She may drink her daily double, non-fat, venti almond latte, but she'll buy whichever laundry detergent happens to be cheapest at the supermarket. Or Marc Anthony: An admitted Prada addict and style maven who has been known to match the color of his sunglasses with his girlfriend's shirt, he wears an inexpensive Kiehl's aftershave instead of designer cologne. Or Ellen Feiss: The apparently stoned teenager from Apple's infamous "Switch" ad looks as if she buys her clothes at the thrift store.

That baked teenager scares the hell out of us marketing professionals. How will anyone be able to convince her to shed her second-hand jeans for Seven for All Mankind low-riders? Why is Apple the brand she deems worthy?

I can assure you it didn't happen by accident.

INTRODUCING THE BRAND HIJACK

Marketing managers aren't in charge anymore. Consumers are. Across the globe, millions of insightful, passionate, and creative people are helping optimize and endorse breakthrough products and services— sometimes without the companies' buy-in. What exactly is going on? Let's call it brand hijacking.

The traditional "big bang" marketing model still works for some— even many—products and services, such as an upgrade to an existing offering. But in order for a brand to stick, for it to have real impact on our culture, it better collaborate with its users.

This is the template set by brands as diverse as Palm handhelds, Dr. Martens boots, and an experimental pharmaceutical—originally developed as an angina treatment—called Viagra. They stand for a simple, bigger-than-life idea that will spread and evolve. These new brands use the market's input to develop a life and a meaning of their own. Starbucks didn't merely introduce America to a new coffee chain; it convinced Americans of the simple notion that no one should have to drink a plain cup of coffee.

Brand hijacking is about allowing consumers (and other stakeholders) to shape brand meaning and endorse the brand to others. It's a way to establish true loyalty, as opposed to mere retention. We're not just talking about creating hype here. We're talking about a new template for going to market. We're talking about a complex orchestration of many carefully thought-out activities. And above all else, we're talking about being willing to collaborate with a group of people you're not used to collaborating with: consumers.

THE NEXT CONSUMER

At a superficial glance, it appears that the brand hijack approach offers a tremendous untapped opportunity for companies: to use the market as eager product developers and low-cost media. In this light, consumers might be viewed as a cheap, innovative, and abundant resource.

But watch out. Let's be careful not to assume that consumers are a bunch of suckers. They don't devote themselves to brands because they want to provide free marketing for corporations. They do it because some special brands offer up a vision that people can identify with, one that they want to involve themselves in more deeply.

In the end, market involvement brings about a better, richer, more sustainable product experience. It garners true loyalty from consumers: an investment on their part to build a stronger relationship with the brand on an ongoing basis. At its best, market involvement creates a cultural benefit, offering meaning in an otherwise chaotic modern world.

THE NEXT MARKETER

Welcome to marketing without marketing: the emergence of the hijacked brand. Don't let the all-too-clever subtitle fool you. Far from representing the absence of marketing, this approach is the most complex sort of marketing possible, as well as the least understood.

Brand Hijack offers a practical how-to guide to marketing that finally engages the marketplace. It presents an alternative paradigm to conventional marketing wisdom, one that addresses such industry crises as media saturation, consumer evolution, and the erosion of image marketing. The purpose of the book is to demystify the modern brand and make the next generation of marketing practical and actionable.

But be forewarned: Following the book's advice will require some untraditional, even counterintuitive, steps on the part of modern marketers. This type of marketing is not for everyone. You must be willing to let the market take over. You must be confident enough to stop clamoring for control and learn to be spontaneous. You must be bold enough to accept a certain degree of uncertainty in the handling of your brands.

Brand hijacking relies on a radical concept—*letting go*. What a frightening, yet oddly liberating thought . . .

A NEW MARKETING PHILOSOPHY

This way of thinking about brands is contrary to many of the marketing industry's current ideas and techniques. Many old-school marketers are already voicing their opposition to marketplace involvement. For instance, Coke's high-profile former head of marketing, Sergio Zyman, recently warned:

> Leaving things up to the consumers' imagination is something you *never* want to do. Customers are dangerous, and if you let them decide how they want to be satisfied, you're going to have a terrible time living up to their dreams. It's better if you can control both the promise and the delivery.

I have a message for Mr. Zyman and all like-minded marketers:

MARKETING WITHOUT MARKETING:
A BRAND HIJACK MANIFESTO

Let go of the fallacy that your brand belongs to you.
It belongs to the market.

Co-create your brand by collaborating with your consumers.

Scrap the focus groups, fire the cool chasers, and hire your
audience.

Facilitate your most influential and passionate consumers in
translating your brand's message to a broader audience.

Be patient. Your brand initiative could take years—or weeks—
to take off.

Be flexible. Carefully plan every step, but be totally open to
having the story rewritten along the way.

Lose control. Free yourself to seize sudden opportunities
that only last for moments.

Resist the paranoid urge for consistency. Embrace the value
of being surprising and imperfect.

Respect your community. Draw the line between promotion
and the adbusting trinity of manipulation, intrusion,
and co-option.

Let the market hijack your brand.

And remember, none of these tenets are *immutable*.

PART II

THE HIJACK

brand hi·jack (<u>brand</u> <u>hī′jak</u>): *consumer takeover* (synonym). The consumer's act of commandeering a brand from the marketing professionals and driving its evolution.

CHAPTER 2

Public Property:
The Serendipitous Hijack

Buckle your seatbelt, Dorothy, 'cause Kansas is going bye-bye.

—Cypher, *The Matrix*

"What were you thinking?!" That was the first thing we asked Shawn Fanning, the founder of Napster, when we met him.

Turns out, he hadn't been thinking about revolutionizing the music industry and inventing file sharing along the way at all. He'd simply been thinking, "How can I get music off the Web with the least amount of hassle?"

You see, Shawn was a college freshman, and he and his roommate had become increasingly frustrated by the many dead links they encountered when scouring the web for rare music. In the "old" days, it was a pain in the ass to search for music in the first place. But imagine hours of searching, and then the link you finally discovered would simply disappear. And on top of all that, Shawn had to endure endless hours of bitching from his roommate. . . . You get the idea.

So Shawn sat down and wrote some code to prove that you could create a real-time online index.

Then he used those fateful and seductive words when he emailed the beta-program to several friends in the hacker community: "Do NOT share this with anyone. This is still in a test phase."

And so it was that Napster (Shawn's childhood nickname) was born. Within months, hundreds of thousands of users were forwarded that e-mail and downloaded the software, making Napster one of the fastest-growing technologies ever.

In fact, in a mere two years, Napster went from start-up to growing brand to global mass brand to nostalgia brand, a life-cycle that usually takes at least thirty-plus years and hundreds of million of dollars in marketing investment. This all happened at the same time as the glamorous and sensational launch disaster of fashion portal boo.com, a fiasco that prompted Randall Rothenberg to comment in *Advertising Age:* "Fast branding doesn't work."

Sure it does. You just can't force it.

AN ACCIDENTAL REVOLUTION

To Shawn Fanning's credit, he didn't abuse the unplanned and unexpected success of Napster. In fact, he used tremendous intuition and instinct in letting the brand take its course. In Napster's first months of overwhelming success, he did not run to an ad agency and demand that it *brand* Napster and advertise it. He did not develop any targeted and complex user-acquisition programs or retention schemes. Rather, he did something extremely smart and rare: He got out of the way and let the Napster community add its own meaning to the killer app.

Napster was an accident. Ethical and legal issues aside, it offers the most fascinating brand case study of the turn of the millennium. Why? Because it had serendipity written all over it. Napster was a brand—or rather a software platform—that was completely hijacked by its users. In other words, there was something inherent in the brand rather than a clever marketing ploy or major budget that connected people to Napster. Napster was market—rather than marketing—driven. Far away from some corporate headquarters, the user base—the Napster community— drove its success and added meaning to what Napster stood for.

And the brand was on fire. Within eighteen months it had eighty million users. All with a marketing budget of just $200,000. (Well, that's not entirely true: We are graciously not counting the two million dollars that Napster wasted on a Limp Bizkit tour sponsorship that it never marketed.)

Why was Napster so perfectly set up for a takeover by the market?

It provided a blank canvas.

Far from espousing an ideology, Napster provided a neutral infrastructure designed to facilitate the sharing and downloading of music. It allowed the users to appropriate this platform and make it their own. They created a community spirit ripe with hierarchies, coded communication, and etiquette.

It offered a non-material incentive to participate.

Napster had a very simple built-in incentive that encouraged users to enlist others: The larger the community, the more music that was available. This was no calculated company scheme (e.g., "Five dollar finder's fee for every new user you bring!").

It made the community feel needed.

Napster's value depended on the behavior and visionary ideas of its users. As soon as they grasped and appreciated the immense potential of Napster, the service took off.

It fostered a sense of belonging.

And even more than just a sense of belonging, Napster fostered committed solidarity. It offered access to one of the most personal and emotional pastimes in our lives: music. Of course, it helped that Napster was under attack by the record companies. The repeated shutdown attempts unified the community, giving them a common cause, an enemy, a rallying cry: "Screw the Man! Your time is over!"

Napster developed into a clique that you either belonged to or you didn't.

It had smart leadership.

Shawn was a righteous kid who never intended to make money off of his creation. He harbored none of the malicious intentions the record industry tried to pin on him. In addition, Hank Barry, Napster's acting CEO and Hummer Winblad VC, was a quick thinker. A former lawyer, he was the ideal leader at the time of the record industry's attacks.

The smartest move Napster's management made was to get out of the way and allow the product to evolve under the brand leadership of its own community.

The Ultimate Public Brand

So, once it evolved, what was it that Napster really stood for? There was an initial misperception that Napster was all about being free. Sure, that was a nice side benefit for most users, and the core benefit for a smaller subset of "freeloaders." But Napster was about much more than free music. To some, it was about taking an aggressive stand against the record industry: It did not force the labels' latest fabricated "artist" onto them, but rather let consumers control who and what they listened to. To others, it was about the music library: At its peak, Napster had virtually every song ever recorded available on its site. Still others saw it as the technological pioneer behind file sharing: It was home to a powerful and loyal P2P community.

In reality, Napster was all those things. It did not offer a single-minded value proposition like traditional brands often do. It had different meanings for different groups of people within the community.

Napster truly belonged to its members. Its majority started a movement to liberate music from the record industry. This was not an internally driven cause but a community driven one.

"No more Britney Spears crap forced on us, that's for sure," was a common sentiment plastered all over message boards in Napster's heyday. It was the great equalizer, giving back leverage to the listener and the artist.

Napster spurred a revolution in music, one driven by the music-consuming public and facilitated by a software program written by a college freshman for personal use.

It was the ultimate public brand: a tool for music lovers that could eventually have replaced record labels. No wonder the record industry drove it into the ground.

INTRODUCING THE SERENDIPITOUS HIJACK

It is extremely unusual for a brand to get hijacked to the point of total control by the market, as Napster was. When this happens, the brand essentially becomes *public property;* it's defined and led by its user community. Ironically, this sort of full-throttle hijack is often an accident. Rarely is it the result of initiatives or campaigns coming out of a marketing department.

> **serendipitous hi·jack** (sĕr'ən-dĭp'ĭ-tē-es <u>hī'jăk'</u>): The act of consumers seizing control of a brand's ideology, use, and persona. It is most often practiced by brand fanatics within subcultures, and is largely unanticipated by—and independent of—the brand's marketing department.

DEFINING (AND DEFYING) GENERATIONS

Napster is by no means the first or the only example of a serendipitous hijack. One of the quintessential brands to have been appropriated by the market is Dr. Martens boots.

The therapeutic shoe was developed by a German doctor, Klaus Maertens, in the mid-1940s to help relieve the pain of an injury he sustained while skiing in the Bavarian Alps. He invented the trademark Airwair technology—which gave the shoes "bouncing soles"—and proceeded to sell his product across Germany to elderly women with foot problems.

The Griggs Company, a boot maker in the English Midlands, heard about the shoe and acquired the exclusive license to produce the air-cushioned sole. Hence, in 1960, the brand turned British.

People who tried the boot loved it. They were delighted to have an alternative to the extremely uncomfortable army boot. Maertens later said, "The shoe was the right answer at the right time."

But how did this functional, unfashionable, general-purpose shoe, used primarily by elderly ladies for gardening, transform itself into the quintessential subcultural icon of the twentieth century?

Timing played a role in Docs' rise. They were introduced in Britain at a time of unprecedented social change and cultural upheaval. In fact, Docs were launched in the same year as the contraceptive pill.

The boot initially caught on with the blue-collar crowd: postmen, factory workers, builders, and so on. Policemen were very fond of the boots, as well. Today, the English Post Office still makes Docs part of its uniform.

Next, skinheads brought Docs into the counterculture. They started wearing Docs as a nod to their working-class roots. (Note: This was the time before skinheads shaved their heads. It was the heavy boots, and not the haircuts, that defined their look.)

How did Docs become the skins' original "bovver boot" (that's taken from the slang for "bother," as in: "Let's look for some bovver")? Sheer luck: The English football police banned Docs' steel toe–capped predecessors as "offensive weapons." So the skins needed a soft-toed boot with the same edgy look.

Another accident further helped Docs attain cult status. In 1972, Stanley Kubrick's controversial film *A Clockwork Orange* simultaneously garnered underground acclaim and sparked public outrage. After sixty weeks in the theaters, the ultra-violent and socially subversive movie was banned, making it a pirate film classic. Rebels started mimicking the style of dress employed by the characters in the film, which included heavy black boots. Ironically, these boots were not actually Dr. Martens. But the mistaken identity further ingrained the brand in bovver culture.

Over the next few decades, the boot continued its journey through several evolutions of youth culture. Starting with hero figures like social-ist MP Tony Benn and The Who's Pete Townshend, Docs soon became the symbol for the punk movement.

In the '80s, Docs passed into mainstream fashion. The boots were particularly popular among British gay men who had adopted elements of the skinhead look. By the early '90s, they'd made their way across the pond, becoming staples for the U.S. grunge and indie music scene. It seems that the hippies were the only major youth movement to by-pass the shoe as part of their look.

Why did the youth movement continuously hijack the Dr. Martens brand, appropriating the boots to define themselves?

The product was practical.

Docs were without a doubt functional, comfortable, and durable work boots. What's more, the boots were "worn in" rather than "worn out"—they improved with age. Therefore, Docs were highly practical shoes for blue-collar workers.

The product served as a medium for self-expression.

Docs became a canvas for self-expression, and the market got busy developing coded communication involving them. You could make a statement by choosing whether to lace your boot with eight, ten, or even twenty eyelet holes on each side. The more holes you laced, the more forbidding the boot looked.

You could also wear so-called "steelies," weapons-grade versions of the boots with steel-tipped toecaps.

The most important statement that you could make, though, was through your choice of laces. *The Deviants' Dictionary* has the following entry:

> Traditionalists insist these should be flat, like soccer boot laces, though the Covent Garden store supplies round ones. As well as lacing the boot, the laces should be long enough to wrap two or three times round the top, which means laces of at least 2m (6') length for 14 hole boots, and these are not always easy to obtain, except, for some unexplained reason, in Edinburgh. The color of laces can also have some significance. Black is supplied and is a safe bet; in certain circles yellow can indicate a preference for sex involving piss; red can mean either fisting (as in common BDSM codes and symbols) or indicate left-wing politics; and white is a known, though by no means universal, skinhead code to indicate extreme right or racist politics.

Finally, Docs were known to gain character as they aged. Over time, they would begin to resemble the personality of their owners. As a result, people frequently developed sentimental affection for their boots, which they wore through important "steps" in their lives.

The company espoused no ideology beyond support for the working class.

One of the most amazing aspects of Dr. Martens' success was its ability to penetrate the entire political spectrum: the extreme right, the extreme left, and most everything in between. No other brand has achieved this feat with such aplomb.

This is probably due to the fact that the company proclaimed no political ideology. The founders were boot makers and soccer fanatics, not activists. Their neutrality allowed each counterculture to make Docs its own.

The only crucial conviction upheld by the boot maker was its support for working-class England. Even today, every pair of Docs is made in Wollaston village in England.

The company abstained from "image marketing."

Before the image-makers took over in the '90s, Docs' marketing remained entirely utilitarian, just like the boot. When Pete Townshend wrote about the boots in his song "Uniform," the company had by no means commissioned it.

Ads provided functional information, ready to be interpreted by consumers as they wished. A typical Dr. Martens ad read like this:

> It's a fact! The working man has never before been offered a really comfortable boot. Hard work—hard boots had to be accepted. The revolutionary Dr. Martens' Air Cushioned soles puts an end to this foot-breaking torture . . . a most pleasant experience for the much-abused foot.

Dr. Martens did a tremendous job of allowing the market to take over. The company let the boots be whatever consumers wanted them to be.

BATTLE OF THE SWILL

At the turn of the new millennium, two pioneers of the beer industry set out to resurrect their respective franchises: Pabst Blue Ribbon and

Miller High Life. Let's take a look at the battle between these two un-likely protagonists. Both brands were former staples in the top brand landscape. Yet both were dying off alongside their aging consumer base. Each needed to find a way out of their identity crisis in order to bring in the next generation of beer drinkers.

And both succeeded—albeit with markedly different approaches. Bubba in one corner, bike messengers in the other.

Marketing Bubba

Sales of Miller High Life, the former flagship of Miller Brewing, dropped to an all-time low in the mid-90s. Miller opted for a big ad-vertising idea as its solution. Its ad agency, Wieden + Kennedy, devel-oped a superb TV campaign celebrating the "high life." Shattering all category-advertising rules, the ads avoided beer clichés like male bonding, women, and sports. They did not preach about the brand's history or heritage or fall into the nostalgia trap (although Miller did eventually do a retro packaging redesign). And they wisely did not go after the holy grail of marketers: twenty-one- to twenty-five-year-old men. Instead, they targeted a neglected group: the working class.

You might say Miller High Life finally came to terms with what the brand really stood for. You might say the folks at Miller finally embraced their inner suburbanite. The ads laid bare the flaws of their core con-sumer group, yet in a disarming, affectionate way, the way a drinking buddy might dish on his best friend. It put a mirror in front of Miller's hapless, older, blue-collar hero by resurrecting the "Bubba" archetype. In so doing, it celebrated the forgotten values the working class holds so dear.

W + K's Creative Director, Jeff Kling, explained:

> We're having fun with Bubba. We've got Bubba in our blood, and miss that part of him the modern world has bled out of us. We're showing details of a fading life that to our minds de-serve attention, elevation . . . And I suppose it's funny that any-one would bother.

As a bonus, the campaign drew in a younger crowd of cynical beer drinkers who interpreted the ads in their own way. They liked that Bubba did not get the irony in these slightly biting fifteen or thirty seconds of TV advertising satire.

In one recent pool-out, a balding middle-aged guy finds himself alone in a kitchen after a get-together, eyeing a near-empty plate of deviled eggs.

> "Hmmm. That last egg is looking really good," says the older, plain-speaking narrator to himself.
>
> "You had quite a few, though. Maybe you shouldn't. But if you make a light choice here *[holding up a Miller High Life Lite]*, maybe you . . . will have room for just one more . . . *[picks up the final, nasty looking deviled egg and savors it]* . . . See there. If you live the High Life you can have it both ways."

Brilliant, creative. And it worked. It stopped the brand's long-term decline. When Miller's marketing department halted the campaign in 2000, sales immediately dropped by 5 percent. So Miller returned with the campaign in 2001. It even started to sponsor such "Bubba" sporting events as bowling and fishing to deepen the archetype's connection. Perhaps getting way ahead of themselves, the folks at Miller, W + K, and documentary filmmaker Errol Morris are even mulling over concepts for a TV show. Imagine Bubba as the next Archie Bunker. Regardless, as soon as the campaign was back on air, sales stabilized.

Hijacking a New Trash Icon

Pabst Blue Ribbon, on the other hand, took no such conventional marketing approach. After several divestitures of the brand to new owners and years of declining sales, a major ad campaign was not in the cards. A lucky break, as it turns out.

Because suddenly, without any efforts behind the brand, PBR started to take off. By mid-2002, PBR had become the fastest-growing brand of domestic beer. Sales grew in double digits, even as its overall segment, called the popular beer segment, steadily declined.

How did this happen while PBR remained part of the brand portfolio for the "consumer from hell"? Old, cheap, and lonely men are not exactly the trendsetters marketers salivate over. These old-timers will buy whichever old-school beer is on sale.

Well, PBR's success resulted from a takeover by a totally new market. It was spontaneously adopted as the beer of choice by a cynical and disillusioned consumer base, with subcultures like bike messengers championing the brand. Progressive regions such as the Northwest started seeing sales growth rates double within a year.

PBR's hijacking was partly a matter of timing. In this day and age, anything that gets in the way of capitalism, from Napster to Linux to *Adbusters*, is dynamite. Within this complicated cultural context, the no-frills aesthetic of PBR fits right in. It's perfect for the self-mocking, "anti-brow" attitude of critics and rebels intent on expressing disdain for mass commercialism.

What were some of the other factors that played into PBR's hijacking?

It is legitimate.

"Heineken? Fuck that shit! Pabst Blue Ribbon!" was the anti-elitist rallying cry made immortal by *Blue Velvet*'s psychotic main character, played by Dennis Hopper. Although the line lay dormant for over a decade, when the time came, it reemerged on the cultural landscape. This provided PBR with legitimacy, elevating the brand's status to that of underground darling. (Look at it this way: If Dennis Hopper had said, "Fuck that shit! Schlitz," fifteen years later the market might've hijacked Schlitz and not Pabst.)

PBR is the beer of choice at art exhibits and music gigs. It's also part of the revival of the speakeasy. As novelist Adam Davies confesses in *The Frog King:*

> Sis's Place is an illegal bar on Avenue B that is in the basement of this old woman's apartment. She doesn't have a liquor license or the right zoning permit or anything like that. She has a fat old fridge in which she keeps all the cans of Pabst Blue Ribbon—the only beer she offers. I think she just buys them at the grocery, retail, and she walks them home and throws them in the fridge.

It is cheap.

PBR ain't bad in terms of bang for the buck. Brian's Beer Belly website gave it a rating of 8.8 out of 10. Epinions rated it three out of five stars. It's the only pint I'm aware of that sells for twenty-five cents on special.

Philly's Tritone bar has created "The Special": one shot bourbon, one can PBR, for a mere three bucks. Bartender Rick D. thinks it works. "It's two bad tastes that taste great together."

It takes you through a time warp.

It's the lighthouse beer representing the old "college days." As one loyal consumer claimed on a message board:

> I have to laugh every time I see PBR. It certainly brings back memories. How many times did I throw up on that magic potion? Let me have one more and take me back to that place.

It carries a rallying cry.

Rumor spread when Pabst closed the Milwaukee brewery that it had gone out of business. That sparked a lot of nostalgia and fervor. People got involved with the brand, rallying for a comeback (as with this message board post):

> You know I blame those damn microbrews. Forget that crap. I say stay with mass-produced beer. Let's unite to save Pabst Blue Ribbon. Stop buying Guinness and buy Pabst for the love of GOD.

It has retro status.

The brand has permission to be "in" again. The current drinkers' parents didn't drink it—their grandparents did. *The Hipster's Handbook* gave it the following review:

> The best tasting domestic beer. Very popular with guys in work shirts and cowgirl hipsters. The only beer that is cool to drink out of the can.

It benefits from product scarcity.

PBR is not widely available. Bumping into it remains a special occasion. One fan told this story:

> We walk a short distance down the street to this hole in the wall. We walk in, I look around. A pool table, but uh, no telltale signs of what cure my ailments. Ask the bartender, "What's on tap?" He speaks the words that put me in heaven: "Pabst Blue Ribbon." YEE HA!

In today's anti-corporate scene, PBR is affectionately known as the "anti-sponsor." People often promote it without compensation or even knowledge by Pabst. For instance, "Knees Up," a Friday happy hour party in San Francisco, offers pints of PBR on special. Not because of any deal they have with the local Pabst distributor, but simply because the brand carries the right image.

FROM UNDERRATED TECHNOLOGY TO TEEN MUST-HAVE

Hijacked brands do not necessarily have to be great products. It's all about the killer experience.

There is a long list of allegedly superior technologies that were beaten in the market by weaker rivals. Let's take a closer look at one of those "inferior" technologies.

I'm talking about the rise of SMS text messaging in Europe and Asia and the subsequent failure of the WAP (wireless application protocol) technology.

Finland. 1991. Nokia and a consortium of other telecom companies had just finished creating GSM, a new protocol that would allow customers of the various wireless carriers to communicate with each other. As a minor part of the protocol, they included a simple technology for text messaging. SMS, for short message service, was developed primarily as a sales tool. The idea behind it was that it would allow carriers to announce promotions to their customers.

Nokia viewed SMS as little more than an afterthought because the target consumers, mostly businessmen, concluded in research that it was of little interest to them. The technology was unsophisticated: Messages were limited to 160 characters that customers punched out on tiny keypads and viewed on Lilliputian screens. Obviously, any rational consumer would opt to call instead.

However, as the good people of Finland adopted cell phones, a funny thing happened. The carriers noticed that the number of sent text messages steadily increased. This phenomenon repeated itself throughout Europe. By 2001, the total number of messages sent reached approximately one hundred billion. Within a decade, SMS had created a whole new convention—the use of cell phones to send and receive short text messages. As a result, more and more players jumped on the profitable bandwagon, offering ring tones, traffic updates, games, and the like.

Worldwide volume for SMS is now estimated at more than three hundred billion messages a year. Texting accounts for about 15 percent of carrier revenues.

How did a completely overlooked and underdeveloped technology meet with such success?

Teenagers took over. And once teens established this new habit, older consumers copied them. Text messaging became a social connector for busy European and Asian professionals, just as Instant Messaging has entered the American workplace.

Here are a few reasons why teens hijacked SMS:

It wasn't hyped.

As teens got cell phones, they discovered SMS on their own. Because it wasn't advertised, they felt ownership and enjoyed coopting it as a secret communications tool. Grown-ups didn't have any clue as to what was going on.

It called for creativity.

To teens, SMS's limitations actually became a challenge, a call for creativity and brevity. Friends created their own shorthand vocabulary and icons, which distinguished one clique from another. Soon, a whole new vocabulary had formed. This coded communication, coupled with texting's immediacy, made it addictive and engaging for teens.

It facilitated an existing habit.

In retrospect, teens were the perfect early market for SMS. Texting is the ideal medium for gossip and banter—popular with youth anywhere—because of its discreetness and technical gadgetry. SMSing quickly became the edgier way to gossip.

Its stars were aligned.

The wireless industry accidentally facilitated SMS usage by targeting teens with several small initiatives. It introduced prepaid phones to reduce the costs of phone ownership. Then it tiered pricing to make text messaging cheaper than calling. Finally, it made receiving incoming messages free so that SMSs were not considered an expensive nuisance by the receiver.

It worked.

The wireless industry ensured interoperability among carriers so that text messaging was seamless.

WAP Loses Out

As SMS grew, it seemed logical to the industry that consumers must be dying for an upgrade. Clearly users would welcome a better protocol, one that would allow them to transmit content-rich data like pictures and color text, as well as give them access to the internet.

So in 1998, when the industry launched WAP—a technology that offered all of these benefits—they thought they had a sure thing. In addition to being more advanced, WAP was bolstered by millions of dollars in marketing support. The WAP Forum and other stakeholders heralded it as the "wireless web."

Everyone thought SMS's days were numbered. Text messaging was like DOS compared to WAP's Windows. But by 2000, it was clear that the more advanced technology had flopped. At the same time, its ugly cousin, SMS, hit the mainstream.

What was the problem with WAP? Rather than facilitating creativity, the carriers dictated usage. They thought people would use WAP phones like PCs. So they tried to create PC-like content. Commercials with taglines like "Surf the mobile internet" showed people easily sending pictures to their friends and downloading data.

But in reality, the experience wasn't anything like the PC: Coverage was porous, content limited, connection speeds slow, and the screens minuscule. According to an industry analyst, "By referring to it as the wireless Web, they really did a disservice to consumers. It's not the wireless Web; it's information you get on a wireless phone."

By training consumers to think of WAP phones as PC substitutes, the industry set itself up for failure. Instead of trading up to the new phones, consumers chose to stay with texting, an "inferior" technology.

Why SMS Failed in the U.S. Market

Of course, a key question is: Why is the United States so far behind in texting?

Some say SMS volume in the United States will never catch up with Europe and Asia because Americans love the PC. We already have instant messaging and email. Text messaging would be redundant.

Others say that we drive too much. Texting is a byproduct of a commuter culture, and as a result would only survive in urban pockets like New York City.

But regardless of the cultural background, what's clear is that the industry itself has not really given text messaging a chance. Under current policies, texting cannot flourish—there's no economic or social incentive.

The six major carriers finally instituted out-of-network text communication in 2002. But it was too little too late. Cheaper pre-paid plans aren't marketed. Most carriers focus on pushing plans that bind consumers to monthly minimums, year-long contracts, pricing that's tiered by peak hours, and minutes that don't roll over. In addition, consumers still pay to receive messages. In fact, it's no cheaper to receive a text message than a call.

None of these factors foster spontaneous text messaging interactions among cash-poor teens. An SMS entrepreneur critiques:

> Everyone has grown weary of the excuses . . . there was the contention that because the Japanese have small fingers, SMS messaging might work in Japan, but not elsewhere. Of course, the Europeans proved that silly observation false. . . . What lack of vision. Who wants to be tethered to their PC, when we have the option of messaging whomever we like—whenever and wherever?

Text messaging is just another reminder of who's really in control. Product quality lies in the eye of the beholder. It's not the engineers' vote that counts; it's the consumers'. The key lesson: Make it easy for consumers to adopt your product or technology.

FUELED BY A SECRET MENU

In-N-Out Burger, the fifty-year-old West Coast burger chain, has done a consistently phenomenal job of allowing their followers to feel that the brand belongs to them.

Tom McNichol described the brand's mysterious success in a recent *New York Times* article:

> The 166th In-N-Out Burger restaurant opened quietly last Tuesday morning on Century Boulevard, hard by the Hollywood Park racetrack. There were no "Grand Opening" banners flapping in the breeze, no food giveaways and no advertisements promoting the event. Still, for a quiet opening, there was a lot of noise. By lunchtime, the restaurant was filled with patrons, and the line of cars at the drive-through window snaked into the street. An In-N-Out employee was assigned just to direct traffic.
>
> "As soon as I drove by and saw it was open, I called my son Sean, who loves In-N-Out," said Margaret Beters, a city employee, who said she lives nearby. "This is dinner," she said,

holding up a white bag containing two double cheeseburgers, one with grilled onions and one without.

In-N-Out, founded on the West Coast in 1948, is that rarest of chain restaurants: one with a cult following. Exalted both by hamburger fans and those who normally shun fast food, it has built its reputation on the rock of two beliefs: fast food should be made from scratch, and the whims of the customer should be entertained.

Even Eric Schlosser, author of the muckraking book *Fast Food Nation*, is a fan. "I think they're great," said Mr. Schlosser, whose less appetizing findings included that some ground beef destined for fast-food restaurants had been contaminated with bits of cattle spinal cord. "It isn't health food, but it's food with integrity. It's the real deal," he said.

To the fast-food industry, In-N-Out is an enigma. The service is extremely slow. There are only four items on the menu: burgers, fries, shakes, and soft drinks. Special items or promotions are unheard of. It lacks ubiquity. And it doesn't go with the times: The last change on the menu appeared nearly ten years ago with the addition of Dr. Pepper to the soda fountain. Little about In-N-Out's food preparation has changed since its inception, either. There are no freezers, heat lamps, or microwaves in any of its stores. Burgers are made from pure beef ground by the company's own butchers. Fries are cut from fresh potatoes in the store every day.

As industry analysts say, In-N-Out is the "un-chain." What it has, though, is all the elements of a public brand: a cult following and coded communication.

Over the years, [the trend of special consumer requests to the limited menu] has evolved into what's become known as the Secret Menu—a list of popular burger variations that don't appear on the menu but are passed along by word of mouth. For example, a burger ordered Animal Style comes doused with mustard and pickles, extra special sauce and grilled onions. The Wish Burger is somewhat simpler to parse—a vegetarian option, without meat or cheese. And the Protein Style burger replaces the bun with a piece of fresh lettuce, for those on a low-carbohydrate diet. And then there's the mighty 4-by-4, with four meat patties and four slices of cheese.

The Secret Menu is not an In-N-Out marketing creation, and its popularity appears genuinely to mystify the company's officers.

"We've never called it the Secret Menu," said Carl Van Fleet, the chain's vice president for operations. "We've always prepared a burger any way you want. Our customers came up with the names like 'Animal Style.'"

The secret menu is not listed anywhere in the store, but each item has a button on the cash register, only visible to the employee behind the counter.

Equally impressive is In-N-Out's advertising effort. Its agency, the T&O Group, uses camp sixty-second radio commercials with the fifteen-year-old jingle "In-N-Out, In-N-Out, that's what a hamburger is all about."

There's no attempt to be as hip as its target audience, just naff (i.e., outmoded, clichéd, unstylish), 50s-style, no-frills reminders.

Let go of the fallacy that your brand belongs to you. It belongs to the market.

CHAPTER 3

The Marketer's Guide to the Serendipitous Hijack

*I have caught word that a child is using his imagination and
I've come to put a stop to it.*

—Principal Skinner, *The Simpsons*

About a decade ago, the powers-that-be at Mattel got all bent out of shape. Consumers had started interpreting the world of Barbie to their own liking rather than following the company's operating instructions.

Across the globe, adult fans of the cultural icon began to do what little girls had done for ages: play with her. They gave Barbie an updated look. They fashioned her new clothes, created accessories, cut her hair, and applied make-up. They threw Barbie-themed parties and formed Barbie clubs. They read Barbie magazines and catalogs. They spent thousands of dollars collecting versions of the little plastic doll and every product associated with her. For a while, fashion show parties were all the rage. Guests would design an outfit for Barbie and make a duplicate for themselves. Then they'd walk the catwalk with their creation.

Mattel must have been thrilled. Or so you would think.

SLAPPing a Hijack

Sadly, the folks at Mattel provide a textbook example of how *not* to handle a serendipitous hijack. You see, they couldn't resist the urge to control the Barbie world. The company launched one of the most aggressive, ill-conceived, and largely unsuccessful campaigns against copyright and trademark infringement to date. In so doing, it passed up the opportunity to let some of Barbie's most loyal consumers direct the evolution of the blonde bombshell into the next millennium.

One of the company's targets was Paul Hanson, a San Francisco artist who exhibited his own sub-genre versions of Barbie at a Castro Street store. When Mattel executives learned about Trailer Trash Barbie and Big Dyke Barbie, they were not excited or even amused. Instead of celebrating this risqué artist for reclaiming Barbie in a tongue-in-cheek, au courant way for a very specific audience, they sued him. Mattel garnered a cease and desist order against sales of the product with an eight-count trademark infringement lawsuit. Even worse, the company demanded that he stop displaying his creative work in art galleries. During the trial, Hanson said he'd grossed about $2,000 in sales on the dolls; Mattel claimed $1.2 million in damages.

Not surprisingly, a federal judge saw through the scare tactics. In his ruling, he chided Mattel for "not having a sense of humor." But in the end, following a year of litigation, Hanson settled and agreed not to sell his alternative versions of the dolls or display them in galleries.

And Hanson was only one of thousands of Barbie fans to be affected by Mattel's attempt to put a stop to the fun.

Shockingly, the company went after its most devoted consumers. It stopped fan clubs from using the Barbie name in charity events. It also tried to put the leading collectors' publications out of business.

In 1995, Mattel sued Paul David, a devotee who was, at the time, one of the largest certified dealers of collector's edition Barbies. David admittedly "ate, drank, and slept Barbie," but he also occasionally critiqued his beloved. For example, in his catalog, David gave the "Ugliest Barbie" prize to the Elizabethan Queen Barbie. Again, Mattel wasn't pleased. In the suit's settlement, the company went so far as to dictate how David could use its product. Any portrayal in the catalog that wasn't "wholesome, friendly, accessible and kind, caring and protecting, cheerful, fun-loving, talented and independent" was expressly forbidden.

Mattel's copyright crusade has won it nothing but bad press, courtroom humiliation, and a "Pink Anger" rebellion from Barbie's alienated fan base. In one trademark infringement case that went all the way to the U.S. Supreme Court, an appellate judge labeled Mattel "Speech-Zilla."

Anti-Mattel websites still litter the internet. Mattel is identified as one of the most flagrant abusers of SLAPP (Strategic Lawsuits Against Public Participation), which has been outlawed in several states.

After two years of refusing to sell the doll, David and his business partner have now put Barbie back in their catalog. But he says thousands of other fans are not so forgiving:

> They [Mattel] really cut off their nose to spite their face. They lost thousands of collectors in the '90s, and they'll never get them back.

The toy giant would have been better off accepting its "plight"—a passionate and creative user base. After all, that is something most companies would love to have.

Flora Skivington, a planner at Barbie's ad agency during the Hanson litigation, says that while Barbie customizations can be seen as trademark infringements, they are not necessarily a bad thing:

> It is also a great compliment to the strength of the brand that people feel able and inspired to make Barbie their own. One could look at these subversions as a reflection of a reality that this brand represents that it is not currently expressing. The customers take it into their own hands and express it for them. Hence the desire for San Francisco to make Drag Queen Barbies in the late nineties.

Mattel simply did not understand the power and inherent value of a consumer takeover. Instead of trying to stop Hanson, David, and others from adapting the brand to fit their worldviews, the company should have embraced its new market of devoted brand enthusiasts. In their misguided attempt to exert control over a forty-something-year-old cultural icon, Mattel missed the boat entirely.

Doing It Right

So, you've got an accidental brand phenomenon on your hands. Now what?

Fueling the momentum of a brand driven by its community is one of the most challenging assignments in marketing. It requires walking that finest of lines between safeguarding the integrity of the brand's soul and keeping its legitimacy within the market community. Success hinges not only on your ability to resist the tremendous urge to do "cool marketing," but also knowing when to turn the switch to mainstream marketing and brand investment.

Whether or not they realized it, the folks driving each of the brands outlined in the previous chapter made solid choices in allowing the market to take over their brands. Based on their experiences and those of a few other hijacked brands, as well as the disastrous example set by Mattel, we can deduce the following principles for how to handle a serendipitous hijack:

Start with the Right Attitude

Don't be afraid of your consumers.

The most important lesson to be learned from Mattel is this: At best, get the joke. At least, turn the other cheek. Companies that aren't afraid of their consumers—or their consumers' creativity—can go a long way.

Your most passionate users will provide you with critical insights into how to evolve your brand. Just listen and respond. If your brand is hijacked, the consumers may take your product or service in unexpected directions: They may choose to reinterpret how the brand fits into their lives (as with the Barbie catwalk) or use the brand for social commentary (as with Dr. Martens). Learn to trust them.

Take Burberry, for example. Its sales doubled from 2000 to 2002. This remarkable growth can be attributed partially to an ad campaign in which supermodel Kate Moss appeared in a teeny Burberry plaid bikini. The ad delivered a bold statement, and it worked to update the image of the once stodgy label.

But there was another reason for Burberry's sudden success. A group of consumers that the label had made no attempt to court hijacked the brand, giving it unexpected edginess and exposure—the hip-hop crowd. Stars such as Jay-Z, Ghostface Killah, and Cam'ron now shell out thousands of dollars for customized styles that are more East Compton than Upper East Side.

It's time to accept a new reality: In this era of the involved consumer, the market sometimes claims brands for itself. Rather than shy away from the trend, why not embrace it as a (mostly) good thing?

And don't be afraid of a little controversy.

Another mistake Mattel made was in taking itself too seriously. Did it really think the appearance of Trailer Trash Barbie in a few San Francisco stores and art galleries would ruin the doll's appeal to six-year-old girls? Develop a sense of humor about your brand—especially if the market is hijacking it. Consumers find it endearing when you show that you can laugh at yourself. Furthermore, don't be afraid of a little controversy. Pushing the usual limits of what's acceptable will serve as a demonstration of how much confidence you have in your brand.

Look at Southwest Airlines, the discount carrier with a better sense of humor than most people I know. The company has agreed to be the subject of an A&E reality series—and has relinquished all editorial control. Letting film crews follow around your employees and openly display your behind-the-ticket-counter dramas takes guts. Southwest president Colleen Barrett explained the decision this way: "I had faith that the viewing public would quickly see why Southwest has ranked No. 1 in terms of customer satisfaction." Faith in the public, yes, but Southwest clearly also has confidence in its brand. How novel.

Or how about Palm? For its "Simply Palm" campaign, then-owner 3COM used a provocative image of a naked woman, artfully concealed, cradling the handheld device. The image was ripe for appropriation, and it didn't take long for web designer Jason Kottke to post a parody of the campaign, called "Simply Porn," on his Web site. 3COM's lawyers quickly caught wind of what was going on and went after the guy for trademark infringement. They won, scaring him into removing the anti-ad from his site.

That is, until Kottke's friends fought back. They posted the parody on other sites. Soon, the media started to pick up the story. When Kottke and his buddies escalated the issue in the courts, 3COM wisely backed down. Perhaps the company wanted to avoid bringing more attention to the fake ad. But perhaps 3COM realized that the well-intentioned parody was doing more good than harm, a symbol of the market's involvement in the Palm brand.

It seems that even the corporate machine at a behemoth like Viacom can sometimes indulge in a little self-mockery. Parent to both Paramount and MTV, Viacom allowed the producers at Paramount to attack its sister company in the surprise hit movie *The School of Rock,* when Jack Black's character went on one of his rampages:

> The Man, oh, you don't know the man. He's everywhere . . . In the White House . . . Down the hall—[school principle] Ms. Mullins, she's the Man. And the Man ruined the ozone, he's burning down the Amazon, and he kidnapped Shamu and put her in a chlorine tank!
>
> There used to be a way to stick it to the Man. It was called rock 'n' roll. But guess what? Oh, no, the Man ruined that, too, with a little thing called MTV! So don't waste your time trying to make anything cool or pure or awesome, 'cause the Man is just gonna call you a fat, washed-up loser and crush your soul. So do yourselves a favor and just give up!

The fact that this line survived the final cut helped lend the movie credibility among critics and audiences alike.

Or take Old Style beer. It used to be Chicago's beer, but it had slowly faded away from the city's cultural landscape. Enthusiasts had given the old favorite several tongue-in-cheek nicknames such as Mold Pile and Doggie Style. Several years ago, I recommended to the company that they put out labels with these names in several of the city's neighborhood bars and stores . . . unannounced. Old Style was in dire need of becoming part of the Chicago nightlife again, and such a move would have created talk-value and endeared the brand to its once loyal following.

Don't panic about a bit of controversy "tainting" your brand image. You've got more to gain from treating it with a sense of transparency, reality, and, above all, humor than from trying to squelch it. It's not like these things aren't out there in the public arena anyway, and taking them head on will likely endear your brand to the public and show off your confidence in it.

Adapt Your Marketing

Figure out why you got hijacked.

In order to capitalize on your good fortune and ensure the ongoing popularity of your brand, it's critical to figure out why you got hijacked. Too often, brand owners try to identify the drivers behind serendipitous brand hijacks through focus groups, quantitative studies, or expensive trend-hunting reports, but these methods simply do not reveal the real causes. The drivers are social in nature and evolve from a myriad of causes.

One way to understand the complexity behind hijacks is by researching the origin of the movement and then tracing its evolution. Put together a timeline. This will help you determine what the brand's different drivers are. But be careful not to oversimplify: There are often more factors involved in the market's decision to take over your brand than you initially realize.

My colleagues and I used this tactic with Pabst Blue Ribbon. The word on the street was that people loved PBR because it was retro. But the same could be said of several other brands of beer. It seemed clear that "being retro" was only one small part of the story. Digging into the brand's history revealed many other factors that contributed to PBR's sudden rise in popularity: Its mention in *Blue Velvet* gave it credibility; its appearance on the speakeasy revival scene provided visibility; its symbolic value as the anti-microbrew provided meaning; and so on.

Docs provide another example of this approach. We made a timeline of the boot company's decades-long relationship with various youth movements. This revealed which major groups had adopted the brand through the ages and why: blue-collar workers for practicality, skinheads for the rebellious message, the American grunge scene for the alternative image already established in Britain, all the way to the adoption by the

Midwest vanilla crowd, which led to its downfall as a countercultural statement.

Who hijacked your brand, and why? Study the historical context. Take the time to understand what a hijacked brand does for its users, and what social factors are driving the brand's success. Essentially, you will become a cultural anthropologist.

Establish a code of conduct to stay true to your consumers and your character.

While hijacked brands can become far more powerful than conventional brands due to the passion consumers invest in them, they can also become extremely fragile if they stray from the core values and belief system of their markets. It is crucial to maintain the respect of your early market by staying true to the inherent values of your consumers and the "persona" of your brand.

That's why it makes sense to invest in educating your entire organization about the hijacked brand's DNA. You can do this by establishing a code of conduct. This code will guide your marketing efforts and ensure that you keep the original spirit of the brand alive.

In order to create a code of conduct, you first need to approach your brand from the perspective of your consumers. What values are most important to your hijackers?

When coming to terms with the complexity and depth of PBR's inner circle, our team hit the library. We studied Naomi Klein's fierce tirade against the ubiquity and power of branding, *No Logo,* Thomas Frank's cynical dissection of the *Conquest of Cool,* George Monbiot's *Anti-Capitalism,* Kalle Lasn's *Culture Jam,* and Travis Culley's *The Immortal Class: Bike Messengers and the Cult of Human Power.*

This reading proved a great platform to identify PBR's battle cry as the "anti-badge" brand. It helped us understand some of the fundamental trends and drivers of the skeptical, anti-corporate modern-day consumer. And, most important, it enabled us to create some marketing rules so that Pabst Brewing would remain the brand of choice for an audience that uses "consumption as protest."

We began to understand, for instance, that members of the PBR inner circle lived according to anti-authoritarian principles: "No one is in charge. Are you kidding? That would spoil all the fun." But they also acted according to a strict code of respect: "You have the right to take any path you choose. Follow your bliss. But you can't hurt other people. That is the only rule." And they treated public space as democracy's last stand: "It's the only space where one can be promised lasting respect and recognition for what one can offer to the community."

Based on these insights, we developed a code of conduct. For example, we concluded that the marketing department had to facilitate market expression: "PBR is a symbol of anti-consumption. Allow the market to appropriate and use this symbol (i.e., leave the Pabst poster girl with her teeth blacked out, let Starve package their CDs with PBR cardboard and duct tape)." It had to reject overt commercialism: "Don't succumb to hype, bluster, greed. Keep it honest and real. At the end of the day, life ain't about the almighty dollar." It had to stop being defensive about the beer's image: "Don't chase after the beer snobs. Some people are always going to look down on PBR. So what?" You get the idea . . .

This code of conduct could then be used to educate the Pabst Brewing marketing and sales team about how to safeguard the respect and support of their crucial early market on an ongoing basis.

Once you have codified the values and principles of your early market, you next need to codify the values and principles of your brand. This is called the "brand persona." Create a synopsis of the characteristics that define what the hijacked brand (as opposed to the hijacker) is all about.

At Napster, this document was a treatise on what not to do, called "10 Great Ways to Kill Napster." It started as an inside joke, born out of the many profit-generating ideas being thrown around at the time.

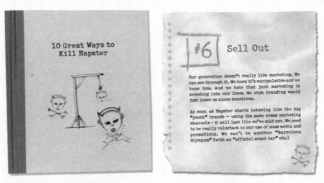

An internal brand bible with "teeth."

Nevertheless, it served a real purpose in committing the brand's identity to paper.

Napster had figured out that every employee represented the brand. A single finance manager selling Napster merchandise online, planning banner advertising opportunities, or—even worse—inking a deal for a Visa Napster card could have done tremendous damage. (Equally disastrous: A PBR sales rep orchestrating "bimbos-in-bikinis" sampling promos.)

As former Nike and Starbucks marketer Scott Bedbury warned: "A brand is the sum of the good, the bad, the ugly, and the off-strategy."

Resist the temptation to do "marketing."

Staying neutral is the toughest job in marketing. We professionals don't like to let go and leave the fun stuff to the consumers. And yet it's exactly this type of behavior that is required with a market-appropriated brand. The hijacked brand manager's key job is to keep the brand neutral—a blank canvas, so to speak—so that the market can fill it with meaning and enrich it with folklore.

In a sense, serendipitous brands are built through *anti-marketing*. Away from pompous campaigns that try too hard, they can get away with an admirable dilettantism that needs to be kept alive.

Therefore, in designing a marketing campaign for your brand, you've got to stick with the spirit of the original hijack: Grassroots. Real. Anti-hype. Transparent yet enigmatic. Even a bit imperfect.

Basically, the campaign should feel as though a bunch of normal folks got their hands on a marketing budget. If it doesn't, it's a sign that the brand has become wannabe to what it used to be. Nothing will turn people off faster. Hijacked brands are in grave danger of parroting back a "marketeered" version of once-authentic cultural associations and statements. Truly cool brands do not say, "We are cool."

Dr. Martens committed this fatal error with the seemingly clever image advertising campaign launched for it by Cole & Weber in the '90s. The campaign—which ironically jumpstarted the careers of quite a few creatives and won the prestigious Kelly awards in 1994—marked the beginning of the end for Docs.

By trying to market an attitude, the brand became the wannabe version of what it used to be. As good as the creative was, it could only

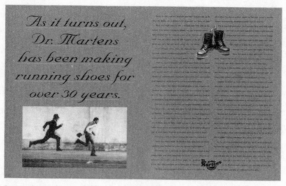

As it turns out, Dr. Martens has been making running shoes for over 30 years.

Great creative. Yet an insufficient imitation of an authentic feeling—and the beginning of the end for Docs as a genuine statement of defiance.

insufficiently imitate the emotional extremes the former symbol of rebellion provoked. As a result, Docs crossed the fine line between being cool and being despised. It had exploited the position the market had developed for it, and had started to believe its own hype.

Today, the Dr. Martens brand is virtually irrelevant. The boot no longer plays an important role in youth culture. The current sentiment is: "Yeah, I used to wear Dr. Martens when I went to shows. . . . They just sort of disappeared."

To be fair, an important cultural development also contributed to the brand's demise: "Defiance" has been devalued by corporate brands such as Mountain Dew. The authentic punk movement has been marginalized to such an extent that it's now a fashion accessory you can buy at the mall. Docs no longer have a credible leg to stand on.

Yet Docs can stage a comeback. The brand still commands respect. However, its marketers must be careful not to cop an attitude or chase after the aspirational cachet of "cool." Instead, they need to return to their working-class roots and harness the charismatic power derived from being true to oneself.

Know when to go mainstream.
The art of managing public brands lies not only in respecting and protecting the values that consumers have created around the brand; it also lies in growing the brand without selling out.

Let's return to our PBR case study. When the consumer takeover first happened, Pabst Brewing didn't know what had hit it. One of its brands was exploding out of nowhere? What should it do?

The company decided to protect its lucky break. Management's ethos became "We don't know what happened, but let's not screw it up." It began supporting its anti-brand community, starting with bike messengers and moving on to snowboarders and the local music scene. Pabst was careful never to force the brand on to a market. For instance, while sponsoring bike messenger races, it would refrain from hanging banners all over the place and it made sure that competing beer brands were served. This counterintuitive move allowed the various subcultures to choose PBR rather than having the brand chosen for them.

However, keeping the fringe momentum going is not enough for a company in desperate need of both volume and profit. Pabst needed to move on to broader markets—without losing credibility with their core consumers.

People consume PBR as an expression of their attitudes against mass marketing and hype. But within this umbrella, there are different shades of meaning and a wide-ranging cast of characters, bike messengers and cheap old men being the starting point.

Pabst has the ability to attract several different types of protest consumers that promise both more volume and a lot more cash outlay than the bike messenger crowd. First and most obviously, Pabst appeals to the retro hipster crowd, where old items are becoming "cool" again. But this group fundamentally doesn't get it. They're only drinking PBR because it is the "in" thing right now. They are not the long-term solution to PBR's growth, since they quickly will move on to the next trend. In many ways, retro hipsters are the apolitical descendents of the old-school geezer.

There is another group that is more ideologically compatible with the hard line messenger crowd: the progressive consumers. They use brand choices as a form of principled dissent from the current economic-political system. These are the people who can genuinely and organically grow the brand, because their values are consistent with the persona and soul of PBR. These are also the people, from school teachers to lawyers and business owners, who could grow the brand and make it profitable.

When a product or service has hit Next Big Thing status, brand managers will need to step in. At this point, they should take back control of the message and switch to conventional above-the-radar marketing methods. This will signal to the mainstream audience that your brand is legitimate and sustainable.

Reclaim your brand, if necessary.

Allowing the market to create your brand image sounds great, doesn't it? However, there may be times when you'll need to reclaim the brand because the "wrong" people have hijacked it. That's when the brand manager must step in to change the brand image or limit its association with a particular subculture.

For instance, alongside Burberry's recent jump in popularity came an explosion in knock-offs. Imitations of the signature Burberry plaid can be found on everything from Corvette upholstery to cell phone covers. Rather than obsessing over the dilution of its brand, however, Burberry has chosen not to publicly criticize or challenge the imposters. Instead, the company has quietly toned down its emphasis on plaid and switched to another pattern—the Burberry stripe.

Ben Sherman offers another example of the phenomenon of brand misappropriation. Founded in 1963, the company's shirts were adopted by skinheads in the 1970s. This association weakened in the U.K. by the 1980s, giving the company hope that their products could appeal to a wider audience. So when the company noticed Neo-Nazis in France, Germany, and Italy re-adopting its shirts in the '90s, it made an uncompromising decision: It stopped distribution to the three countries. "We walked away from those distribution channels, which meant walking away from a hell of a lot of business," says Andy Rigg, the shirt-maker's marketing manager. The company also diminished the role of its traditional button shirt, a skinhead favorite, in its overall line.

For Ben Sherman, the issue was clear: The right wing was not a tolerable user base. So the company opted to forego this lucrative yet ethically questionable market. It reclaimed its brand in a stealth way.

THE SERENDIPITOUS HIJACK IN A NUTSHELL

To you, the owner of a buzzing brand that became cool without any apparent doing of your marketing team: Congrats, you manage the purest form of a hijacked brand. Perhaps it is one of the cases mentioned earlier: Napster, Dr. Martens, PBR, SMS, or In-N-Out Burger. Perhaps it is Krispy Kreme, Hush Puppies, Carhartt work wear, or LOMO cameras. Perhaps it is a brand emerging right now. The market made you look like a marketing genius—now prove it.

Below are some key characteristics of this type of hijacked brand and recommendations on how to treat it. Each case, of course, has its own rules and peculiarities.

	SERENDIPITOUS BRAND HIJACK	CONVENTIONAL BRAND
Type of Brand	Utilitarian, no-frills	Conventional, competitive
	Values-driven	Benefit-driven
Brand Leadership	Appropriated by the marketplace; brand owner facilitates	Controls the brand
	"Owned" by subcultures	Chases subcultures. Thrives in the mainstream
Brand Meaning	Means different things to different groups or people	Strives for a simple and single-minded proposition through a major campaign
	Blank canvas; battle cry developed by the market	No higher cause—come on, it's just a brand
Marketing Approach	Exclusive grassroots movement	Push-down image mass-marketing
	Driven by brand folklore; keep communications neutral and exclusive	Nuanced broadcast media

But enough of these accidental brand hijacking success stories. Most of us will never stumble into that kind of success. We have to create it ourselves.

CHAPTER 4

A "No Marketing" Illusion: The Co-created Hijack

It's not what you do. It's what they do with what you do.

—John Grant, *The New Marketing Manifesto*

"No new product has ever failed this convincingly." That was the verdict reached by the research firm hired to test a new beverage concept with consumers. Initial results were abysmal. The thin color of the drink appeared "unappetizing." The sticky texture and taste were "disgusting." The "stimulates mind and body" concept was irrelevant at best. "Don't quit your day job," they advised the middle-aged entrepreneur who sat before them.

But Dietrich Mateschitz was past the point of no return. He had exited the corporate world exactly three years earlier to create Red Bull, a beverage styled after energy drinks popular in Asia. And in some ways, the devastating consumer reactions to the drink were only the beginning of his troubles. Mateschitz was already locked in a drawn-out battle with the Austrian food and drug authorities: Getting approval for the first energy drink in a European country was no easy task. And in the "add insult to injury" category, the friend who Mateschitz had hired to handle advertising couldn't come up with a single good campaign idea. "Those were the worst three years of my life," Mateschitz says today.

Of course, Red Bull now holds a place in the marketing hall of fame alongside such enigmatic miracle brands as Hotmail, Palm, eBay, and Starbucks. It beat the odds by throwing conventional marketing wisdom overboard and developing a powerful new go-to-market template.

Red Bull was an innovative—even disruptive—product. It established a new category: the legal, yet "hip" stimulant. And it placed absolutely no importance on taste. (In fact, it's safe to say that Red Bull tastes like melted gummy bears mixed with cough syrup. The industry blog BevNet gave the drink a generous D+ in its initial taste rating.) But that didn't stop Mateschitz from selling Red Bull at an ultra-premium price point—about eight times higher than Coke—without any higher authority's endorsement to justify the steep margin.

As you might imagine, an expensive, funny-tasting soda/stimulant hybrid can make for a complex pitch to consumers. But Red Bull's marketing approach never shied away from complexities.

A BULL ENTERS THE BEVERAGE MARKET

Although Red Bull sets the gold standard in terms of how to launch innovative food and beverage brands, its magic sauce never really has been identified. Nor have the large bureaucracies of its conglomerate competitors managed to mimic its success. This is partly because Red Bull is understandably hush-hush about its strategy. Why give away the farm and let competitors in on your intellectual capital? Red Bull has refused to enter industry competitions such as the prestigious IPA Effectiveness Awards, which require a thorough description of marketing efforts. It also has successfully avoided being the subject of any thorough case studies. But it's also difficult to imitate because Red Bull fundamentally changed the go-to-market model. That's why it's worth a closer look.

How has Red Bull become one of the most remarkable brand success stories of the modern era? It has rewritten all the rules.

It serves up an intoxicating cocktail of rumors, hype, and reluctant denials.

Before the company could ever sell a drop of the stuff, the drink's ingredients needed approval from local food and drug authorities in each market. In several instances, the harmless but unusual main ingredient, taurine, slowed this process and resulted in a waiting period.

As frustrating as that may have been for Mateschitz, the waiting period turned out to be ripe for generating rumors.

It took five years for the company to gain permission to export into Germany, Red Bull's second market (after Austria, where it is headquartered). When it did, Germany became the foundation for the brand's success and the cash cow for further expansion. But a black market started flourishing in Munich, which is close to the Austrian border, long before the approval process concluded. During this time, consumers started asking intriguing questions: Why was the drink illegal in Germany? Was it speed-in-a-can, a legal drug? Was its taurine extracted from bulls' testicles? Was Red Bull an over-the-counter Viagra? The list of innuendos and insinuations went on and on. Rather than trying to squelch the rumors, Red Bull shrewdly added a "rumors" section to its Web site to keep the mythology growing and evolving.

Red Bull has moms to thank for further contributing to the hype. Once the product finally launched in Germany, a group of concerned mothers campaigned to have it banned, claiming that the drink was associated with drug use. The product did happen to launch just as all-night raves and Ecstasy consumption were entering mainstream awareness. Red Bull was well stocked in clubs, where it became the drink of choice for ravers looking for non-alcoholic fuel. The company's marketers encouraged this association by sending subtle cues, like tossing empty Red Bull cans onto the floors of club bathrooms. They cleverly realized that drug culture cachet combined with parental meddling was an instant recipe for cool. As authors Pountain and Robins point out in *Cool Rules:* "Kids want simultaneously to be acceptable to their peers and scandalous to their parents."

Thanks to the boycott and long FDA approval process, Red Bull became not only cool, but also a hotbed for rumors, urban myth, hype, and anticipation. The company itself wasn't prepared for the consequences; it ran out of product within the first three months of its German launch. And yet this only served to send yet another positive signal to the market: The sellout alerted the mainstream to the Red Bull craze. Soon, more and more people were jumping on the bandwagon.

As the drink spread to other markets, its reputation came with it. By

1995, London newspapers were telling tales of a financial district "fu-eled on Red Bull," and reporting a surge of Red Bull–addled bar fights and vandalism. The company execs resisted the temptation to release widespread denials. It wasn't until a bogus medical report claiming the drink caused insanity began to spread on the internet that Red Bull released detailed evidence proving the drink was safe.

Causes insanity? Legal speed? Made from bulls' testicles? Obviously, this stuff is too good to have come from the agency offices on Madison Avenue. Red Bull's early consumers have their fingerprints all over the company's public persona. But that doesn't mean the company just got lucky. Leadership had the wits to let the rumors fly, to not answer the boycotting moms with fervent denials, and to encourage its target consumers to believe what they wanted about the product. In his 2001 article "Liquid Cocaine," *Salon* journalist Jeff Edwards concluded, "The more rumors of Red Bull's potentially dangerous, over-stimulating effects spread, the more the drink sells." He credits this "cultivation of mystery" with earning Red Bull its cultlike following.

Even folks at headquarters enjoy playing into the myths. "I always have to fly to Pamplona to source bulls' testicles," jokes Mateschitz. "Those rumors have never hurt," he adds joyfully. (FYI, taurine was found in bulls initially, but it has long since been produced synthetically.)

It seeds early markets.

Red Bull's early success sprouted from a challenge: As a self-funded start-up, the company simply did not have the capital to spend heavily on advertising. But just as the company knew how to facilitate an urban legend, it also understood how to turn the market into willing participants in building the brand.

The company's marketers became pioneers of seeding early markets. Seeding refers to a company spending its money and efforts to go after an exclusive group of consumers in a profound way. Red Bull's executives targeted several groups at once, allowing each to become involved in creating the product's identity. They treated every subculture with the same intense, creative effort that other brands reserve for their mainstream consumer base. In so doing, the drink company essentially helped the market hijack its brand.

When Red Bull launched in the United States, it focused its

pre-seeding efforts on New York City, where the city's large European population was already familiar with the brand. The first thing the company did was make the product available under the radar to the staff of hip bars—a group of people in need of a boost on the job. Red Bull insisted on delivering the product by cab, thereby earning taxi driver support. The drink became an instant hit with these tastemakers and influencers of bar call choice. The tipping point came when Demi Moore overheard local bar staff bragging about the brand at a time when it was not yet officially available there. She went through quite an effort to get a hold of cases of Red Bull for herself.

But, wisely, Red Bull is not an image chaser. It isn't afraid to court the loyalties of any group that might need a pick-me-up, be it celebrities, ultra-cool ravers, extreme sports fanatics, or hard-working office employees. To seed the truck driving market in Britain, the company commissioned a study from a group of sleep researchers and safety advocates. The media reported the group's findings that energy drinks could help drivers stay awake and decrease their number of accidents. At the same time, Red Bull began advertising on pumps at gas stations, letting drivers put two and two together themselves. It worked. Truck drivers are still one of Red Bull's most dedicated fan groups.

It engages in intimate marketing.

Red Bull understood another rule of brand hijack marketing: Get up-close and personal. Executives realized that deep personal experiences and peer endorsements would trump ad campaigns any day. "Red Bull is willing to invest a lot in making sure people become believers in the brand through hands-on experiences," explains a Red Bull event planner. It uses intimate marketing to get groups of consumers—whether they are average Joes or superstars—to credibly endorse the brand.

For example, Red Bull dedicates a senior manager full time to look after celebrities and make sure that every Red Bull experience they have is a great one. The company doesn't do typical celebrity endorsements. It won't pay for VIP support for anyone other than extreme athletes. Instead, it tries to position Red Bull as part of the celebrity lifestyle. One very smart approach it took to accomplish this was to regularly give free product to studio production staff. In this way, many celebrities became acquainted with the brand and developed a genuine relationship with it. Even Madonna has had Red Bull on stage at quite a few concerts, and yet the company has never paid her an endorsement fee.

Formula One racer Jensen Button wasn't even recruited by Red Bull employees, but rather by his racing buddy Eddie Irvine, who was a fan. When Button met with the British marketing team, he was surprised by the nature of the "endorsement deal." The company made it clear to him that there would be no contract and no fee. All it wanted was his enthusiasm and it would reciprocate with free product, VIP access to events, and so on. The difference is that Red Bull garnered genuine loyalty from Button rather than attaining the typical force-fed celebrity endorsement.

Red Bull subtly goes after the clubbing community by running a Music Academy for aspiring DJs. Talk about a new twist on the traditional marketing model. Instead of sponsoring concert tours like other "cool" companies do, Red Bull brings in top DJs from around the world to teach workshops at its Academy every year. *Brandweek*'s Ken Hein describes the latest Academy held this summer in New York's Lower East Side:

> The collection of 60 aspiring deejays from Croatia, New Zealand, Slovakia and, of course, the U.S. were invited to learn from masters like Derrick Carter, who taught the "art of holding the 10-minute bend." Herbert held forth on how to "funk up that bag of crisps" and David Steele spoke about "law and the music industry." Artwork adorning the walls was provided by Freddie C, a well-known graffiti artist from Los Angeles.
>
> The Academy, now in its fourth year, previously held classes in Berlin (twice) and Dublin. Its purpose is to give these kings of clubland, where Red Bull is often consumed, a once-in-a-lifetime chance to meet their heroes.
>
> Unlike other efforts, where a liquor company hires the 10 hottest deejays and packs a club with 10,000 people, the school is more personal and intimate. When these students return to their respective countries and dance floors, they will often speak of what they learned and who they saw at the Academy.
>
> They won't be asked to push the drink or hand out T-shirts and key chains. Actually, they aren't required to do anything.

> But when they regale deejays and club-goers with tales of their pilgrimage, the words "Red Bull" are likely to leave their lips, giving the brand its vital word-of-mouth hype.

But the intimate marketing tactic isn't reserved for celebrities and hipsters alone. Red Bull even made an effort to market to me. I threw a bunch of parties for about twenty or so soccer fanatics in San Francisco during the 2002 World Cup. The Red Bull sampling team somehow got wind of this and surprised us during the Germany vs. U.S.A. quarterfinals match. At 4 A.M., three bubbly members of the sampling team arrived, providing just the energy boost we needed. Of course, the Germans won in the end, but for all of us crazed soccer fans, the game will be more readily forgotten than will the appearance of the Red Bull team. No broadcast campaign could ever replicate that sort of personal experience.

Consumers are asked to use their imagination to truly fit Red Bull into their lives. This intimate marketing encourages hands-on participation in the brand that has a far more powerful and longer-lasting impact than does passively processing an abstract communication effort.

It uses traditional advertising in a very limited way.

Mateschitz learned in the pre-launch years that advertising would play a very specific and limited role in the marketing of his complex brand: It is used to reinforce, not introduce, the brand experience. Red Bull only aired ads after the launch phase, and they remain a small part of the overall marketing mix.

Initially, Red Bull's agency, led by Johannes Kastner, could not even come up with an idea for an ad campaign. But once they realized that the ads' only purposes were to build brand awareness and likeability—and not to do the overall marketing job (i.e., establishing and increasing the understanding and acceptance of the energy drink category)—the task became much easier for the creatives.

In a now well-known last-ditch effort, Kastner's team came up with the "Red Bull gives you wiiiings" campaign. The odd cartoon with a problem/solution message has been run consistently since 1988 on TV and radio throughout the world.

The company is also clever about the more subtle aspects of media planning. For instance, the brand stays off-air during the peak summer months, when share of voice would sink significantly anyway. In order to reach the right audience, its media planners focus on progressive and innovative TV and radio stations. Also, Red Bull doesn't use print media to convey its brand message. The flatness of the medium doesn't connote energy, which is the key Red Bull message.

It defines itself by its function, not its image.

Here's the big idea: Red Bull is a drink that actually *does* something. The company has never backed off its initial claim that the drink provides a quick boost of energy. (Note: It's up for debate whether Red Bull actually works in a unique way or not. Nutritionists argue that Coca-Cola's combination of sugar and caffeine produces the same short-term effect. But that's not the point here.) This claim—the sort of thing usually confined to the over-the-counter pharmaceutical category—is always at the heart of its marketing. Red Bull embodies energy and stimulation in everything it does.

Fundamentally, Red Bull was one of the first modern brands to turn away from an aspirational image. This was a daring maneuver considering that Mateschitz wanted to compete in the soft drink category, a place where image—particularly a shallow aspirational image—rules. But Mateschitz didn't want to market Red Bull as just an OTC nutraceutical, either. So he set up a marketing template that showed how the drink fit into people's lifestyles: Never let consumers forget the message that Red Bull actually works, when they need a boost.

It creates a persona rather than a proposition.

Steve Henry, founder of London's radical HHCL ad agency, argues that the definition of a brand's character is more important than any one proposition about it. He contends that character definition, which he calls the brand's "Unique Selling Persona," is likely the key to successful marketing and advertising.

The advantage of taking this approach is that, unlike most brands, Red Bull doesn't have to deliver a single selling proposition to its consumers (i.e., Tide washes whiter, Bounty—the quicker picker-upper). Instead, the company has been incredibly successful, both over time and across geographies, in standing for something broader and more flexible: energy and stimulation. The result is that Red Bull can mean different things to different people. Consumers can interpret the brand in their own ways without affecting its core function. *Brandweek*'s Ken Hein explains:

> Ask someone to define it and the answers will vary. For instance, *The Fire Island* (N.Y.) *News* has dubbed it "The new sex drink," while a 13-year-old boy in a local deli said, "Me inspira a bailar" ("It makes me dance"). And, according to a waitress in a New York City wine bar, "If you mix it with cough syrup, it makes your cold go away."

From truck drivers to clubbers to extreme sports enthusiasts, Red Bull weaves itself into the lives of very different groups of people without ostracizing any of them. It effortlessly crosses socioeconomic boundaries. The company delivers the message that there is no right way to use Red Bull, no code of conduct—for consumers, that is.

However, the one aspect that remains constant is the brand persona: the spirit, look, and feel of the brand. Red Bull has gone to great lengths to develop a brand bible and to provide a brand coach for each region to ensure that its managers understand intuitively whether a specific activity or event is true to Red Bull's character.

One event that captures the energetic, offbeat spirit of Red Bull is the Flugtag, German for flying day. Every year, in picturesque spots like Wellington and Santa Monica, Red Bull sponsors a contest in which amateur pilots are invited to create wild and wacky flying machines. They attempt to launch their giant lemons and fly their homemade helicopters off a pier or dock and into the air. Most end up belly flopping into the water.

Flugtag regularly draws crowds in the tens of thousands. But the point isn't whether or not the event is successful. The point is that it embodies the Red Bull character. The company rewards participants not just for how far they fly, but also for their creativity and showmanship. "Outrageous is what we want," say the organizers, "something that both physics and common sense tell you has zip chance of flying."

Red Bull's unwavering commitment to the brand's efficacy as an energy drink underpins its popularity among both its employees and the public. The company's consistent message is undoubtedly a large part of the reason why consumers shell out a huge price premium without demanding a single shred of evidence that Red Bull stimulates anything other than profits.

It always offers the product in context.

After being told that his product was a complete failure among consumer testers, Mateschitz walked away with a key lesson: Context is everything. Small wonder the product had failed in the sterile environment of a research studio. Red Bull didn't need to be tasted; it needed to be experienced. Just as Gatorade only succeeded in taste tests when participants were dehydrated and the drink was served ice cold, Red Bull would never score high points with consumers in a lab setting. Red Bull was at its core a functional drink, intended to provide a boost of energy. And so it had to be delivered within the context of fulfilling that need.

Instead of launching a mass marketing campaign or blanketing the airwaves with commercials, Mateschitz went with what traditional marketers call a "below-the-line" approach. Since Red Bull needs to be experienced in the right context—wherever people are tired, staying up all night, or otherwise in search of a pick-me-up—creating that context became the driving force behind all the company's marketing efforts. To this day, from product sampling to sponsoring and hosting events, Red Bull fanatically sticks to this agenda.

Here's a dramatic example from the early days, before the company had written its go-to-market guidebook. One day, the German field manager discovered a dangerous misstep: Red Bull had started offering samples of the beverage out of plastic cups in supermarkets. She abruptly quit her job. When Johannes Kastner, head of Red Bull's ad agency, heard about what had happened, he immediately reinstated her. He then codified the brand's sampling guidelines to ensure that the drink was only sampled in the appropriate context. For example, Red Bull could never be served in cups, but only handed out as unopened cans so that consumers could decide when and how to drink it. Also, it could only be sampled in places where its function as a stimulant would be appreciated, such as bars and sporting events.

It creates an air of exclusivity.

Passion cannot be bought or hard-sold. Hijack brands win consumers by aiming at the heart, not the head. They seduce, they charm, and, as Red Bull demonstrates, they never come on too strong. At most every turn, Red Bull dodges aggressive in-your-face push tactics, price-offs, and instant ubiquity—the sort of tired techniques that dominate the beverage category. Instead, Red Bull's marketing is designed for the subconscious. It seduces, making the consumer feel in charge.

One major seduction tactic employed by Red Bull is exclusivity. Is there anything you want more than the thing you can't have? Red Bull knows the answer, of course, and is sure to make it hard for the market to experience the Red Bull rush—at least at first.

For one, Red Bull keeps its sampling efforts focused on exclusive subcommunities. It doesn't care how many people sample the product; it's who and how that matters. The company focuses on creating a deep experience for the consumer, one that will demonstrate the drink's function. So it targets bars, raves, and movie sets (where, as we've seen, it gives free product to staff during production)—any place where people are in need of a real boost.

Red Bull also creates a sense of exclusivity by limiting access to its branded merchandise. It only gives out T-shirts and the like to its sponsored athletes. Consumers don't have access to anything. Keeping tchotchkes out of consumer reach flies in the face of beverage marketing convention. And yet it's worked wonders for Red Bull. Murray Partridge, the former Creative Director of TBWA London calls this tactic making the merchandise "nickable," the British term for stealing. The idea is to force consumers to work hard to get a hold of any Red Bull merchandising, so that when they do, they cherish it like a prized possession. And just as important, they will tell friends and acquaintances about their misadventures, thereby adding to the mythology of the brand.

Finally, Red Bull adds to the air of scarcity by deliberately limiting distribution of the product when it first enters a market. Even the trade hears, "No, you can't have it yet!" a definite first in the packaged goods world. When Red Bull comes to town, they initially select just a handful of outlets to sell the brand. Compare this to the beer industry, for instance, a market that hasn't seen a new brand succeed since the deliberate launch of Sam Adams a decade ago. Instant distribution, awareness, and intrusive promotion tactics (like those used for A-B's fleeting Tequiza) can't charm an early market or make them feel ownership of the brand.

Red Bull views distribution as a branding tool, not just a volume outlet. Just as Gatorade developed a conceptual approach to distribution by prioritizing "points of sweat" (making sure that Gatorade is available wherever athletes are active), Red Bull focuses on distributing to places where it knows it will be appreciated, like clubs, bars, and extreme sporting events.

While broad availability is usually used to create demand for new brands, Red Bull flips this convention on its head by creating demand before broadening availability. All of this exclusivity encourages consumers to feel special, as though they've discovered something different—a rarity in this chain store, cookie cutter marketplace. Perhaps Hein says it best:

> It's no wonder that rival beverage companies and analysts alike are so mystified by Red Bull's success, where sales seem to sprout from cracks in the pavement. The fact of the matter is, there is a party going on and the people who travel by day haven't been invited yet.

Its employees believe in the brand.

And then there are those throwing the party. Red Bull employees are another breed altogether. To them, Red Bull is on a mission. Everyone who works for the company—even every vendor—is totally on board. It's an internal culture driven by a sense of being the overachieving underdog with an amazing survival instinct.

This type of company has a spiritual aura. But unless you have dedicated buy-in from your employees, partners, and vendors, as well as retail sales personnel, the vibe will never cross over to your consumers. Employees serve as credible role models, aligning the internal values of the company with the external values and principles of the brand. You need to move your own people before you can touch a removed audience. Red Bull employees really believe in the product. And this belief carries through the organizational structure with a dedicated education and coaching approach rivaling that of Nike's *Ekin* team. (That's the sales education team named after the brand spelled backward that has the swoosh tattooed on their ankles.)

Red Bull employees also thrive on its entrepreneurial structure. "Management by organized chaos," is how Mateschitz describes the hierarchy-free organization. Red Bull employs a fully committed team hired primarily for its passion about the product and non-conformism.

It has a passionate and charismatic leader.

Red Bull is a personality-driven organization, with the charismatic, life-embracing Mateschitz at its helm. Mateschitz leads by example: He makes sure to work only three days a week so that he can live the life of extreme sports that his brand endorses.

Mateschitz has so far resisted the temptation to go public. Without pressures from a board and shareholders focused on quarterly profits, the company is free to concentrate on doing what's right for the brand and the business in the long term. How fascinating and old-school. Imagine a company that can actually manage its brand rather than its stock price. Patience is crucial when it comes to co-creating a brand with your market. The U.S. success was five years in the making. There is hardly a conglomerate around that would have allowed such a time-consuming marketing scheme to unfold. And yet look at how Red Bull dominates the American energy drink market now.

To Mateschitz, a company, above all else, should be about producing a quality product and coaching its people. "If someone preaches profit-maximizing as a company's highest goal, then that's simply wrong. Hell, it's criminal," says Mateschitz. Before you start giggling about such naïveté and lack of worldliness, let me briefly remind you that Mateschitz's personal wealth is estimated at about $5 billion. Amen, brother.

Selling Out

The marketing team at Red Bull does not have a perfect record by any means. It screws things up, just like the rest of us.

In the late '90s, Red Bull went into an innovative placement deal on a Playstation game called WipeOut 2097. When Playstation launched in Europe, it was one of the hottest games around. It was packed with super graphics, adrenaline-pumping game play, and a killer soundtrack including such faves as Prodigy, Daft Punk, and the Chemical Brothers.

Red Bull integrated itself into the game in a fashion consistent with its functionality theme. By clicking on a Red Bull icon, players could provide themselves with extra energy and improved reaction times.

A cute idea at first glance. But it backfired. Players complained that it felt intrusive and unnatural. Most either ignored it or became quite irate. A typical online review, this one by "Archimedes," read as follows:

> Fast, Elegant, Sell out????? Wipeout XL is a great game to play over and over. The thing that bothers me the most about it is the advertising to Red Bull drink. The companies that the game made up for itsself are cool enough. The fact that they took Red Bull drink into the game kinda makes you feel like you're no longer on the raceway but in an advertisement. If you can just ignore it then the game is great but it is an eyesore to see "improve reaction time Red Bull" every time you're waiting for the game to load.

The good news for Red Bull is that by giving the overall impression that it respects its community, mishaps are more easily forgiven and forgotten.

ME-TOO MARKETING TANKS

With the success of Red Bull, the big boys—Pepsi, Coca-Cola, and Anheuser-Busch—jumped on the energy drink bandwagon. All three companies tried to copy Red Bull's low-key marketing approach, but so far have met with limited success.

Coke and A-B launched their drinks, KMX and 180 respectively, in 2000, trying to emulate Red Bull's distribution and sampling strategy.

Coke launched KMX in gas stations, convenience stores, and night-clubs in only a handful of markets. It targeted the electronic music scene, becoming a sponsor of festivals such as Area One, HiFiBi, and Sunsation. A-B selected bars and c-stores throughout its distribution system for 180, and leveraged its sports properties for marketing opportunities.

The suits in the boardroom must have felt confident they'd be having Red Bull for breakfast. All they had to do was copy the template and overpower it with bottomless resources and a world-class distribution network. What could possibly go wrong? Plenty.

These brands have failed to facilitate a consumer takeover because:

They went for a top-down approach instead of collaboration.

Instead of seeding their brands slowly within relevant subcultures, KMX and 180 entered the alternative music and sport scenes in the traditional marketing manner: as sponsors. Here is what one attendant wrote about an Area One concert:

> There were people all dressed in orange promoting a new energy drink called KMX, and offering free samples to everyone in little test tubes. They were everywhere!

The big companies haven't tried to earn their communities' adoption of the drinks. They've tried to buy it. And so they haven't been as effective as Red Bull, which used marketing tactics that sometimes took years to unfold in order to garner the long-term loyalty of its consumers.

They've been chasing "cool," but ignoring function.

One of the major misconceptions about Red Bull is that it chases cool. Instead, it simply targeted anyone in need of an energy boost. It became cool because of the way it was marketed, not to whom it was marketed.

A-B and Coke have decided to court "cool" subcultures. Coke wants to be associated with more sophisticated "social energy," whatever that means. In doing this, they've abandoned the functionality message and returned to the old soft drink branding game of image selling.

They haven't been honest with consumers.

The big guys are trying to hide the fact that these energy drinks are their creations. KMX bottles are printed with the name Delaware Punch Company, which is a Coke subsidiary, but make no mention of the soda giant. KMX is missing from a list of Coke brands posted on the Coca-Cola Web site. This approach only incites cynicism, not loyalty. Here's a typical message board post:

> KMX is an energy drink made by Coca-Cola. I'm sorry to say, but Coke makes enough money. HELP OUT THE LITTLE GUY!

They try to maintain too much control.

Ultimately, Coke, Pepsi, and A-B have entered the energy drink category by attempting to mimic Red Bull's tactics. Although they got a lot of the particulars correct, they couldn't copy the spirit of Red Bull. As a start-up company, Red Bull learned to roll with the punches. From rumors to smuggling, Red Bull understood that it could benefit from the unknowns in the market.

The big corporations haven't learned to tolerate such uncertainty. They've tried to control participation in the brand. Check out KMX's Web site. In the "Speak Up" section, consumers are invited to give their input, but only in predetermined categories: new flavors, events, and serving suggestions. Input is only welcome as long as it is easily formatted to serve as free market research for Coke.

INTRODUCING THE CO-CREATED HIJACK

A hijack does not have to be serendipitous. It can be planned. But it requires the mindset of allowing the active involvement of the market to discover, to engage with, and to help shape a brand's larger meaning.

---

co-created hi·jack (kō_krē-'āt'd 'hī'jak): the act of inviting subcultures to co-create a brand's ideology, use, and persona, and pave the road for adoption by the mainstream.

AN OVERNIGHT SUCCESS—YEARS IN THE MAKING

Red Bull's success was a cocktail of an innovative product, keen seeding, ballsy management, and a healthy shot of good luck. But hijackings can be orchestrated even without some of those advantages. In fact, they can be pulled off without the innovative product.

Let's talk about *The Blair Witch Project*. It was a mediocre "horror" movie with no stars, almost no scary parts, and, at least at first, no distributor. It's the kind of thing born every day in film schools throughout the country.

And yet perhaps no one has ever co-created a hijack quite as expertly as the folks behind *Blair Witch:* filmmakers Daniel Myrick and Eduardo Sanchez. The pair used a tight budget to their advantage. Rather than marketing the movie, Myrick and Sanchez marketed a big idea—the myth of the Blair Witch. Three years later, that urban myth grossed $241 million. Not bad for a movie that cost just $35,000 to produce.

The path to the $241 million in box office revenues was a tactical masterpiece full of many small initiatives, techniques that played to a subconscious level. Some of these techniques were borrowed—okay, stolen (we'll get to that later). But many were new to the movie industry. And the marketing team demonstrated incredible forethought and patience in implementing its plan.

Let's take a closer look at how *Blair Witch* so effectively executed the co-created hijack of its brand.

It pre-seeded the market with a myth.

The most radical marketing strategy *Blair Witch* introduced was a two-year pre-seeding phase before the movie itself was even announced. During this time, the filmmakers created a new urban legend.

Instead of spreading a message about the movie, they spread questions about its premise: Did the Blair Witch really exist? Did three film students actually die in the woods while trying to find her? Was *Blair Witch* a snuff movie or not? Instead of appealing to audiences with a typical trailer that gave away most of the plot, they tapped into a time-tested social phenomenon—gossip. Humans are wired for casual social conversation: It's how we bond, build ties, and establish hierarchies (those in-the-know rank higher). Positioning Blair Witch as an urban myth played perfectly into this human tendency. It made people talk about the movie while simultaneously leading the audience to believe that it controlled the buzz surrounding the film. Of course, in reality the buzz was built piece-by-piece, at what in marketing time amounts to a snail's pace.

The marketing team then carefully facilitated the spread of the myth by blurring the line between fact and fiction. For example, the first movie clips were introduced as actual "found" footage rather than a preview of an upcoming film. Prior to the early screenings at colleges, three-person teams would blanket the campuses with mock "missing" flyers of the "lost" filmmakers and spooky stick figures (something the Witch makes to scare the characters in the movie), adding to the film's mystique.

In 1998, Myrick and Sanchez launched a Web site. Although there's some debate as to whether or not the duo planted discussion boards during this time, what's clear is that legitimate threads did develop, debating and spreading the mythology. Later, Artisan posted "evidence" about the case to the *Blair Witch* Web site: pseudo-interviews with the police, pages supposedly found from the missing filmmakers' journals, etc.

Artisan also co-produced a "documentary" with the SciFi channel about the curse of the Blair Witch, which they aired late at night a few days before the film's release. The mockumentary not only further contributed to the excitement surrounding the Blair Witch myth; it also made those who watched it feel special, like they had discovered privileged information.

All of these activities served to reward the most loyal fans and feed the growing buzz about the myth of the Blair Witch.

It targeted the right early market.

Myrick and Sanchez knew that *Blair Witch* initially would attract interest only among the fringe crowd. So in their early marketing efforts, they targeted people like themselves—internet junkies, horror freaks, and film buffs. Once the story gained traction within this inner circle, the promoters facilitated chatter among art house filmgoers and the

Hollywood elite. Hence, it created a ripple effect that moved gradually toward, and eventually engulfed, the mainstream.

Although the media liked to play up the filmmakers' newcomer status, it often failed to mention that the two had the backing of an indie film veteran, John Pierson, who had invested $10,000 for the filming. Pierson gave the Blair Witch myth its first public exposure in August 1997 on his *Split Screen Show,* an insider's program on Bravo and IFC. He also encouraged his fans to debate the truth about the Blair Witch on his Web site. These early events attracted the attention of the indie aficionado and horror film crowds.

In the months leading up to the movie's release, Artisan kept its insider communications exclusive to these markets. The first trailer for *Blair Witch* appeared on the then-obscure film insider site Ain't It Cool News. The movie was first screened on forty college campuses rather than in NYC and LA theaters, which is the industry norm.

But Myrick and Sanchez didn't just go after the fringe. When the time was right, and the film had started to gain traction in the film buff crowd, they started to court the industry cognoscenti. The duo insisted on treating members of the film elite like just another audience. This was a seemingly obvious yet potent innovation, because it is the Hollywood movers and shakers who help films find distributors and, later, control the buzz. After gaining access to the Sundance Film Festival for a midnight screening (thanks to John Pierson, who happened to be a member of the Sundance Film Festival Committee), the filmmakers put up their "missing" leaflets all over Park City, Utah. The ingenious tactic worked: Artisan bought the rights to the film after the festival.

It carefully timed its use of ascending media.

Myrick and Sanchez used the film's Web site as their primary medium for promoting the movie up to the week of its release. Here, they posted additional information about the Blair Witch myth, encouraged fan participation with discussion boards, and offered clips of the movie. But *Blair Witch*'s success was not entirely Web based. The filmmakers and, later, the distributor, allowed the media to keep building as the film's audience grew broader—from the Web to cable TV, independent weeklies and radio, and finally on to broadcast TV and major newspapers.

THE EVOLUTION OF THE BLAIR WITCH

Pre-Movie Announcement (1997–1998)		Post-Movie Announcement (1999+)	
CREATING THE MYTH	**ANTICIPATING THE FILM**	**LAUNCHING THE FILM**	
		Becoming the "Next Big Thing"	Building Momentum
	Seeding the Film		Mass release
Growing the Myth		Limited release	
Seeding the Myth	Switching message from myth to movie		· *Wide-release in 2,000+ theaters*
The rumor spreads		· *Debuts at NYC's Angelika Film Center*	
A rumor starts	· Introduced at Sundance during midnight screening	· *Limited distribution, creating long lines and great PR*	· *90% of advertising budget spent during this phase*
· *Second clip is shown on* Split Screen Show			
· Myrick and Sanchez appear on John Pierson's Split Screen Show	· Artisan buys distribution rights for $1 million	· *Advertising starts in phases, print, radio, and then TV*	· *Comic book, CD, and book released*
· *Pierson invites viewers to debate the rumor online*	· Pre-screened at 40 colleges with students, but not with critics		· *Film racks up $224 million at the box office*
· *They show eight minutes of footage claiming that it was found in the woods*	· *Blair Witch Web site goes live*	· Mentioned on Ain't It Cool News Web site	· *Web site gets 650,000 hits a day*
· *The rumor of the missing students is planted*	· *Team spreads misinformation and drives traffic to Web site*	· Trailers shown on Ain't It Cool, MTV and after Star Wars movie	· *Media jumps on bandwagon, directors appear on cover of Time magazine*
		· Add more "evidence" to the Web site, created fake fan sites	
		· Curse of the Blair Witch "mockumentary" airs on SciFi Channel	

It fostered a sense of exclusivity.

Artisan knew that it needed to keep the momentum going through the film's opening. And so it decided to make the viewing experience exclusive by limiting distribution of the movie in theaters. "It's a difficult ticket to get, which was part of the concept. People do have the experience of going and not being able to get in," explained Artisan co-president Amir Malin.

This exclusivity tactic worked to create long lines and sold-out theaters, which only served to heighten the buzz surrounding the film. As a side benefit, the long lines ensured that early word-of-mouth would be mostly positive. Who else would endure the lines except for the most hardcore fans, people predisposed to liking the movie? And who would admit that the film wasn't all that after having wasted hours trying to get tickets?

A Painful Aftermath

In the end, *Blair Witch* became one of the most profitable films in history. But even marketing coups of that magnitude don't necessarily end up reigning supreme for long.

Five years after Myrick and Sanchez rewrote the movie-marketing template along with their distributor, Artisan, the two filmmakers themselves could appear on their mock "Missing" posters. Their attempt at a *Blair Witch* follow-up film died in preproduction, and both have struggled to get back into the business. Along with the actors and the distributor, they're officially venturing into "Where are they now?" territory.

The folks at Artisan can primarily be blamed that *Blair Witch* did not turn into a franchise. They did not seem to fully comprehend the magic behind the film's success. If they had, they would have never sold out when creating the sequel. Rather than employing the co-created hijack tactics that caused *Blair Witch* to become an international sensation, Artisan returned to traditional marketing techniques. As a result, the sequel tanked, grossing a mere $26 million. Artisan's former president, Amir Malin, admits to letting success obscure the lessons learned from *Blair Witch:*

> From a business point of view the company had started out with the strategy to operate efficiently, with no bloated overhead and smart decisions. Then all of a sudden with the success [of *Blair Witch*] and all that money coming in, all the principles that had been engineered upfront were thrown out the window.

Had they wanted to milk the franchise any further, Artisan's executives should have stayed true to the spirit of the original film and fought to keep the Blair Witch myth alive. Instead, they simply released a typical big-budget sequel, with none of the pre-seeding and myth-building efforts of the original and, therefore, none of its buzz. The cover was blown. The mystery no longer existed. It was purely a film, not potentially an extreme, real documentary. Without the intrigue, the sequel was exposed as a second-class copycat, and even the original *Blair Witch* lost some of its charm.

The Facts Behind the Myth

*The Web site . . . looks anything but low-budget. The Story
and Synopsis are fantastic; when we first came upon this site,
we thought that the movie was a documentary—they've done
that good a job of creating an extensive background to their
story! Okay, so maybe we're just naïve. Either way, this is a
site you should definitely check out. Make sure you download
the trailer.*

—The Wild, Wild, Web, August 1997

If you think this review is referring to the much-vaunted *Blair Witch* Web
site, you're wrong. Notice the date: It was written over a year before *Blair
Witch* launched its Web site. The truth is, *Blair Witch* wasn't as innovative as
its backers wanted us to believe.

This "Wild, Wild, Web" review refers to the Web site of *The Last
Broadcast,* an independent film that came out in 1998, a year before the release of *Blair Witch*. While the mainstream press was busy falling over itself
praising the innovation of *Blair Witch,* citing everything from the filming
technique and the plot to the Web site and the marketing tactics, the indie
film press investigated the suspicious similarities between *Blair Witch* and
its predecessor.

- **Plot**
  The plot of *Blair Witch* is strikingly similar to the plot of *The Last
  Broadcast. Broadcast* is about four members of a cable access show
  called *Fact or Fiction* who venture into New Jersey's Pine Barrens in
  search of the Jersey Devil. One by one, the crewmembers disappear
  or are murdered. The video footage of their gruesome demise is
  found. The film is a mock documentary tracing the history of the
  lost crew, mixing "the found footage" with interviews of friends, lo-
  cals, etc.

  The film's directors, Stefan Avalos and Lance Weiler, weren't too
  miffed by the similarities in plot between *Blair* and *Broadcast*. "No,
  we're not going to sue, man," they said. "Storyline—there's no such
  thing as original or innovative."

(cont'd)

In addition, *Broadcast*'s directors felt like Myrick and Sanchez had made an honest effort to reduce the similarities between the two films. In the summer of 1998, as *Broadcast* was touring independent festivals, Myrick and Sanchez were editing *Blair Witch*. They scrapped all the interview footage, opting instead to make *Blair* a movie of the found footage only.

- ## Web site

Much has been made of the cleverness of the *Blair Witch* Web site. However, contrary to popular belief, it is not an original concept. In fact, it is almost an exact reproduction of *Broadcast*'s Web site, which came out fifteen months earlier. The 11thHour.com noted:

> *Both Web sites encourage the viewer to believe the respective film is real, with features that include a timeline of fictitious events, biographies of the lost "filmmakers," an introductory summary of the occurrence, fabricated "interviews" with those involved and grainy evidence photos from the "crime scene."*

The irony is that the *Broadcast* site itself borrowed heavily from another film site, a documentary called *Paradise Lost: The Child Murders at Robin Hood Hills*. Avalos freely admits that he copied from this site, but Myrick and Sanchez have been less forthcoming about the source of their inspiration. When pushed, they admitted to Diane Sawyer that they did see *The Last Broadcast*'s Web site during the making of *Blair Witch*, but they would not admit to anything else.

- ## Marketing

Avalos and Weiler also came up with the innovative trailers and flyers that *Blair Witch* imitated. Because the two filmmakers didn't have a lot of money, *Broadcast*'s trailers weren't like typical Hollywood promos with smooth voiceovers, a score, and so on. The *Broadcast* trailer was just a clip from the movie, simulating the cinéma vérité quality of the script. Of course, Artisan did this as well. Who can forget the famous *Blair Witch* trailer with the face of Heather Donohue up-lit by a flashlight, eyes bloodshot and terrified, her panicked voice and heavy breathing echoing into the camera?

In 1998, *Broadcast* went to five film festivals. As part of the promotion, Avalos and Weiler created flyers about the missing film crew. "We had people handing out flyers—weird flyers, you know? 'Four people went in and no one came out—what really happened?' Our flyers were always set up as fact as fiction."

So, if the two movies were so similar, why did *Blair Witch* succeed when *The Last Broadcast* failed? (*Broadcast* never made it to the big screen, although it has done well in video thanks to the *Blair Witch* controversy.) Perhaps it's because Avalos and Weiler did not pre-seed the myth of the missing crew and the Jersey Devil. Even though they created a clever Web site and rogue marketing for film festivals, these efforts were only intended to promote the movie. If the filmmakers had built a larger context for *The Last Broadcast*, they might have garnered more attention outside of the independent film crowd.

Which brings us to the final coincidence. *Broadcast* was actually a fairly successful indie film. In 1998, Sundance planned to premiere the movie in their midnight slot. But at the last minute, the film was mysteriously rejected. *Blair Witch* took the spot instead. The rest, as they say, is history.

ANOTHER CURSED COPYCAT

John Hegeman, Artisan's marketer behind *Blair Witch*'s success in distribution claimed, "The marketing can never be re-created because the stars will never be aligned the same way again." Whether or not Hegeman is right, there are a whole lot of people—both inside the entertainment industry and out—who have tried to copy the *Blair Witch* blueprint and failed.

One such copycat is *Man on the Moon,* the 1999 Andy Kaufman biopic starring Jim Carrey. In several interviews, Universal Studios alluded to the fact that *Blair Witch* provided the template for its marketing efforts for the film. Unfortunately for Universal, it seems they came to the wrong conclusions about why *Blair Witch* succeeded. In retrospect (always a nice position to be in), the studio missed the mark on several levels.

What went wrong with the marketing of *Man on the Moon?* How did the attempt at a co-created brand hijack fail?

It misunderstood the role of the Web site.

Sure, the *Blair Witch* Web site was cool, but it was only important because it built a full-blown mythology around the curse of the Blair Witch. By blurring the line between fact and fiction, the site facilitated gossip. Capitalizing on the status they gained from being "in the know," fans eagerly spread rumors about the film that they'd read on the Web site, generating a tremendous buzz. They didn't talk about the Web site per se; they talked about the inside information they found on the Web site.

Universal (and a lot of other studios) did not grasp this critical distinction. When the marketing executives attempted to apply the *Blair Witch* model to *Man on the Moon,* they thought to themselves, "Ooh! We need a cool Web site!" And so they built one. But they failed to find a compelling big idea about Andy Kaufman that a mainstream audience could eventually latch onto and enjoy talking about. Instead, Universal designed a Web site to lure in the lingering Kaufman fan community. Called AndyLives.org, the site helped fuel the rumor that Kaufman might have pulled off the "ultimate stunt" in convincing everyone that he'd died when he hadn't. It also served as a place to seed rumors about Jim Carrey's Kaufmanesque behavior on the set. For the relatively small number of existing Kaufman fans, it was admittedly a fun site. But the myth that "Andy lives" just wasn't interesting gossip for the mainstream market. And so buzz for the film never evolved.

It didn't target the right early market.

Although *Blair Witch* became the "in" movie of the summer of 1999, the brand didn't start out by chasing trendsetters. It targeted the fringe first, then moved on to court the cognoscenti, and eventually hit the mainstream.

Universal went for a similar seeding effect with *Man on the Moon*. But in targeting both trendsetters and highbrow Andy Kaufman devotees, it did not pick the right early markets to pursue.

Perhaps Universal recognized that the Kaufman fan-base was too narrow a target audience, because it chose to target "trendsetters" with its seeding campaign as well. It hired popular DJ Swamp to remix Kaufman's signature song "Mighty Mouse," then sent the 7-inch vinyl to the club set. It plastered city streets with wild postings, hoping that urban hipsters would get excited and talk about the new movie. It commissioned guerrilla artist Shepard Fairey to immortalize Kaufman in stickers and posters. The problem was that Andy Kaufman meant nothing to the twentysomething crowd—they were too young to remember the early days of *Saturday Night Live*. And so Universal's attempt to get them excited about *Man on the Moon* fell flat.

Universal pursued the wrong early markets: one was too narrow, the other too removed. What's more, the two target audiences did not communicate with one another, and so winning over one (long-time Kaufman fans) had no impact on the other (twentysomething trendsetters). There was no ripple effect, no linear progression of the story, as there was with *Blair Witch*—the message did not spread. By seeding the movie among Kaufman fans and then following with another, more broad-based but overlapping group, Universal could have succeeded in generating an early buzz that would have spread slowly but steadily to the mainstream. Instead, the studio missed its opportunity to make the (rather good) film prosper.

Falling Short

Eventually, *Man on the Moon* died on the vine, bringing in a mere $34 million for Universal. It was, at the time, the lowest grossing of any Jim Carrey feature.

Man on the Moon's marketing initiative wound up little more than a cheap imitation of *Blair Witch*'s clever hijack. Where *Blair Witch* skillfully cultivated interest in a new urban legend, *Man on the Moon* manufactured hype that no one really cared about. Where *Blair Witch* patiently spread its message to a wider and wider audience, *Man on the Moon* tried too hard and failed to draw an early market in.

Whereas co-created hijackings like *Blair Witch* propose fresh and broad ideas, those who miss the mark, like *Man on the Moon,* are often strangled by the narrowness of their proposals, and not by the limitations of their products.

———

Co-create your brand by collaborating with your consumers.

CHAPTER 5

A Dangerous Attitude

"Whoa. Is this like The Weather Channel?"
"Yeah, eh heh heh, the forecast is partially cool."

—Beavis & Butthead

Can Birkenstocks ever be made cool? Believe it or not, the shoemaker tried to revamp its image to go from granola creature uniform to hipster style in 2003. Seems that the Birkenstock management team got caught in the marketer's twilight zone: chasing after the most elusive of marketing aspirations. Cool brands have the "it" factor—that certain attitude, style, and appearance to which people are magnetically drawn. This leads ambitious corporate executives to constantly demand of their marketing teams, "Make my brand cool."

THE FALLACY OF COOL

But in chasing cool, these guys are playing a dangerous game.

cool ('kül): An oppositional attitude adopted to express defiance to authority.

Do the suits in the boardroom really want their brands to be defiant and oppositional? No, what they're most likely striving for is mainstream acceptance laced with some topical cachet.

Therein lies the fallacy of cool: It's not really what you want to chase. There are several reasons why:

Cool limits growth.

While a cool cachet may initially spark your brand's growth, it eventually limits it. By definition, cool will only appeal to a minority, never the mass-volume mainstream. Larry David, arguably the coolest comedian on TV, built a following by mocking minutia and telling jokes about nothing. Yet he says of his early career as a stand-up comic, "I was not for everyone. I was for the very few."

Cool is temporary.

Cool is temporary, as attitudes are ever changing. Think of the "In/Out" and "Hot/Not" lists that appear in magazines on a monthly basis. Marketers often have fleeting fads sold to them as the Next Big Thing, only to find out that the fads have already passed. Even when they can figure out what they need to do to make a brand cool, most companies find that cool moves too fast for them to keep pace. By the time they've brought the initiative to market, the market's idea of cool may have already changed.

The only thing that stays consistent over time is that today's tastemakers reject what the mainstream and earlier generations deemed cool—that is, until it comes back around again (after skipping a generation). Very few brands attain lasting, sustainable coolness. If they're successful, the brands eventually achieve mainstream popularity . . . which makes them uncool. Their original, die-hard fans usually turn against them. It even happens to quintessential American icons like Elvis. As social critic Kalle Lasn points out:

> Over a twenty-year period, Elvis Presley evolved from the avatar
> of American cool to the embodiment of American excess.

Cool is indefinable.

Most people can only define cool as, "I know it when I see it." It is an extremely finicky concept. It's often ambiguous and always subjective—it lies in the eye of the (cool-hunting) beholder. The definition of cool has changed many times since the term originated in West Africa (where it meant "gentleness of character") and found its way through the Romantic irony of nineteenth-century poets. Today it's the painful wanksta-style of Ali G in his bright-yellow jumpsuits, Hilfiger skullcaps, and wraparound shades. Tomorrow, who knows?

Cool is unquantifiable.

To make matters even worse, in a corporate world of constant data tracking, cool is inherently difficult to measure. It's an attitude that can't be captured with conventional market research. In asking your most loyal supporters whether (and why) they think your brand is cool, you risk losing them by trying to make them feel self-aware about a subconscious feeling. And getting an answer from just one or two people who are capable of articulating their feelings about your brand's cachet won't be of much help, anyway; most marketers want their data in quantity. (You can monitor eBay, however. The number of listings for a brand and the value of the bids serve as good indicators for how passionately fans feel about it.)

THE CAPTURE OF AN ELUSIVE ATTITUDE

At this point, you may be asking yourself, "Is cool even attainable?" Superbrands consultant Marcel Knobil went so far as to create a "Cool Council" to find out. His conclusion:

> Cool is indefinable and unable to be chased. It is primarily in the hands of consumers, is reliant on word-of-mouth, is difficult to maintain and requires constant renewal. It is extremely tough to achieve, but it is achievable.

So if the limitations of cool haven't scared you off yet, and you're willing to do the hard work, let's take a look at how you might achieve this elusive goal. Now remember, the rules of the cool game are constantly changing. We're just talking about some of the ways in which today's brands achieve cool:

Cool brands dare to be imperfect.

While cool brands are unique, they are by no means perfect. In fact, their limitations and eccentric flaws are part of what makes them cool. James Dean was the epitome of cool partly because he constantly struggled with a restlessness that eventually ended in tragedy. Apple has long attained cool partly because users must battle compatibility issues and confront second-tier developer status. Harleys remain cool partly because the bikes are such a pain to ride. Larry David is a surly, middle-aged neurotic who is cool partly because he steals forks from restaurants, traumatizes little kids, and awkwardly admits to getting "naughty" massages. Imperfection breeds cool.

Cool brands excel at leveraging heretical values like "unpolished" and "inconsistent," values that make them endearing and enduring. This breeds credibility in an ever more skeptical, anti-hype marketplace. What a contrast to "15-minutes of fame" brands like the PT Cruiser, a car purposely designed for cool and hype appeal. In spite of its conspicuous Chicago gangster design, the PT Cruiser disappeared from the scene as quickly as it appeared.

Cool brands are visionary.

Cool brands see something others don't. They are extremely observant and intuitive. They have their finger on the pulse of society, and they're not afraid to challenge the norms. As a result, they lead, pushing us into new ways of seeing things.

Brands that redefine categories are cool. Mini regained cool status by celebrating smallness in a category where bigger is better. Viagra has become the hipster's party accessory by breaking taboos.

Cool brands are selfish.

Early in his career Larry David walked out on stage, surveyed the comedy club's audience, said "Never mind," and walked off.

Cool brand owners' most important customers are themselves. Sure, they're trying to make money and sell product. But they don't really care what people think of them and would rather focus on doing their own thing.

Larry David's TV persona is uncompromising and unchanging.

He's never softened the biting tone of his humor to accommodate tastes, even when that tone earned him a *New Yorker* profile that posed the question, "Is Larry David funnier than everyone else, or just more annoying?"

Net, cool brands are detached outsiders who won't sell out.

Cool brands have nothing to prove.

Cool brands are led by people who are trying to bring something they love and appreciate—an experience, a product, an environment—to others. They stand up for their beliefs, even if that means they won't appeal to the masses. These brands follow a set of convictions and a distinct sensibility to create an experience they feel personally passionate about.

Computer designer Jonathan Ive reintroduced cool to the computer industry through his Bauhaus-inspired designs for Apple. But he wasn't going for cool when he did it. He considered simplicity, function, aesthetics, and who knows what else, but never the reactions of a *tastemaker* focus group. Even if he only reached a minority of computer buyers with his designs, that was just fine with him and his boss, Steve Jobs.

Cool brands are like the opposite of the anxious party hostess who spends so much time flitting around making sure things are "perfect" that she makes everyone feel uncomfortable: They are calm and confident that if they stay true to their vision, consumers will come to them. This is bold, brave, and authentic. Cool.

Cool brands fill a need.

Cool brands fill in cultural gaps. Our Creative Director Mark Lewman explains:

> There is something missing, a new thing comes along and addresses that need, and a movement arises. Part of the energy that makes "cool" is from the novelty of its newness, the fuel of creativity as people discover it, interact, and add to it. But somewhere at the root of the movement is . . . need.
>
> Thrift stores were for people who couldn't afford (or refused to buy) off the rack fashion. Punk filled the gap left wide

open by "legitimate" arena rock. Action sports were the anti-
dote to playing on a team. Graffiti writers painted on trains because they couldn't get into galleries.

THE CULTURAL MARKETER VS. THE COOL HUNTER

Many marketers start the search for cool by enlisting the assistance of a
cool hunter, which often ends up in a wasted effort. The most progressive cool hunters team up academics with sixteen-year-old trend spot-
ters. And yet even their findings remain shallow. Global PR powerhouse
Hill & Knowlton enlisted the services of a University of Utrecht
professor only to learn that yes, the iPod was the hottest gadget in
2003 and, get this, celebrities are hot again—especially those with
drama in their lives. (See Nicole Kidman's divorce or 50 Cent's hard-
knock life.)

While discovering that "smirting" means smoking and flirting on
sidewalks or that "Russians are hot" (they pop up in trendy nightclubs,
especially in London) may make some trend-hunters rich, it won't get
your brand hijacked.

The real insight as to what drives successful orchestrated hijacks is
this: These brands take advantage of a significant cultural opportunity,
a need that they realize they can fulfill. It's up to the cultural marketer,
and not the cool hunter, to figure out just what that opportunity is.

FCUK Cool Hunting

Let's play out a hypothetical scenario to illustrate the difference between a fad-generating tactic and a sustainable cultural opportunity.

Take the turnaround of French Connection U.K. in the late 1990s.
It did not materialize because a cool hunter in the form of a seventeen-
year-old hipster from Brighton or South Beach reported seeing college
students wearing sarcastic brand parody T-shirts (which read, for example, "Aberzombie," "Devil Inside," "Just did it," or my personal favorite
"Postal," a shirt illustrated with a Post Office logo battered by gunshots).

The turnaround was guided by a more substantial understanding of a larger cultural phenomenon. French Connection's marketers recognized a major cultural divide in fashion and branding: A growing number of young adults were tired of being walking billboards for mainstream brands. They wanted to stand out and make a personal statement through their clothing choices at a time when fashion lines were all but differentiated by their logos.

And so, French Connection invented a new mantra: *FCUK fashion,* or in less controversial words, *don't be a fashion victim.*

Exploiting the innuendo of the company's initials was ingenious, but quite serendipitous. French Connection had already been using the shorthand in correspondence between the company's London (FCUK) and Hong Kong (FCHK) offices for decades. It just took an opportunistic advertising exec to point out the potential of the abbreviation.

But the brilliance of the mantra was that it was so much more than a provocative play on words. *FCUK fashion* did not become just another hyped slogan or T-shirt line; it became the company's new identity. Iain Webb, *Elle*'s fashion director, recalls:

> When I first saw [FCUK fashion], I was shocked by how such a simple message could be so provocative. It perfectly encapsulates the culturally aware aesthetic of modern youth.

Fashionistas seized the opportunity to make that personal statement with their brand of choice. In just four years, FCUK more than doubled its sales and tripled its operating profit.

Today's brand manager has a tough new job that needs to be well defined. However, it most certainly does not involve philosophizing about topics such as, "If blue is the next black, what is the next blue?" And it should never involve shelling out thousands of dollars to cool hunters to predict, for example, that short haircuts will be the next fad among Seattle hipsters. Cool chasing is definitely not in the next marketer's job description.

The Coolhunter

by Mark Lewman

I prepare trend reports for Fortune 1000 companies.
I am paid to play
the disenfranchised against the disrespected
make the F1000 feel connected
to the cognosumers who reject them,
stuck in the cultural crosshairs.

I package the questions and organize the answers,
emailing the butcher, blackmailing the baker,
sharing the bone marrow with clandestine video game maker.

I tell them about funky black barbers in Memphis
using fire to cut hair.
Swedish teens bored to tears
soaking their tampons in vodka
to get juiced in school.

Crispin Glover joins the Wu Tang Clan
and nobody bothers to understand
but everybody says
dude that's cool.

The revolution
is a bunch of white kids
addicted to database pollution
yelling slogans, brandishing upside down crosses
bearing inverted icons;

Pillsbury wants to update the dough boy and make butter "younger,"
stick that fucker with a fork and call your mother,
scrape the lard from the fat of the land
and leave it smoking in the pan.

And some guy in a conference room in Ohio says into his speakerphone:
"Tell me more about the Krautrock movement and the abstract bands."
I spit out details to counteract,
and wipe my face with my cuff,
generating more fluff,
without concentrating on the end result,
just the next step which is an orchestrated effort to tap into tech step
to sidestep the fact that all packaged goods are the same,
only the name changes.
and the game rearranges and the world Wayne lives in
can be divided into stages, phases, trends, fads, and crazes.

Declare a war on a demographic,
paying top dollar for a guerrilla campaign of street posters placed in
prime places
where kids congregate and pedophiles masturbate to juvenile faces,
services provided by an eco-terrorist graffiti artist specializing in
revitalizing heavy metal.
His brandalism spreads the viruses we peddle:
Kids in custom vans should crave candy and chemicals, rejecting
morals and resting on their laurels,
making fun of Pauly Shore
as they get addicted to death and keep whoring for more.

And some guy in a conference room in Ohio will smile. "This is teen cool
AND mom cool."

What's hot, what's right, what's not in the spotlight?
Hold a focus group and retool, train the pilots to tame the planes
and get ready for a midair refuel.

Do kids really think black is the new brown?
or is platinum the new black?
Who do we assassinate, and what era is ripe for a comeback?

Do you trust me to keep the world on track?

© 2001, Mark Lewman

CHAPTER 6

The Marketer's Guide to the Co-created Hijack

It takes a lot of work to get accidentally discovered by the right people in the right way at the right time.

—Richard Kirshenbaum

Without exception, a hijacking rewrites the job description of a traditional brand manager. The new job is, in a word: *facilitator*. Successful managers enable an ongoing conversation between an engaged consumer base and a distinctive brand. This requires finesse, patience, and a solid understanding of your brand's purpose.

The marketing department as facilitator or gatekeeper. Sounds good. But what, exactly, does it entail? How does a company pull off a co-created hijack? How do you get the market involved in building your brand?

Lead with purpose.

Conventional brands position themselves as providing certain benefits to their consumers. The nuanced marketing of these virtually interchangeable products and services relies mostly on the creation of an *aspirational* image. In other words, the brand owners try to convince you that using or wearing a certain brand will make you, say, seductive or successful.

Hijacked brands, on the other hand, offer consumers something much bigger—meaning within a broad cultural context. As a result, they play a far more *inspirational* role in people's lives. A co-created brand like Harley Davidson signifies a way of life. The famed English soft drink Tango cops an attitude. *Blair Witch* invented an urban myth. Apple sells an entire worldview. Starbucks stopped at no less than creating new social norms.

Brands like these have an inner feel to them, a soul that is brought to life with a distinct persona and distinct sensibilities. They seek to represent an experience and a vibe rather than an image—a purpose. And, as we saw with the example of Red Bull, this message needs to be placed in the right context to be fully understood. Researchers Wendy Gordon and Virginia Valentine call this creating the brand's "moment of identity."

Explore the deeper meaning your brand will have within your community's lifestyle. Then build a sense of belonging around your specific rallying cry.

What that greater purpose is, well, that's something each brand must figure out for itself, either through its visionary leader or with its audience.

Adopt the attitude that everything matters.

When attempting to create a brand that becomes a part of the culture, even the tiniest nuances matter. It's the personal touches that make the difference. So pay attention to detail. Think of your brand like a favorite birthday present. For most of us, it's not the most expensive or extravagant item but the most personal and thoughtful one, such as a handmade card, that leaves the biggest impression.

Starbucks takes this attitude to an extreme. Their former marketing chief, Scott Bedbury, tells this story:

> I once asked Dave [Olsen, the company's Chief Coffee Guru] what was most important to Starbucks. What was the brass ring? Was it the coffee, was it the store, was it the people? He thought for a moment and emphatically answered, "Everything matters."
>
> It occurred to me that Olsen had distilled the entire company and the brand itself into just two words. It was refreshing to hear someone who worked endlessly to procure the world's best product take the broader view, when many companies are

content to take refuge behind their product's features and benefits as their reason for being.

Bedbury labels the Starbucks approach "brand environmentalism." He calls their coffee shops "branded showrooms." Nothing you see, hear, touch, or feel in them is an accident. The company is fanatical about maintaining the highest quality atmosphere in its stores. And so it has deconstructed everything that might stand in the way of the customer having an optimal in-store experience. It banned cigarettes to protect the coffee beans from the odor. It insisted on keeping the less profitable shorter cup rather than introducing a "biggie-size." It even ensured the highest quality of the toilet paper provided in its bathrooms.

Knowing full well that regulars view the stores as a haven for relaxation, Starbucks has, in an ever so subtle way, even changed the way people stand in line. Ever notice how the baristas chat you up while you wait to place an order, and they prepare someone else's concoction? Rather than becoming annoyed at the wait, as you usually would, you're so pleasantly distracted that you hardly notice the six people in line ahead of you.

That's the level of commitment co-created brands demonstrate to their consumers.

Embrace your brand's complexity.

One of marketing's immutable laws has been to keep things simple. To keep them single-minded, focused. Yet the more you get involved with something, the deeper you want to understand it, and the more you want to know of it. That goes for hobbies, for people, and for hijacked brands, as well.

Every brand with a deeper meaning has a timeless story to tell, a hundred different ways of telling it, and millions of willing participants to enhance that story. It is precisely this folklore surrounding a brand that makes it so precious.

Hence, the advantage of hijacked brands lies in their complexity. Embrace it. This empowers consumers to interpret the brand to fit their needs, so that they don't feel like they're being forced to swallow the company line.

Friendster understands this concept well. The big idea behind it was to be "like real life." Its creator, Jonathan Abrams, explains:

> In real life, people wouldn't want to go to a party where everyone was desperate. They want to meet people through people they already know. I wanted to create a way for people to meet over the Internet that was more like real life.

What Abrams has invented is a complex beast. Friendster is a service that means different things to different people, and has many different selling points. It is a dating site for some, a tribal gathering place for others. And some folks simply use it to reinvent themselves, creating a whole new identity. While the gallery may be the preferred feature for people who like to feel as though they are in a human candy store ("Look at all these hot single chicks!"), others gravitate toward the testimonials section. Here, users can pretend like they're back in high school again, writing funny endorsements for their friends that are reminiscent of what they used to say in yearbooks. For those folks who use it to keep in touch with their social network (like our former office manager, who posts for her environmental and animal preservation cause), the bulletin board becomes the most important feature, a way to keep their network up-to-date.

Friendster can serve other functions, as well. Supporters of Matt Gonzalez, San Francisco's Green Party scare to the Democrats in the 2003 mayoral race, used it as a political medium. They posted a profile of him that listed his ambitions (apparently without his knowledge). I found out because I use Friendster for marketing research, and the posting had listed "Doc Martens" as one of Gonzalez's interests. You see, Friendster may well be the next great market research tool for recruiting brand enthusiasts and composing in-depth character studies of them.

Friendster does not have a single-minded value proposition. It has no tag line. It's up to the users to find their own applications for the service. That's why Friendster works.

Next, complexity makes people get deeper into the experience and makes them feel that the brand truly belongs to them.

Create a distinctive voice.

Whereas serendipitous hijacks require a neutral, or at least light, touch, it is important for co-created hijacks to have an innovative yet consistent voice in all their marketing communications. The goal is to signal to consumers that the brand is special and even disruptive.

Most co-created brand hijacks are oppositional in nature, and therefore communicate a shade of rebellion in their voice. Yahoo *yodels*. Tango *shocks England's suburbs*. Nike lives its *intense passion*. Red Bull's *nerdy* cartoon characters grow wiiiings. These are all instantly recognizable signs of the respective brand's persona. A few seconds into a commercial or any other marketing material, and you know which brand is being signaled. All of these communications were groundbreaking in their respective categories (as compared with the naff advertising of completely appropriated brands like In-N-Out). They introduced a new marketing language, and hence stood out.

Since consumers add their own meaning and interpretation to participatory brands, marketing communications should be driven by a tone that is consistent with the brand persona. Hence, a key challenge for the marketing department becomes nailing down the brand voice and sticking to it.

THE CO-CREATED HIJACK IN A NUTSHELL

Welcome to the co-created brand hijack. As we have seen, there are no true accidents here. The brand owner is ultimately responsible for leading a carefully planned and well-structured marketing charge that facilitates the market's collaboration.

The table below summarizes some of the key characteristics of the two types of hijacked brands in comparison with conventional brands. Note that while a serendipitous hijack requires that the brand stay neutral, a co-created hijack requires just the opposite—that the brand stand for a big idea and communicate this purpose in a mold-breaking way.

	SERENDIPITOUS BRAND HIJACK	CO-CREATED BRAND HIJACK	CONVENTIONAL BRAND
Type of Brand	Utilitarian, no-frills	Disruptive, innovative	Conventional, competitive
	Values-driven	Purpose- and persona-driven	Benefit-driven
Brand Leadership	Appropriated by the marketplace; brand owner facilitates	Lets the marketplace in to co-create brand initiatives	Controls the brand
	"Owned" by subcultures	Adopted by subcultures first, then by main market	Chases subcultures; at home in the mainstream
Brand Meaning	Means different things to different groups or people	Celebrates its complexity through many smaller initiatives	Strives for a simple and single-minded proposition through a major campaign
	Blank canvas; battle cry developed by the market	Deeper meaning lead by visionary brand owner	No higher cause; come on, it's just a brand
Marketing Approach	Exclusive Grassroots movement	Sequential target audience and media, from grassroots to mass	Push-down image; mass-marketing
	Driven by brand folklore; Keep communications neutral and exclusive	Collaborative marketing; mix of mold-breaking communications and folklore to a selective audience	Nuanced broadcast media

PART III

THE HIJACK, CORPORATE STYLE

CHAPTER 7

Brand Hijack Candidates

*We're selling more than a cracker here. We're selling the salty,
unctuous illusion of happiness.*

—The Onion

Not every brand is ready to get hijacked. But on the flip side, a hijack candidate does not necessarily have to be a brand targeted at a youth or lifestyle movement. It could be a new technology. It could be the relaunch of an adult beverage. It could be a pharmaceutical (as in the case of Viagra). Nor does a hijack candidate necessarily have to be the product of a company with a maverick or entrepreneur at its helm. Well-established corporations can—and should—adopt the brand hijack mindset as well.

However, that having been said, there is no need to seed the flanker launch of Tide's new fresh scent. That's a competitive move. Incremental improvements to existing products or services do not require the involvement of early markets.

Rather, collaborating with subcultures is an important move for *breakthrough* brands. These are brands that create entirely new markets or have a major cultural impact.

DIFFUSING THE BREAKTHROUGH BRAND

Why do breakthrough brands require a different go-to-market template than traditional brands?

Either because they are so disruptive and new that they will initially scare off the mainstream, and therefore will be adopted only by the most brave and novelty-oriented consumers at first. Or because they require people to make a significant change in their behavior or shift in their outlook.

A top-down approach does not work with breakthrough brands because nothing is more ingrained and harder to change than basic patterns of human behavior and "common sense." Sociologist J. B. Thompson differentiates between the *mediated experience* of mass-communication, which is less relevant to the context of daily life, and the strong, immediate *lived experience,* the "reality" of which consumers take for granted. Breakthrough brands must take the latter approach—they must allow themselves to be hijacked. As John Grant states: "Customers learning and teaching each other is the make or break step in adoption."

Dictating change won't work. Change must evolve out of the marketplace itself.

ARE YOU NEXT?

There are two types of breakthrough brands: the functional "must-have gadget" and the social badge. They represent different types of brands and they involve their consumers in different ways. But both need to open up to collaboration with the marketplace in order to succeed.

THE MUST-HAVE GADGET

The must-have gadget presents a breakthrough in *performance.* It is an unexpected product that over-delivers and enhances the quality of people's lives. We're talking about brands like TiVo, Hotmail, and Viagra. These products are intended for personal use in a relatively private setting. As such, they are not primarily badges; consumers do not use the brands to convey a social message to others.

Early markets play a specific role in the development of functional

FUNCTIONAL MUST-HAVE GADGET	SOCIAL BADGE

■ Offers a breakthrough in performance
  • Establishes a new category
 	
  • Changes the mental map of a category
	■ Is the Next Big Thing
	  • Owns an occasion, attitude, or mood
	  • Becomes part of a particular lifestyle, association, or activity

■ Intended for personal use
  • The brand is driven by consumers' quest for authentic innovations
	■ Highly visible brand
	  • The brand is driven by consumers' desire to be "in-the-know"

■ Early markets test ride the brand and translate its usage for the main market	■ Early markets are trendsetters

breakthroughs: These consumers are the first to test ride the products and translate their usage to the main market.

Must-have gadgets break through in one of two ways:

They establish a new category.

Hotmail was a functional brand that established a new category by offering this breakthrough benefit: free Web-based e-mail service.

Hotmail provided users with an email account for life that they could access from anywhere in the world at no cost. Traditionally, your e-mail had been tied to one PC, either at work or at home. Now, e-mail became mobile. Traditionally, your e-mail address had been temporary. If you changed your job or your service provider, you lost your e-mail address. Now, you could sign up once and never have to worry about your address changing again. Traditionally, your e-mail address had revealed your true identity. Now, you could choose your own screen name and invent a personal profile—you could be whomever you wanted to be.

These benefits were truly revolutionary. Hotmail had what the Japanese call "quality that fascinates" (*miryokuteki hinshitsu*) rather than mere "quality that is expected" (*atarimae hinshitsu*), the absolute minimum that consumers will accept or they will feel cheated.

Much has been made of the advertisement posted at the bottom of each e-mail sent from a Hotmail account: "Get your free e-mail at

Hotmail.com." Marketers often describe it as the trigger for Hotmail's explosive growth. But according to Steve Douty, the company's original head of marketing, such was not the case. Less than 3 percent of users attributed their knowledge of Hotmail to the tagline.

Rather, Hotmail's key growth driver was the unexpected superior product experience it delivered to consumers. This is what led early converts to tell everyone in their personal networks to try out the brand. This is why Hotmail got hijacked.

Douty explained Hotmail's success to me this way:

> It was the reward/reinforcement stimulus. . . . It was truly word-of-mouth that made things jump.
>
> What I mean by reward/reinforcement is how quickly the story is meted out for a particular consumer. That is, one of our key design points for Hotmail was that the time between first learning of it and productively using a Hotmail account was less than one minute. Secondly, we promoted two features—InBox and Compose. So sending messages was also very easy. This caused excitement with the users, and also validated/reinforced the message delivered by the trusted party (word of mouth).
>
> In a way, buzz is essentially a pervasive feeling or communal reputation of a product that is caused by the goodwill of fulfilled expectations. That is, something like "Hey, this really DOES work!"

They redraw the mental map of a category.

While Hotmail offered a new solution, Netflix offered a better solution. It did not establish a new category, but it did redefine the rules of an existing one. Netflix established itself as the better way to rent movies by creating a system that took the frustration out of the traditional rental process.

Let's face it, the Blockbuster store in your neighborhood has serious limitations: an incomplete selection, no guidance as to what to rent, a relatively high charge per rental, and—most annoyingly—late fees. Netflix's business model started with exactly these limitations and offered solutions to each one of them.

While internally billed as a software company (it even did the quintessential tech/dot-com IPO), Netflix is essentially in the customer service business. Its overarching goal is to delight its users. It offers more than twelve thousand titles to choose from—virtually every DVD ever released in the United States. It provides algorithms to provide online guidance, as well as title reviews and pre-grouped browsing. And it ensures idiot-proof returns: A well thought out prepaid envelope comes with each movie rented, so that all the customer has to do is enclose the DVD, seal the envelope, and drop it in a mailbox.

Above all, Netflix charges no late fees. This simple concept has revolutionized the movie rental experience for consumers. Netflix lets customers keep their three DVDs at a time for as long as they want. The company merely waits until a DVD is returned before sending out the next selection in the queue. But it doesn't charge customers a cent for keeping the films they have for a couple of weeks or even a couple of months.

Thanks to Netflix, what used to be an often frustrating, impulsive act can now be interpreted as a relaxing occasion to view a film that you already have on hand. Netflix redrew the mental map of renting movies.

And it did so with a unique marketing approach very appropriate for a breakthrough brand. Foregoing any branding-type marketing, Netflix had the insight that "a great customer experience is the brand." Marketing VP Leslie Kilgore, a former P&G and Amazon employee, focused her entire effort on free trials and peer-to-peer recommendations. "Seventy percent of our trials come from word-of-mouth," she said.

Kilgore makes sure that the trial is easy to sign up for and has no catch. It's a straightforward two-week program, which customers learn about from a "Tell a friend" button on the Netflix Web site, coupons on the inside sleeves of the return envelopes, strategic partnership deals with Web sites such as DVDeasteregg.com, and promo inserts in new DVD players—all no-brainer mechanisms.

Yet that trial—the experience of a tangible difference to the category norm—is what converts people. A whopping 90 percent of trial users become paying members. Kilgore says, "For most people, the light goes on when they return a movie and forget about it, and a couple of days later their next movie is in the mail."

That is the power of delighting your customer with a breakthrough product or service. That is what makes a strong brand hijack candidate.

THE SOCIAL BADGE

The second type of breakthrough brand ripe for hijacking is the social badge. A social badge is a Next Big Thing in waiting. It is a brand that primarily lends status to consumers or allows them to make a statement. It is highly visible and occasionally socially risky. It relies on attaining insider cachet and allowing early markets to define its role.

These brands are trendsetters, dictating, in the words of RoperASW's Ed Keller and Jon Berry, "where to eat and what to buy."

Social badges break through in one of two ways:

They own an occasion, attitude, or mood.

It is no accident that for years the Gap owned "business casual"—it helped invent it. The San Francisco retailer encouraged the casual dress movement and pushed khakis as the movement's uniform of choice.

First, the Gap had to elevate the perception of khakis, which had been viewed as blue-collar or seasonal attire at best. The cloth was originally manufactured for U.S. army uniforms and used as work-wear by civilians. But the Gap pre-seeded the concept of khakis being a classic through its "Legends" campaign. The black and white ads featured old-school stars and celebrities in their khakis. This made the entire concept of wearing khakis to the office acceptable to the mainstream.

Next, the company instituted a program to educate corporate HR departments about the dos and don'ts of casual dressing. This initiative culminated in a highly visible marketing coup when, in 1997, the Gap hosted a casual Friday for the three thousand traders at the New York Stock Exchange. The televised event signaled to the rest of America that business casual was here to stay and that the Gap was at the vanguard of the movement.

Finally, the company followed up with its now famous khakis TV commercials, which featured young office workers dancing and jiving in their beige cotton pants. The "Khakis Rock" campaign captured the optimism of the dot.com era and its casual new dress code perfectly.

Consumers enthusiastically went along with the business casual movement and the Gap's role in it. The initiative fueled the Gap's growth in the late 1990s, helping double category sales to $1 billion in three years (that is, until the Gap bought into its own hype and lost its position as cultural leader).

They become part of a particular lifestyle, association, or activity.

Mountain Dew Code Red became synonymous with black urban youth culture when Pepsi executed a co-created hijack of the brand in 2001. Instead of going for the hard sell, Pepsi started small and created a sense of authenticity for the brand. It made the drink available only in urban convenience stores, and only in single-serve sizes that were conducive to trials and the on-the-go lifestyle of urban teens. More important, it seeded the brand with the right trendsetters, sending samples to sports insiders and DJs. Through the Pirate Radio Tour, urban youth could listen to their favorite local DJs, dance, and chill out as they tried the new drink.

Only later did Pepsi launch a conventional media campaign. It recruited hip-hop stars Macy Gray and Busta Rhymes and NBA stars Chris Webber and Tracy McGrady to help write and star in radio and TV ads. Though the delay was unintentional, it actually served to help foster Code Red's insider, low-key image, which was appropriate for the target market's lifestyle.

Does your brand qualify for a hijack? And if so, how will you ever pull it off, if you happen to work within a large corporation?

CHAPTER 8

The Marketer's Guide to the Corporate Hijack

You must unlearn what you have learned.

—Yoda, *The Empire Strikes Back*

Is corporate America excluded from pulling off brand hijacks? We've seen how brand hijacks happen mostly in entrepreneurial, independent environments. Is it possible for large corporations to win consumers over and convince them to participate in the creation of brand meaning?

Managing a breakthrough brand is not the same as maintaining a conventional brand. It requires a more intuitive, unconventional approach, one that has not been broadly codified in the marketing literature or by corporate training departments. When they try to engage in a hijacking, many corporations discover that it's not as easy to commit marketing heresy as they originally thought. This is one of the reasons so many companies sitting on potential brand gold mines cannot turn that potential into sustainable success.

Big companies tend to be hindered in their attempts at brand hijacks by the ghosts of conventional marketing. They easily fall prey to the following mistakes:

They misinterpret the reasons for success.

Unconventional brand success stories tend to stump large corporations. While many of the giants have tried to understand the magic behind hijacked brands like Starbucks, Red Bull, and Napster, rarely have they discerned or aptly applied the lessons.

That doesn't keep corporate marketers from routinely citing these examples in an attempt to inspire the rank and file. Corporate marketing departments read the case studies of breakthrough brands like bibles. The problem is that most of their analyses are riddled with misinterpretations.

The Blair Witch Project, for example, has probably wreaked more havoc on the world of marketing than any case study since Bill Bernbach's groundbreaking advertising work for VW in the '60s. A former senior exec at P&G admitted:

> P&G went through a state where it was all about seeding and unconventional approaches. The BIG case study was *The Blair Witch Project.* Several brands then tried this approach, including Physique [a premium-priced line of hair care products] in the U.S. After a year, they looked at the data and concluded— shit, we've got incredibly low awareness!
>
> I think it all depends what you are trying to achieve. Physique wanted to be a major player—and hence needed a more conventional approach. But if you're starting a new category and are willing to be patient, then the stealth approach makes every sense.
>
> The risk of big bang is that you spend all the money and it doesn't work. Risk of stealth is that you never get off the ground.

One aspect of *Blair Witch*'s success that P&G may have missed with the Physique campaign is that a seeding strategy must go mainstream after its launch. While the initiative should begin with getting an exclusive early market deep into the brand experience through subconscious techniques, the strategy must change over time to draw in the mass market. When the brand is ready to hit the mainstream, conventional marketing techniques should be used to create awareness and reassure more risk-averse consumers.

They rely on "proven" managers.

Big companies often place breakthrough brands in the hands of "proven" managers—executives who have earned their status by sustaining or growing static or evolutionary brands in a traditional marketing fashion. But if a hijacked brand is managed with a "business as usual" mentality, it is sure to fail.

Executing a brand hijack requires a whole new skill set. It takes facilitation, an intuitive sense of the early market, a confident patience, and a light touch. These are not the sorts of skills taught in business schools or marketing textbooks. Which means that corporate marketing departments—no matter how well intentioned the staff—are often ill equipped to handle breakthrough brands.

They measure success by the wrong standards.

When launching a new brand, most companies typically look at traditional measures such as brand awareness, sales volume, and weighted distribution. But these metrics are irrelevant when disseminating a brand idea through early markets, before reaching the mainstream. For hijacked brands, growth happens in a curve: slow at first, exploding exponentially only once the mass market has bought into the trend. So if the performance of breakthrough brands is judged by the old standards alone, the hijack is doomed to be put to halt before it even has a chance to succeed.

For instance, it is considered sacrilege for a company to ask a salesperson to forego a sale. And yet that's exactly what Puma did. In its successful bid at a consumer takeover, Puma refused to allow its shoes to be sold into discounters like Footlocker. The company felt that offering the shoes on sale would diminish the brand's cachet. Certainly this decision negatively affected sales volume and distribution numbers over the short term. But over the long term, the counterintuitive tactic worked—Puma has reemerged as a major player in athletic wear. Claims Puma's CEO Jochen Zeitz, "One of the reasons we are successful today is because we went a completely different route."

Managers planning a hijack must establish new internal and external benchmarks to evaluate its likelihood of success. Internal measures— like whether the company's management buys into the unorthodox go-to-market template and whether corporate behavior and mindset have changed—should tell the manager whether a hijack is even possible within the company's structure.

External measures should be qualitative and attitudinal, indicating whether or not a brand idea can gain Next Big Thing status. As such, they should monitor whether the selected early markets show an affinity for the brand, and whether the brand has the ability to gain scale within these markets to "tip" toward ever-larger markets.

TOSS OUT THE "IMMUTABLE LAWS OF MARKETING"

It's true that most of our previous examples of brand hijacks, both serendipitous and co-created, came from entrepreneurial companies. But the basic principles still can be applied within the established corporate context. For the most part, big companies attempting a brand hijack should follow a similar path as start-ups. They just should anticipate requiring a hefty dose of passion, patience, and a willingness to battle convention along the way in order to see the initiative through.

Corporations will need to develop an entirely new mindset when using this approach to launch a new product. First and foremost, it requires a willingness to let go. . . . But beware, there are many more heretical headlines forthcoming:

A brand hijack cannot be controlled, only guided.

PepsiCo's Mountain Dew Code Red is not only the most successful launch of a brand in the company's history, but it may also serve as an internal, and even external, case study for how to launch brands right. But—without taking too much away from the marketing team's efforts—it must be said that *the hijack really happened by accident rather than by design.*

Code Red's launch had been carefully planned. But a major element of the brand's success came about as the result of an *involuntary* delay in TV advertising. Initially, Pepsi and its agency, BBDO, could not agree on an ad campaign. Once the ad was shot, the companies could not obtain release signatures from members of the cast. And so the release of the ad was postponed. Instead of relying on traditional TV advertising, PepsiCo seeded the product in the inner city. Its early adoption by the urban market contributed substantially to Code Red's eventual mainstream popularity.

When a brand uses an early market to help disseminate ideas into the mainstream, marketers give up the driver's seat. Market involvement requires flexibility and tolerance for inconsistency. The consumers' portrayal of a brand may not always match what was planned in the meeting room. Dealing with each new incarnation requires brand managers who have the willingness and imagination to reinvent the brand at the drop of a hat. Not an ideal scenario for the standard set of control freaks in the marketing department.

Remember, a marketing department may be able to control its agencies, but it cannot control the market.

A brand hijack requires patience to achieve broad results.

"How long will this take?" is a reasonable, but not especially helpful, question to ask when pulling off a hijack. Time frames cannot be predicted. Sometimes things take off in no time, as was the case with Hotmail, Mountain Dew Code Red, and the British positioning of IKEA at the center of modern taste. Sometimes they just appear as instant successes, even though they took years to prepare. Krispy Kreme, for example, was an overnight sensation seventy years in the making.

Gerard Tellis, a professor of American Enterprise at USC, conducted a study on the takeoff time of new products. He measured how long it takes, on average, for a product to suddenly accelerate toward the main market after slow initial sales with early adopters. The shocking result: six years. Timing depends on variables such as how interconnected the early market subcultures are and how viral the product is. Tellis warns: "Managers may pull the plug on a product before it has a chance to take off."

Companies following a "seeding" campaign strategy will have to demonstrate commitment, learn to be patient, and not go mainstream too early, or they'll ruin all their good work.

Entertainment insider Bob Lefsetz illustrated this concept in one of his rants against a record label:

> The key is not to do a John Mayer. As many people as LIKE John Mayer HATE him. Because he's been shoved down their throats. Looked goofy in videos. Been on the Grammys. I mean how much can you believe in the guy, he seems to be molded by his handlers.
>
> But if his album had been released without fanfare, and

there were NO videos, and NO effort at Top Forty radio, god, he'd have a cult of BELIEVERS! They'd be telling EVERYONE they knew. God, have you HEARD this guy? He's fantastic!

And they'd spin the CD for you. Now you don't spin the John Mayer CD for anybody. Everybody's HEARD IT! Oh, not at first. He WAS broken on the net. But, the label put the metal to the pedal.

An Exercise in Patience: A Political Hijacking Case Study

Major corporations looking to encourage a consumer takeover should take a cue from perhaps the most high-profile brand hijack in political history: the 2004 presidential campaign of Howard Dean.

A political unknown just one year before the campaign began, Dean had already been seeding his ideas with die-hard Democrats who were searching for a fresh face for years. As early as 2000, he made exploratory trips to New Hampshire to hobnob with key party activists in a state notorious for making or breaking a presidential candidate's hopes.

Once he'd decided to make a go of it, Dean turned to his natural early market (or in this case, constituency): the gay community. As the first governor ever to sign a law acknowledging same-sex partnerships, Dean gained early credibility with this population. His advisors later told *The Washington Post* that gay men and women organized every fundraiser Dean attended outside of his home state of Vermont in 2002. The community spread the Dean message peer-to-peer. According to his finance director, Stephanie Schriock:

> *[Gays were] the first to recognize Dean's strength of character after his leadership on Vermont's civil union legislation, and because of that they were the first to open up their homes for events and ask their friends and colleagues to give money to this endeavor.*

In early 2003, Dean made a play at another group of trendsetters and rainmakers: the Hollywood elite. The entertainment industry was the fifth-largest source of cash for federal candidates in the 2002 election, and more than 80 percent of those funds went to Democrats. Getting early backing in Hollywood

(cont'd)

was crucial for a candidate whose name three-quarters of Democratic voters didn't recognize. Dean won the support of Martin Sheen, Rob Reiner (a $4.5 million man in the 2000 election), and others. These funds helped move Dean away from fringe-y Kucinich territory to top-tier status.

Then something happened that enabled the mass market (or mainstream voter) to truly participate in building the Dean brand: Dean's first campaign manager quit and was replaced by Joe Trippi. The Silicon Valley vet made sure the operation was wired for blogging and raising money online, not so much as a point of strategy, but as one of financial necessity. Never mind that Dean himself asked, "What's a blog?" The campaign relied on listservs, Web logs, and Web sites to organize its constituents. Joe Trippi's regular morning e-mails to supporters were, for many, the official face of the campaign.

Members of this internet-based support group talked incessantly to each other. They didn't wait for direction from the campaign to take action, either. A bunch of fans in Atlanta made their own "Georgians for Dean" business cards and passed them out freely to reporters. Supporters argued online about what campaign fliers should say and where they should be passed out. A special lingo even developed. Deanheads: hippies for Dean. Deanie Babies: young Dean fans out on their first campaign. Deanocrats: old-timers drawn to Dean's firebrand liberalism.

It took a business magazine to point out what was happening. *Fast Company*'s Linda Tischler wrote:

> *The campaign's strategy is one that nimble companies have been using for years: give staffers on the ground the authority to make decisions tailored to their markets without having to check back constantly with the home office. But it's a radical, and some would say risky, way to organize a campaign, where control is usually fanatically guarded. "Most campaigns have real top-down controls," says Carol Darr, director of the Institute for Politics, Democracy and the Internet, at George Washington University. "They're apoplectic about people not speaking for the campaign, afraid that somebody will say something that will reflect badly on the candidate."*
>
> *But letting go of that control has benefits as well. By unleashing*

thousands of people to spread the word to friends, neighbors, and fellow citizens, a campaign could grow faster and more viscerally than through any other medium.

Once fully hijacked, the Dean campaign became a completely different animal—one that the centrist, NRA member, Wall Streeter-turned-doctor could not have predicted. The louder Dean turned up the volume on his antiwar rhetoric, the more support he got. The fact that he'd entered the race as the health care candidate was quickly forgotten. So it was that Dean became the anti-war, internet, insurgent candidate. A candidate with a "movement" behind him. A candidate who was on a roll . . .

But then Dean made his pivotal blunder. By August 2003, the mainstream press had picked up the Dean story and plastered it everywhere. Dean appeared on the cover of *Time* and *Newsweek*. Why was this a problem? Still four months out from the first test in Iowa, he could no longer pull a Jimmy Carter (whose Iowa campaign slogan had been "Jimmy who?" and after whose 1977 campaign Dean had modeled his strategy)—Dean was now the frontrunner.

Hijacked because of his fresh, daring, and fringe appeal, Dean thought he could continue to play "the democratic wing of the democratic party" as the lead candidate. Instead, he became Al Gore circa 2000—and he was getting the same treatment from the press. His every whoop and holler played into his live wire, hothead image. By the time the Iowans caucused in January, Dean's faults and flubs were common knowledge and his face was considerably less fresh. He placed a dismal third place, and second in New Hampshire a week later. The next day, Trippi resigned from the campaign, and a Washington insider was brought in as a replacement. The period of innovation was over. The campaign spiraled downward from there.

Had he been able to stay under the radar longer, Dean well could have become the ultimate hijack case study.

A brand hijack thrives on a big social idea rather than detailed positioning.

It's time to say good-bye to the value proposition. When I worked at P&G, we judged advertising ideas by whether they were distinctive, provocative, and sustainable. We looked for a clear, if marginal, difference from the competition: "*Better than . . . because . . .*"

Marketing managers simply will have to let go of the question, "So, what is the differentiating positioning?" because hijacked brands tick differently. They tap into basic ideas that are so fundamental they seem mundane, like Starbucks' "You deserve a better coffee experience," Nike's "We better be court-worthy," and Apple's "Man should be above systems and structures, not subordinate to them." And then they deliver on the promise of that idea with fanatical attention to detail.

Diesel Jeans lives up to its "The World According to Diesel" mantra by aiming to be "one hundred percent Diesel" to make their dream of *Successful Living* a reality. Says Diesel's visionary, Renzo Rosso:

> You need to be perfect in every aspect—in the window, in every square foot of the store. Even ten years ago it was enough to just create the product and the advertising. Now you need to produce a total environment, a world in which everything fits together. We started selling jeans, and now we are selling a way of life.

A brand hijack requires major orchestration, from start to finish.

Successes like those of Saturn, Starbucks, *Blair Witch,* and Viagra don't happen by accident. They are extremely well planned events, which are orchestrated years before the actual launch with an attention to detail that would surprise most outsiders. Joe Kennedy, Saturn's EVP of Marketing and Sales, took on that position a full five years prior to the product's launch at General Motors.

The greatest misunderstanding conventional marketers have about hijacked brands is the appearance of lack of marketing investment. Even though a brand like Starbucks may not have funded major ad campaigns, its brand development budgets rivaled those of any major brand in the United States. They just chose to spend their time and money creating an invaluable, personal consumer experience rather than developing impersonal mass-marketing tools.

A brand hijack utilizes the medium as message.

Media has come a long way from the days when it was nothing more than a GRP-counting afterthought. It will soon be at the center of marketing planning. It has become part of the message, underscoring the brand persona and providing the necessary context to understand what role the brand plays in people's lives.

Nike's *Book of Lies* is an ironic supplement appearing in European women's fashion magazines. It lists a false female athlete stereotype, such as "I don't care about winning or losing, I just want to participate," and juxtaposes this with a contradictory photo image, such as that of Mary Pierce holding up a trophy. The campaign has single-handedly brought credibility to the brand in a submarket that had thus far rejected Nike.

Media planning is evolving into a conceptual, creative, and intuitive discipline at the heart of the marketing plan, rather than a back-end execution. In the future, media planners will likely be the most dynamic part of the marketing communications sector, taking a center role next to brand planners and creatives as the strategic sparring partners for brand owners.

When asked what she would like to change about the advertising industry, ESPN's marketing chief, Lee Ann Daly, replied, "I would challenge them to use the media strategy as the driving force for the work they do, as opposed to the creative idea."

I believe that the media roadmap is becoming an important tool in planning. The roadmap lays out the sequence of events for seeding an initiative. It begins with outlining how the brand managers will facilitate early markets in discovering and helping shape the brand idea, and concludes with the point at which they turn the switch to mass marketing. As with *Blair Witch*—whose marketers orchestrated every aspect of the media from the first rumor-spreading Web site and TV mention of the myth to the eventual cable feature "documentary"—the roadmap becomes part of the message and determines its evolution.

A brand hijack lets go of the conventional definition of quality.

In a brand hijack, quality is still crucial, but redefined. It's not about the better technology; it's simply about the better experience. It's brand ideation, but not from the product developer's perspective.

Take the LOMO, or rather the *Leningrdskoye Optiko-Mekhanicheskoye Ob'edinyeniey*—an outdated Russian camera with four frames per exposure that requires no preparation before taking shots. The camera was suddenly adopted by Viennese hipsters around 1991, and soon become the darling of the alternative art world, finding supporters in such celebrities as Brian Eno and David Byrne. Rather than using it as a conventional camera, users took advantage of its low-tech approach to create a unique style of photography. One of the art movement's leaders, Matthias Fiegl, explains:

> Lomography has an anarchic approach to the world of pictures. It's about fast shots, impossible perspectives, gloomy and spectacular colors, anonymity. The whole Lomo thing doesn't care if it's art or not.

A brand hijack requires the ideators to forget their engineering backgrounds and think about how their product can benefit the community. According to this definition, a high-quality product is one that has carefully fine-tuned what meaning it wants to have with specific groups, and then is executed with that goal in mind.

A brand hijack embraces the consumer as peer rather than as "target."

Consumers of hijacked brands are looking for a meaningful connection to the product. This connection is established through a common value system rather than a common demographic denominator, or even a psychographic one. Hijackers establish communities around a brand because they believe the brand believes in them.

Marketers therefore need to humanize their targeting exercises. After all, you can't collaborate with a statistic. You can't co-create your brand with a "twenty-one- to thirty-five-year-old white, suburban, college-educated professional." But you can collaborate with a group of people that share a set of values.

Furthermore, it is hard to define an audience for hijacked brands, especially through traditional segmentation techniques. Take the Coachella music festival, for instance. How could you possibly segment that market? How does the sixteen-year-old raver kid fit into the same segment as the forty-year-old music lover dying to see a Pixies reunion one last time?

Not by fitting them into any of our preexisting "target audience" boxes. The lesson here: Don't define your audience. Create them.

My team was working on a project for a major brand of whiskey. Our goal was to reestablish the custom of drinking scotch. Rather than going after the typical whiskey target market of over-thirty-five-year-olds, we took a look at what common values whiskey drinkers might share. Our team identified as our target consumer the "reluctant grown-up," a Peter Pan, arrested development-type caught in the struggle between living life large and being a responsible adult.

Next, we explored this conceptual consumer community in more depth. We found literature that described our Peter Pan in a charming way—Dan Zevin's *The Day I Turned Uncool*. This hilarious parody revealed precisely the mindset we were hoping to capture with our campaign:

> Out of nowhere came the day we developed a disturbing new interest in lawn care. The day we ordered Pinot Grigio instead of Pabst. The day we refused to see any concert where we could not sit down.
>
> I speak, of course, of the day we turned uncool.
>
> Not too long ago, if you asked me to hook you up with free tickets, or a fake ID, or a summer sublet, I'd give you ten people to call off the top of my head. Now I find myself recommending exterminators. Need a roofer?
>
> To tell you the truth, I can't believe I've turned into that type of individual. I still think of myself as young and with-it, which, obviously, I am not. I mean, reread that last sentence. Who says "with-it"?
>
> I tell you who. Practicing members of the adult-oriented lifestyle—a crowd I've never felt particularly comfortable with.
>
> I suppose I am what you'd call a reluctant grown-up, living in a perpetual state of astonishment that, yes, it is really me who has somehow become one of those responsible neighbors who always buys enough Halloween candy.

Reading Zevin made our consumers real to us, personable and part of a community we would like to be part of ourselves, rather than abstract targets. We then moved on to identify their media habits. We learned that the reluctant grown-up tends to read both *Maxim* and *Good Parenting*. And that said it all. In this way, we began to truly understand our partners-in-crime and became genuinely interested in working with them.

A brand hijack preserves its magic rather than exposing it.

A brand hijack is driven by a distinct community that creates folklore around the brand. Something special and magical happens to these brands. It might seem that the logical next step would be to acknowledge that community and market its folklore to a larger audience so that they could share in the magic. But doing so could be a mistake.

Brand strategist Ivan Wicksteed points out that brands with highly valued social groups, like BMW or Mercedes, often appear to do very little to recognize their community as a whole—preferring instead to address them as individuals. The fact is, nobody likes to be treated like a number. But even more so, acknowledging the group would betray much of both the brand's and the community's magic. Once you expose how special a hijacked brand is, you remove all that is magical about it, and ruin it for its insiders.

Take Starbucks' 2004 initiative to "Customize Your Cup." It is an in-store event supported by a print campaign, which is intended to educate the general public about the rituals (and snob-appeal) of Starbucks. And it will likely backfire. Brad Stevens, a Starbucks marketer, justifies the program this way:

> There are still a lot of people to whom we can introduce the joys of espresso. And [an initiative] like this will help our new customers understand and uncover the fun of being a fan of espresso. It's really about fun.

Actually, it is about betraying the special status loyal insiders have built up over time to be part of the inner coffee circle. Salon writer Dale Hrabi rightfully asked: "Are Americans too dumb to order their 'grandes' and 'ventis' without a 22-page instruction manual? Starbucks says yes!"

Ad Age's editor-in-chief Rance Crain puts a final spin on it:

Each person takes away his or her own experience with a brand, and advertising often has a difficult time mirroring that experience. That's why Starbucks doesn't often use traditional ads, and when it does, it actually has a negative influence.

The Counter-Intuitive Nature of Brand Hijacks

ROUTINE BRAND MANAGEMENT	HIJACKED BRAND MANAGEMENT
• Is about *branding*	• Is about subtle *seeding;* branding comes later
• Is about volume and profit	• Initially sacrifices volume and profit for getting the *right* people *deep* into the experience
• Is inclusive and aims for as many users as possible	• Is exclusive, making it challenging for people to experience the brand; this will foster deeper passion
• Is about one-way broadcasting through mass media	• Is about letting the market participate as co-creators of their brand initiatives

CREST SMILES

Every so often, large corporations get it right. Corporate hijacks are sometimes driven by a lucky break (like Mountain Dew Code Red) or by necessity (like Saturn's need to distance itself from Detroit's self-destructive way of doing business, or Kamel Red's search for new marketing channels). But sometimes companies actually let a team of innovators loose on a hijackable initiative.

Just look at the triumph of Crest Whitestrips, P&G's most successful product launch in twenty years.

When it introduced the do-it-yourself teeth-whitening product, P&G threw out the old marketing model. The brand manager, Vince Hudson, fresh from his stint in e-commerce sales, convinced executives to use the web to distribute the new product before it was available at retail. Hudson thought this would allow word-of-mouth to develop, creating a buzz.

Plus, information the company collected from the site would help P&G discover and go after its target markets. The Crest team around Oral Care GM Ayman Ismail also engaged in many other small yet carefully planned initiatives, which helped spread product awareness.

By the time of the retail launch in May 2001, P&G had already created a 35 percent awareness level of Whitestrips. Sales of the product reached $200 million in the first year. P&G also was able to democratize a previously costly and inconvenient personal care regime and, in so doing, create a whole new category in the dental care industry.

Just how did P&G pull it off?

It pre-seeded the concept behind the brand.

At the time the product was developed, teeth whitening was hardly a widespread practice in the United States. Less than 5 percent of the population had ever undergone a treatment. Therefore, P&G had not only to generate awareness for Whitestrips; it also had to sell Americans on the concept of teeth whitening.

In order to do this, P&G recruited dentists to sell the whitening kits in their offices. The company figured that patients would be more receptive to the concept of teeth whitening if they were in a context associated with dental care. Moreover, they'd be more likely to try the product when a trusted authority figure was backing it up.

In addition, P&G engaged in a PR campaign targeted at health and beauty magazines, encouraging them to cover the new teeth-whitening trend. The PR agency estimated that it generated around 400 million media impressions before the retail launch.

It let the consumer "discover" the product.

Whitestrips were available on the internet a full eight months before their retail launch. This long lead time proved critical in allowing the early market to feel as though it had discovered and championed the product on its own.

The strategy was simple: Get the word out about the website, and let consumers take it from there. To build web traffic, P&G spent over $2 million in print advertising and cross-merchandised with other Crest products. Over the next eight months, visits to the site increased, indicating that the early market had taken the bait. In fact, the site's conversion rate grew to 12 percent, four times the industry average.

These enthusiastic early consumers also played a crucial role in promoting Whitestrips to others. "The best salespeople are the users," said P&G manager Rich Kiley. The average consumer referred five friends.

It targeted specific subcultures.

In public, P&G downplays how much money it spent to support the retail launch of Crest Whitestrips—$50 million. But instead of going after Middle America (like the old days), the company focused its early marketing initiatives on several specific subcultures.

Through its Web site, P&G had discovered that gay men, brides, teenage girls, and young Hispanics were its most ardent consumers. So those are the groups it initially went after. Jim Stengel, P&G's marketing chief, explained:

> All four of those targets you can go after laserlike. We were all over bridal shows. We were very targeted wherever we went. If we see an event where bright smiles will be noticed and newsworthy and consumers will be watching, we want to be there.

P&G took a holistic approach in its wooing of these subcultures. Take, for example, how it targeted the gay community. It put up print ads, posters, and postcards in bars, restaurants, and health clubs. It used the Smile Team, a group of hunky men with beautiful smiles, to spread the message in gay neighborhoods like the Castro in San Francisco. It sent a sampling team to the New York Gay Journalists Association holiday party. And it also sponsored film festivals and Pride Parades in various cities.

It kept momentum going with several small initiatives.

P&G did not rely on any one tactic, but instead used several small initiatives to generate word-of-mouth and awareness. An online program gave consumers three dollars off for each friend they referred. A Web-based "Reveal Your Whiter Smile" contest encouraged existing users to stay engaged with the brand over time (which was crucial since Whitestrips need only be used every six months). In 2001, P&G gave gift boxes to the Academy Awards nominees a few weeks before the big night. A few celebrities showed off their freshly sparkling teeth and mentioned Whitestrips on television.

Within two years—and an unusually stealthy launch—Crest had turned the teeth-whitening category from a $50 million business to a $600 million business.

The Corporation That Cares

Alongside the internal management hurdles, corporations wanting to pull off a hijack may face consumer perception problems. Sure, it's easy for a young upstart like Napster to appear altruistic and consumer driven—it started with a blank slate. It's not so easy for a Fortune 500 company to erase years of history. Still, consumers' stereotypes can be altered slowly over time.

Having consumers perceive you as a "corporation that cares" is often a precursor to co-creation. But what does this mean? Harvard's *Mind of the Market Laboratory* studied consumers' expectations for corporations that have "consumers' best interest at heart," and came up with a list of characteristics.

We can venture to say that a company with these characteristics is best positioned for a hijack:

It appears to be evolving.

The company continuously develops and fine-tunes the relationship between the consumer and itself. This involves believing that the relationship is enduring and dynamic, as well as a "two-way-street." The company and consumer learn from one another and adapt their behavior accordingly.

It appears honest.

The logic here is obvious: If a company provides straightforward and truthful information about its products, consumers will appreciate its honesty and be more loyal to its brand.

It appears innovative and creative.

The company attempts to continuously develop new products or services that improve its ability to satisfy consumer interest and needs. If a company demonstrates an ability to think differently, to switch frameworks and function in a range of situations, consumers tend to believe these things are done on their behalf. Innovation shows openness to unconventional ideas instead of rigorous adherence to the status quo.

It appears to have strong moral character.

The company recognizes the potential good and bad outcomes of its business practices, and acts ethically.

It appears to have a proactive orientation.

The company tries to preempt any problems by looking ahead, keeping in mind all possible outcomes and preparing accordingly.

One other crucial characteristic not mentioned in the study but found in all our analyses of hijacked brands is:

It appears to have an altruistic nature.

The company seems to have a loftier goal in mind than mere short-term profits and stockholder values, and it acts accordingly. That's the difference between "*The Cult of Mac*" and *Micro$oft*. As *Wired*'s Leander Kahney explains:

> There's a common perception that Gates is in business for every penny he can get, while Apple exists to create great technology—to change the world, in Steve Jobs' words. For Apple, turning a profit is secondary.

Letting the market collaborate in the management of your brand may be counterintuitive, especially to conventional brand managers. But the fact is, it builds stronger brands. Instead of *communicating*—or rather dictating—brand meaning to the market, brand hijacking *communes* with—or rather guides—the market to a common understanding.

It's a new brand era. It requires a new mind-set.

CHAPTER 9

The Dawn of the Next Marketing Era

Everything else has been reinvented—distribution, new product development, the supply chain. But marketing is stuck in the past. While consumers have changed beyond recognition, marketing has not.

—*The Economist*

An obvious question left to explore is: WHY? Why do consumers hijack brands? What are the factors contributing to the need for us to take a fresh look at marketing and its *immutable* laws?

To start with, let's explore the social context we live in and come to terms with the new state of the Western world.

LIVING IN A CONSUMER CULTURE

Consumer culture, a culture in which brands create purpose and give our lives meaning, is replacing popular culture, a culture in which brands serve merely as a form of entertainment. In this day and age, that statement is neither radical, controversial, nor, necessarily, critical.

Take Pets.com, for example. The company may have been a business failure, but the sock puppet had his fifteen minutes and more. He marched in the Macy's Thanksgiving Day parade and was interviewed on *Good Morning, America.* A Budweiser float appeared in President Clinton's inaugural parade. Our sacred love for college sports now climaxes with the likes of the Chick-fil-A Peach Bowl and the Crucial.com Humanitarian Bowl. Many people profess to watch the Super Bowl for the commercials rather than for the game itself.

Meanwhile, just look at what's happening in the music industry. Coca-Cola has indeed taught the world to sing. In Europe, Levi's was able to catapult virtually every song it used in its ads throughout the '90s to a Top 10 hit. It didn't matter whether the song was an oldie making a comeback, like Steve Miller's "The Joker," or a newly released one-hit wonder, like "Underwater Love" by Smoke City. In fact, Levi's agency, BBH, incubated a music-publishing firm for unsigned talent, called Leap.

Busta Rhymes was single-handedly responsible for the reemergence of an Allied Domecq Cognac with the release of his 2002 hit single, "Pass the Courvoisier." And he did it without any financial support from the distiller.

We gon' tell that brotha, pass the Courvoisier
We gon' tell that brotha, pass the Courvoisier
Everybody sing it now, pass the Courvoisier
Everybody sing it now, pass the Courvoisier.

The irony is that Busta actually drinks Hennessy, yet preferred how the name Courvoisier sounded in his lyrics. Which begs the question: Is the brand co-opting the artist, or is the artist co-opting the brand?

Recording artist Alana Davis serves as another illustration of what it means to be living in a consumer culture. Disillusioned with her contract and "The Man" in general, she left Elektra Records, and immediately found herself a more appealing home. Of it, she said:

You want everyone to like you, and you don't want to sell out. For me, to be able to sing a great song and not have someone hire a choreographer or have to worry about my image—it's much purer.

This "purer gig," this alternative to "selling out," happened to be making a recording of Crosby, Stills, Nash & Young's classic song "Carry On" for a Sony Camcorder TV commercial.

No wonder San Francisco's cutting edge marketing shop Agenda attained notoriety by creating *American Brandstand,* which tracks all the mentions of brand names that appear in the lyrics of Billboard Top 20 songs. The rapper 50 Cent appeared most brand-obsessed: He dropped the names of thirty-one different brands into his six 2003 hits, ranging from AK assault rifles to Payless Shoe Stores, the Maybach luxury car, and Ramada Inns. On the brand side of the equation, Mercedes blew away the competition with a whopping 112 mentions in hit singles throughout the year. Among entertainment marketers, *American Brandstand* has become a key barometer of brand relevance in youth culture. It's enough to "make Naomi Klein choke on her Fairtrade mochaccino," mused *The London Sunday Times.*

Brands as Culture

Branding has clearly crossed the cultural chasm. Ads have become art, and art has become advertising. Think Andy Warhol. Think Absolut Vodka. Think *The Bulgari Connection,* a book that the jewelry maker commissioned bestselling author Fay Weldon to write. Think TV soap operas, so called because they were created and produced by Procter & Gamble as a vehicle for reaching housewives.

We live in the age of commercialism. America is no longer a country but a multi-million dollar brand. Says Kalle Lasn:

> American culture is no longer created by the people. Our stories, once passed from one generation to the next by parents, neighbors and teachers, are now told by distant corporations with "something to sell as well as to tell." Brands, products, fashions, celebrities, entertainments—the spectacles that surround the production of culture—*are* our culture now.

Some of our craft's efforts may be deemed irresponsible. But marketing as a catalyst for cultural development is not necessarily a bad thing. People like to be entertained by advertising and marketing as a whole. Furthermore, they are clearly passionate about hijacked brands.

At a 2003 *Ad Age* conference, Coca-Cola's Steve Heyer stunned his audience by admitting that Coke sees itself as both entertainment and vehicle for influencing pop culture. The bottle is a medium, he said, "to open a movie, popularize and sell new music . . . and maybe . . . charge [the entertainment and media industries], like [they] charge us."

Branding can no longer be reduced to differentiation, a simple attempt to get consumers to either conform or distinguish themselves within their peer groups. Brands have infiltrated our lives more deeply and are driving the very shape of our culture.

Brands as Moral Signposts

Once upon a time, in the days before mass media, heightened superficiality, and consumerism, life was easy. Our social roles were handed down to us from previous generations in the shape of norms and respected institutions. We each had a clear, predetermined identity and role in society that shaped how we lived.

But then we rebelled and set ourselves free to choose our own lifestyles and our own identities. And with this freedom came a hefty price tag. According to sociologist Anthony Giddons, we now are threatened by a number of "dilemmas of the self," like uncertainty, powerlessness, and commodification. We are lost, struggling with a "looming threat of personal meaninglessness."

And that's where our consumer culture fits in. Brands provide an answer to our identity crisis by giving us meaning. They help us construct our social world. In other words, in our search for place and purpose in life, consumer culture is replacing tradition.

WELCOME TO THE NEXT GENERATION OF MARKETING

It should come as no surprise that while consumers are increasingly looking to the marketplace for meaning, the job of the marketer is shifting dramatically. More than ever, we've become arbiters of culture and facilitators in the search for identity.

As a result, we marketers need to replace our old *immutable laws of marketing* with a new set of guideposts:

	STATUS QUO	WHAT'S NEXT
Marketing Toolbox	Mediated experience	Direct experience
Role of Brand	Make an emotional connection	Provide a larger purpose
Consumer Behavior	Receptive bystander	Active participant

Let's take a closer look at what each of these changes means.

THE *NEXT* MARKETING TOOLBOX

Consumers are demonstrating an increasing immunity to conventional marketing. Here are some reasons why:

They distrust marketers.

It seems that no space has been left unbranded, from the inside of taxicabs to cows being sold as billboard space in Swiss pastures. The London-based "ambient" agency Cunning Stunts has even created a database of five hundred "good-looking" college students ready to paste logos on their foreheads for about seven bucks an hour to become the agency's ForeheADS medium.

It also seems that no deceit, no attempt to manipulate, has gone untried. Some debate arose about celebrities such as Rob Lowe, Lauren Bacall, and Kathleen Turner appearing on talk shows like NBC's *Today* and CNN to praise prescription drugs without disclosing that they had been paid by the drug makers to do so. But the most appalling part of it was that the debate, which took place in respected publications such as *Time* magazine and *The New York Times,* centered on the effectiveness of the tactic, not on its ethics.

Finally, most cultural happenings have been coopted. As soon as a new art form emerges, a marketer will come around offering to buy it rather than support it. Woodstock II comes to mind. Show organizers sold out to both greedy promoters and insensitive brand sponsors to such an extent that they destroyed the spirituality and tradition created by the original festival.

All of these examples serve to demonstrate how marketers repeatedly cross the line. Small wonder consumers distrust us: We've earned it.

They're suffering from media overkill.

Media Dynamics estimates that we are exposed to 142 significant ad messages each day. Other estimates put that number at more than 3,000 commercial messages a day (and that's excluding internet ads and junk e-mail). Americans are spending more than twice as much time in front of the TV than their parents did, and remembering 70 percent less of what they see. Ad messages have become omnipresent. The U.S. Indoor Billboard Association reports that bathroom advertising grew 15 percent in 2002 to nearly 200,000 spaces. Good news for emerging agencies like Flush Media, bad news for the rest of us.

Media planner Ken Sacharin argues that the days are over when we could assume that we had people's attention, so all we needed to do was persuade. To him, media's new dilemma is "how to get attention without contributing to the problem of getting attention."

Retaining Authenticity

I am not an opponent of advertising by any means. Even as our world evolves, advertising will continue to remain an imaginative and powerful part of the brand story, and traditional media (especially TV) will continue to engage us. But the effectiveness of classic broadcasting has deteriorated, and it can no longer take center stage. Traditional media will have to find its role within the overall, more intimate marketing mix.

The many examples of hijacked brands that we've seen so far, from eBay to Friendster, have demonstrated one critical success factor in today's marketing environment: Let your consumers help shape your brand. And yet, in isolation, conventional marketing does not facilitate such behavior. David Lewis wrote in *The Soul of the New Consumer*:

> One cannot mass-produce authenticity. Rather, it has to be introduced on an almost person-to-person basis, with individual needs, desires, expectations and interests being fully accounted for.

Non-traditional media will find a more prominent place in overall media plans in large part because it engages consumers at a much deeper level. According to Oxford's marketing professor Richard Elliot, a larger symbolic meaning is constructed through a lived experience:

> Certainly there is considerable empirical evidence that attitudes formed through direct experience are stronger, more accessible, held more confidently and are more predictive in nature than those derived from mediated experience through advertising.

Harley hosts motorcycle rallies. Red Bull hosts wacky flying contests. These brands actually *create* experiences for their consumers rather than just *talking* about those experiences to them.

Perhaps *The Cluetrain Manifesto* hits closest to the bone when it describes markets as conversations:

> Thesis #18: Companies that don't realize their markets are now networked person-to-person, getting smarter as a result and deeply joined in conversation are missing their best opportunity.

The next marketing toolbox will consist of a mix of participatory media and storytelling techniques. "Through a story, life invites us to come inside as a participant," explains writer Stephen Denning. The next marketer will engage the consumer in conversation.

THE *NEXT* BRAND

In his influential book *The New Marketing Manifesto*, John Grant calls brands "the new traditions." They do more than establish an emotional connection with the consumer. This new type of brand stands for something grander than product performance and image.

The classic brand model of aspirational image is being challenged by consumers' rising indifference to it. Has capitalism succeeded? We seem to have created a culture of overabundance. Supermarkets stock an average thirty thousand items each. Income has doubled during the past forty years. We have come close to the American Dream of material fulfillment. Even luxury is no longer an effective status symbol because it's more accessible today. Charles Handy calls it "the culture of having enough." A BMW is not special anymore. It may take some creative financing, but many millions of us can afford one. As a result, it has become extremely difficult for marketers to make people care about their brands based on image plays.

The current generation of consumers is more self-directed than those of the past century. They aren't as easily persuaded by iconic brands. The success of the networks' reality shows, from *Jackass* to the star-on-a-pedestal shattering *The Osbournes,* indicates that today's consumer seeks extreme reality, not false gods. (Although anyone who actually utters the term "today's consumer" without a hint of irony is in grave danger of not getting it themselves.)

In his follow-up book, *After Image,* John Grant links brand image to the fairytale of the "Emperor's New Clothes." His chart on aspirational brands points out that "once post-modern ironic distance arrived on the scene, then image brands were in immediate trouble. . . . Brand image was usually promising something that wasn't true."

THE BRAND LIE	THE DAWNING TRUTH
Chanel makes you seductive	Chanel makes you smell like your mom
Fosters makes you a good bloke	Fosters makes you loud and sweaty
Nike makes you a hero	Nike makes you $100 poorer

In other words, brand image has been exposed and devalued.

The next type of brand will provide consumers with a higher purpose. Think of brands like Apple and Linux, which have been elevated beyond their functional and emotional performance. Their purpose, if not political, is at least of a social nature. The next type of brand will declare a worldview, not just an individual benefit, and play a meaningful role in people's lives.

THE *NEXT* CONSUMER

The era of the media-savvy consumer dawned long ago. When your focus group can identify your marketing strategy (something most of us have experienced to our amusement, embarrassment, or shock), it's time to take the next logical step and include them in the creation of your plans.

But just because we've had some time to figure out that consumers are media savvy doesn't mean we've really figured them out. A September 2001 article in *The Economist* declared: "Consumers have changed beyond recognition." Let's take a look at what that means.

The "Whatever" Generation

Today's critical consumers are quite different from the idealists of the 1960s. They have experienced the decline of trust in tradition. Some of them are old enough to have lived through Watergate. All of them experienced Enron, 9/11, the end of job security, and a high likelihood of growing up with divorced parents. These factors, and many others, have all but shattered the myth of "middle-class security"—a state of mind that fueled American consumer behavior for decades.

This is the first generation to have been marketed to since birth. The first to have realized that consumption can have detrimental consequences. These consumers witnessed the end of the Cold War. The last century's most significant social movements—civil rights, environmentalism, women's rights—were fought and won for them. They grew up with their victories already in place. *Fight Club* author Chuck Palahniuk writes:

> Our generation has had no Great Depression, no Great War.
> Our war is a spiritual war. Our depression is our lives.

These are the psychological drivers of today's consumers, whose disillusionment has helped foster ambivalence. Or in the words of one Napster user, who was explaining how fans were very engaged with the brand's stand against the record industry yet had no problem with its necessary (but blocked) move to a paid subscription service: "That's why we're the 'Whatever' generation."

Coming of Age

Modern marketing has gone through several major stages of evolution in the past fifty years, during which the relationship between brand owner and consumer has completely flipped:

The Marketing Age. During the 1950s through the '70s, manufacturers discovered consumer needs, and the marketplace was grateful for it. Both brands and marketing were new and different. They largely endeavored to be useful to consumers. Think laundry detergent ads playing during "soap operas."

The Age of Aspiration. During the 1980s and '90s, consumers became image conscious, competing with "the Joneses" for status symbols, as people's main concern was what others thought of them. Brand owners responded with clever image advertising that encouraged consumers to aspire to social ideals and distinguish nuanced differences between products. Think slick, good-looking men modeling watches and hair gel in *Esquire* and *GQ*.

The Age of the "Professional" Consumer. With the mid-90s arrived the cynical consumer, someone who was fully aware of the strategy behind the marketing campaigns. This time period brought about an unprecedented media and s.k.u. explosion. There was a short window of an "I-know-that-you-know-that-I know" celebration of the hypocrisy of marketing, culminating in Sprite's "Image is nothing. Thirst is everything," campaign (which, by the way, got away with murder when Sprite entered into a $285 million sponsorship of the NBA).

The Age of the Empowered Consumer. The role reversal is now complete. We live in a world of parity products. A recent JD Power study proclaimed that there is no longer such a thing as a bad car—they are all good. Consumers know they have leverage. It is their choice which of the forty-seven different bleach products available in the average U.S. supermarket they will purchase, if any.

Consumers are in charge, and they have proof of their power. A successful boycott forced Nike to invest in ethical manufacturing standards. Harsh criticism and vandalism of McDonald's outlets inspired internal awareness training and a subsequent change in corporate responsibility regulations. The idea of Linux has been turned into a NASDAQ-traded reality. And the tools of marketing have even been used against itself—as exemplified by Adbusters' "Buy Nothing Day" campaign, inspired by Vancouver artist Ted Dave.

The next consumer will be an active participant in shaping brand meaning and marketing the brand to others. This will no longer be the sole responsibility of the marketing department. According to market researchers Wendy Gordon and Virginia Valentine:

> The reality of brands is that human beings create their meanings. Brand owners do not. Of course brand managers are responsible for sending out signals about the brand, but the way these signals are put together and interpreted are often not the same as that which was intended. Brands live in people's heads and hearts.

———

Non-traditional marketing tools, brands with a higher purpose, consumers who want to help create the brand: We are indeed at the dawn of a new marketing era, one that will require us marketers to make some fundamental changes to our behavior and approach. Still, we have yet to explore the most fundamental question of all: Who exactly is hijacking our brands?

PART IV
THE HIJACKER

CHAPTER 10

The Consumer Collective

There was no such thing as the Pepsi Generation until Pepsi created it.

—Richard S. Tedlow

How can such insanity go undetected? Nike fanatics tattooing themselves with swooshes; crowds of thousands flocking to annual festivals at Saturn's Springfield plant. These days, tales of Harley rallies overrun with accountants have reached such mythic status that they've become cliché. Surely we must presume that these rumors and stunts were the handiwork of clever corporate PR departments.

But I don't care how crafty its PR department is, no company is responsible for the 353 babies named Lexus in the year 2000 alone. No brand manager can take credit for the 298 pint-sized Armanis out there. Kathy and Jason Curiel of Corpus Christi, Texas, named their little boy after his dad's favorite pastime because it sounded nice and Dad is a rabid fan, not because a suit talked them into it. Let's just hope little Espn likes sports.

Call them acts of dedication or evidence of cultural deterioration, but every year millions of people—acting freely, independently and, one can only presume, with the use of most of their faculties—incorporate brands into the most personal and intimate parts of their lives. They make wedding cakes out of Krispy Kreme donuts and hand out mini-glazed gifts to guests. They enlist the services of George F. Fiske III, a funeral director in Massachusetts who takes the hog loving deceased for "one last ride" on a Harley-turned-hearse. They embark on brand pilgrimages, like Halimah Rasheed's trip to Sweden to visit the site of the first IKEA store, or John Winter Smith's plan to cross the threshold of every corporate-owned Starbucks on earth (3,712 and counting).

Meet Uncle Griff, the Vermont man who, through force of personality, savvy computing, and perhaps a minor addiction, turned himself into a celebrity in the eBay universe. In the early days, Uncle Griff was ubiquitous on the site. He logged thousands of hours bidding and selling, helping new users find just what they were looking for, and giving tips for firing up the bidding wars. Uncle Griff's advice covered the site's bulletin boards . . . as did other indications of Griff's talents. (To one of the more personal bulletin board inquiries, Griff described himself as "a large, older hirsute Vermont dairy farmer with a penchant for his mother's clothes, cavorting around the cow pastures while imagining himself to be Julie Andrews.") While other companies likely would have disassociated themselves from apparent cross-dressing users of the brand (see Mattel), the folks at eBay knew they had a gem on their hands. In 1998, they hired Uncle Griff to run their customer service center, which he had sort of run unofficially anyway. From there, he launched an eBay career. He is the author of *The Official eBay Bible*, hosts his own weekly eBay radio show, writes an eBay column, and is dean of eBay University, a traveling training session for auctioning newbies.

Conventional brands don't have Uncle Griffs. They don't inspire baby-naming levels of devotion or donut-themed matrimony. They just don't go that, uhm, deep. But hijacked brands allow enthusiasts to feel like they're part of something bigger than themselves. Their fanaticism about the brand gives their lives meaning.

What's more, brand fanaticism is not a fringe phenomenon. Smith explained his Starbucks quest as an opportunity to do something no one has done before. But he and many other brand fanatics quickly learn that they are not alone. Rasheed waited in line with nearly five thousand others at the opening of an IKEA in Palo Alto. After naming their son Espn, the Curiels discovered that he shared the network namesake with at least one other unfortunate tyke.

Which is why, while it's easy to mock, this trend should not be dismissed. It is a clear indicator of the fundamental change in how consumers relate to brands. A change that goes way beyond mere brand fanaticism.

THE UNDERCOVER TRIBE

The consumer is in charge. That's quite an adjustment for marketers to make as it is. So brace yourself for the punch line: She no longer acts alone. Brands are not being hijacked by individuals. Starbucks, Red Bull, PBR, SMS; these brands were all hijacked by groups.

Do you think Uncle Griff developed his passion in isolation? The increase in brand fanaticism is a direct result of the emergence of the tribal consumer. Uncle Griff was not an individual eBay user; he was an icon—the underdog as spiritual leader—within the eBay tribe.

Modern marketing has taught us to view consumers as individuals, to seek insights from consumers as individuals, and to communicate with consumers as individuals—as though they existed in isolation. But in reality, consumers are influenced by a complex web of interpersonal interconnections.

And in today's world, consumers' decisions are driven more often than not by their memberships in loose social groups that form in a manner similar to the way ancient tribes used to form. However, whereas *geography* and *survival* were the common threads that bonded together ancient communities, modern tribes are bound together by common *hobbies* and *value systems*.

---

brand tribe ('brand 'trīb): A group of people who share their interest in a specific brand and create a parallel social universe ripe with its own values, rituals, vocabulary, and hierarchy.

The reappearance of the tribe is not just a brand phenomenon. Social tribes, or cliques, in general are starting to replace the traditional role of the family. San Francisco writer Ethan Watters discovered the tribe phenomenon while investigating the way young urbanites live and love in modern America. In his book *Urban Tribes*, Watters explains that he was part of a group of people united by little more than their shared interest in each other. During the course of his research, he was shocked to find a country populated with hidden "urban tribes" just like his.

Our whole social fabric has endured a radical change in the past few decades. Trust in mass media and religious and political institutions has eroded and traditional structures, from job security to marriage, have broken down. As a result, previously rigid institutions have lost their authority.

This lack of stability and diminished level of social interaction has revived our ancient tribal instincts. We are seeking ways to reconnect with others. The French marketing professor Bernard Cova sees the formation of tribes as a sign of individuals attempting to assert a sense of local identity over the facelessness of globalization, spirituality over cold reality, and synchronicity over disunity. In his words, "People who have finally managed to liberate themselves from social constraints are embarking on a reverse movement to recompose their social universe."

Why, then, did this large-scale trend go undiscovered for years? Because the formation of tribes takes place in a social universe that's inaccessible to the uninitiated. As Watters explains, "These groups would escape notice of others because the very thing that bonded them . . . was meaningless to those not in the group."

So, unless you're in the tribe, you will likely miss its significance. That has several implications for us marketers. For one, we must start to live in our brand world and hire from within the tribe. And we can't rely on our traditional markers any more. The tribe, as it originates and evolves, cannot be defined by conventional segmentation techniques. Any demographic or psychographic criteria will only insufficiently capture the group's characteristics. In order to define our tribe, we'll have to create it.

The Individual Within the Tribe

We consumers, as tribe members, are increasingly likely to conform to the influences of our peers. Studies show that social groups influence 80 percent of all purchases. Danish consumer behaviorists Per Østergaard and Christian Jantzen put it this way:

> The individual is no longer viewed as an independent self who is trying to collect ever more experiences. Instead of being based on personal emotions, the consuming individual is a member of a tribe.

This tribal behavior seems to fly in the face of conventional wisdom, which tells us that people are becoming more individualistic. But several researchers see a connection between the two trends. Yes, people are becoming more inwardly focused, less concerned with what other people think of them. But underneath this veneer of apparent individualism lies a strong trend toward convergence.

Researchers Janine Lopiano-Misdom and Joanne De Luca have clarified this convergence by introducing the concept of the "collective I." One New York student with whom they spoke explained:

> When I say "I," I collectively mean a lot of people who have the same mind frame as I do . . . a lot of people with the same goals, the same sense of communal responsibility, the same motives, and the same morals.

Wired magazine calls it the "hive mind."

In this day and age, individuals need to be defined in terms of their peer groups, their tribes.

REACH OUT AND JACK SOMEONE

The concept of the "brand" has evolved from functional product and personal experience to tribal tool and cultural symbol. This statement sounds so . . . naïve and idealistic. But the simple fact is that brands represent something more meaningful within a tribe setting.

Ivan Wicksteed illustrates this point by pulling out his MP3 player:

> As an individual my iPod allows me to organize my music more efficiently and carry it with me wherever I go. As a social tool it allows me to be a respected member (musicologist, DJ, party organizer) of the Apple music club.

The iPod is a highly schizophrenic brand, being at once both extremely antisocial and collaborative. As such, it provides an excellent example of the brand tribe phenomenon.

On the one hand, the iPod helps people tune out. Michael Bull, a professor of media and culture at England's University of Sussex, has studied the effect of the iPod on urban life. His verdict: "The potential for continual play means you never have to tune in to the environment you're in. You're perpetually tuned out." A New York art dealer confesses that the tiny gadget is "the next best thing to being transported from place to place in a pneumatic tube."

Isolation may be what users stuck sitting in the stiff Sussex teacher's lounge or wandering anonymously on Fifth Avenue are seeking, but there is a whole other world out there. One in which the iPod plays the part of public symbol and collaborative tool.

Let's start with the design. Much has been made of the player's simple and intuitive functionality. But the most important part of the iPod may be the highly visible white ear buds. These distinctive headphones let anyone know, from far away, who is part of the iPod club . . . and who's not. The signature item draws quite the antagonistic response from the non-iPod crowd. One Craigslist blogger comments:

> I have no problem with anyone using the iPod. What does bother me is people who continue to wear the white earbuds. They suck, but they [use] them so other people would know they have an iPod. We should sell the earbuds without iPods so people can make other people think they have an iPod when in reality, it's attached to, say, nothing. But hey, they will look cool. At least to girls wearing Uggs, who have Ph.D.s.

Love them or loathe them, these ear buds—public symbol of belonging to the "club"—have facilitated new rituals. From public parks in New Jersey to the campuses at Cambridge, Oberlin, and Pixar Animation Studios (surely as a nod to Big Brother Steve Jobs), iPod users not only acknowledge each other; they have started jacking into each other's devices to discover each other's playlists. What started out as subtle recognition of other users has turned into an immensely intimate encounter among tribe members. "We listened for about thirty seconds. No words were exchanged. We nodded and walked off," is how a puzzled fifty-one-year-old engineer described one such meeting to *Wired's* Leander Kahney.

Cultural critic Douglas Rushkoff views iPod sharing as an extension of file sharing. "It's kind of a stoner's ethic, really, the way you pass the joint at a Dead show." Blogger Andrew Orlowski from Britain's *Register* takes this thought even further:

> [iPod sharing] could have fairly dramatic social effects. You could get promiscuous with strangers: You could pair and exchange a song on the same short bus ride. You could create short, ad hoc personal broadcasts, to anyone else with a Bluetooth iPod. You could have a "What am I listening to?" menu option and share your choice within a discoverable range.

A further evolution of sharing among the iPod community is actual swapping of the devices. The *Village Voice's* Izzy Grinspan calls the iPod "The 21st century mix tape."

She explains:

> Listening to someone else's iPod is an intimate, almost invasive activity. On a scale of personal exposure, it's not exactly trading diaries, but it's much more revealing than a mix tape. For example, I never would have expected the [new] boyfriend to have an ethereal cover version of "Leaving on a Jet Plane," mislabeled Björk, as his most recently played track. It also quickly gets self-referential: When I got my iPod back, I put on the "Recently Played" list to see what bands he'd checked out. My iPod then dutifully recorded me listening to the songs he'd heard.

Sharing your iPod is a risky practice, somewhat akin to bearing your soul: There is the potential for great reward if you're regarded as a music connoisseur, yet there is immense social risk in letting people judge you by your personal music collection. Stephen Aubrey, a Wesleyan University student, has already given the judgment of someone else's taste in music a name: *playlistism*. In a column for the school newspaper, he explains that playlistism is "discrimination based not on race, sex, or religion, but on someone's terrible taste in music, as revealed by their iTunes music library." This puts a whole new spin on social implications of brand usage . . .

The most communal aspect of the device may be the emerging iParties, where anyone confident enough in their exquisite music taste can plug their iPods into a bar's audio system. Whether facilitated by DJs like APT's AndrewAndrew, or left as free-for-alls, many members of the club are beginning to bring their iPods out on the town for such events.

There are a lot of MP3 players out there. Why the iPod? Because of the tribe.

Brands are consumed differently today. It's getting harder and harder for them to differentiate themselves functionally. The capital of many brands today is social. And the most powerful of today's brands are the ones with the highest social value, the ones that inspire the creation of a fanatical brand tribe.

Concludes Grinspan, "Intentionally or not, Apple's MP3 player realizes its true potential as a personal device only when it's shared."

MARKETING TO THE TRIBE

Understanding the trend toward tribes as primary social units is crucial for marketers because tribes are now forming around brands. Cova identifies these brand communities as *the* emerging social trend in the new millennium. He explains that they are united by a common passion, like in-line skating, Burning Man, or lomography, rather than by tradition or location.

These tribes are ephemeral; they are constantly forming, dissipating, and re-forming. Nevertheless, they readily embrace, adopt, and alter brands in the marketplace. As Østergaard and Jantzen put it, "Product symbolism creates a universe for the tribe." Companies that learn how to feed and foster these brand communities will find themselves with an invaluable resource.

Often what unites brand enthusiasts into a community is a version of gossip. The folklore, the beliefs and practices passed on through peer-to-peer storytelling, legend, myth, ritual, and symbolic gestures:

These are some key ingredients that go into any brand primed for a tribe hijack.

Brand tribes select products differently than individuals do. They seek brands for their social, not functional, value. They want brands that can facilitate group rituals and experiences, products that establish connections and define the group identity. Members are constantly on the lookout for symbols and signs that will distinguish them from non-members.

Perhaps most important for marketers who are attempting to get their brands hijacked, tribes do not accept brand meaning as dictated by the brand owner. In fact, they actively seek to reconstruct and appropriate brands for their own symbolic usage. Cova explains: "The meanings of tribal symbols do not exist in isolation, but are constructed within the tribal culture, negotiated and interpreted by individuals in that specific subculture."

The emergence of the brand tribe will dramatically alter how we marketers relate to consumers. Product development will no longer strive for mere engineering excellence, but rather for the best way to facilitate communal belonging: *"The link is more important than the thing."* Marketing research will no longer depend on traditional consumer interviews, but will require an anthropological approach to understanding subcultures, their rituals and consumption patterns. Marketers will no longer broadcast to individual consumers, but will interact with tribe members to further develop brand meaning.

The result of this next iteration of our craft—tribal marketing—will be a more powerful brand. It will be a brand with a social function that is not based on *aspiration* but rather on *association*. Within this context, the success of brands like Starbucks and eBay no longer appears so puzzling, does it?

The Tribal Marketer's Core Challenge

Fellow tribe members aren't necessarily people with whom you have close personal relationships. In fact, a degree of intentional anonymity and distance, it turns out, is often a key trait of the brand tribe. It is common for tribe members to know little more than a face they see at conventions or—in the virtual brand world—a screen name or an e-mail address. Author Michael Lewis reported on a conversation he held with one of the leaders of the Gnutella movement, Daniel Sheldon, whose online alias, the_dr, would always draw immediate welcome messages once he entered a chat room:

> "Have you ever met any of these people?"
> "No."
> "Would you ever want to?"
> "Not particularly. I'd rather keep it impersonal."

Why do people seeking belonging choose to remain anonymous? I went back to the experts to explain why folks who have a common bond—their love for a specific brand—prefer to remain faceless.

Leander Kahney, the author of *The Cult of Mac*, argues that anonymity doesn't actually preclude intimacy. He says that he sees plenty of online examples in which identities are fluid, vague, and semi-anonymous but the relationships between these identities are real and personal. Anonymity, Kahney posits, often allows people to be even more intimate with each other than they otherwise would be.

John Grant takes a different approach. He points to "consumer cubism" to explain brand tribe members' preference for anonymity. People do not want to allow one single tribe to dominate their identity. (Why be just "punk" or just "mod," when you can be a Mac-using, Harley-riding punk?) "If I love and affiliate with X, it's just one small part of the fractal enigma that adds up to me," explains John. Maintaining anonymity within each one of those respective tribes we belong to allows us to have multiple selves, each with different characteristics, needs, and moods. And it encourages an impressive degree of self-definition. Yet these invented identities and avatars are often more "real" to us than the names our parents chose for us. Take Subgenius Bob (the radio DJ), aka 00afro (the electronic musician), who is known to his parents as Mr. Kola Ogundipe. Pop quiz: Do you know the Pope's given name?

Douglas Atkin, the author of *The Culting of Brands*, says that membership in a brand community involves a leap of imagination. People who identify strongly with a brand often do so because they imagine people similar to them are doing the same thing. They are driven by the overwhelming compulsion to be with others who are like them—even if only in the abstract. The fact that these "others" are at best anonymous, and potentially nonexistent, doesn't matter. Just think of the way a BMW owner will drive down the freeway checking out the drivers of other BMWs: He doesn't want to get to know these strangers, he just wants to see if they're up to snuff.

Bernard Cova takes Atkin's insights a step further. Cova has observed brand tribe members actually preferring to keep things anonymous even when meeting face to face. Cova studied interaction at brand-centered festivals and found that while people wanted to be in the presence of other tribe members, they didn't necessarily want to interact with them. Tribal "bonding" occurred just by being there—standing, smiling, and exchanging the occasional friendly comment did the trick.

Despite this apparent preference for anonymity, I believe there is a huge opportunity for brands with an intense following to remove the facelessness and make the tribe even stronger.

Just look at Harley-Davidson. Threatened by the invasion of superior Japanese motorbikes in the early 1980s, they survived bankruptcy with what was, at the time, a technologically inept product. The brand's success was propelled by the sheer will and energy of its community, the HOG (Harley Owner Group), which now claims 400,000 members in about 1,000 chapters. Harley localized the tribe and made it personal. Rides and rallies have become the social glue of the community, a tribe in which riders know each other by name and establish real friendships.

It's worth noting that Apple never attempted to transform its flagship stores, which serve as sites for tribe pilgrimages, into community centers. Imagine if, instead of allowing brand fanatics to wander alone about these essential temples, Apple encouraged them to interact with one another. What if, for example, they held creativity workshops in the stores? Imagine what such a tight-knit social network of Mac users could accomplish for the brand and for each other.

The more intimate it is, the more the tribe can accomplish for the brand. Which leaves us with an obvious challenge: How do you make the tribe more intimate?

CHAPTER 11

The Inner Workings
of the Brand Tribe

My name is Linus. And I am your God.

—Linus Torvalds

Brand tribes sound a bit cultlike, don't they? In fact, the "innocent" activities that take place in the world of branding are not so different from those of religious sects.

Just like cults, brand tribes offer their members a greater sense of purpose. They both have initiation processes, rites of passage, and devotion to a single ideal (or brand). Individuals can earn higher status in these groups by investing their time and energy in learning the customs, codes, and rituals. They're rewarded for their efforts by attaining increasing levels of insider status. Eventually, both cult and brand tribe fanatics become apostles, spreading the message to others.

John Grant and I decided to explore the similarities between the behaviors of brand communities and those of religious cults in depth. We looked at how several famous sects recruit, retain, and deploy their members. No doubt, we hesitated before heading down this road. Likening effective marketing to cult recruitment is, in this day and age, unseemly at best. But we felt that we couldn't fully understand brand tribes without investigating analogous groups.

Our research made us squeamish at times, and it will likely do the same to you. However, we believe the results of the study justify it: The comparison of cults to hijacked brands is mind-blowing. As a result of this work, we've been able to create a model for how to facilitate the formation of tribes around brands, and how to make the relationship between the two more intimate. Also, I'd like to emphasize up front that these techniques all involve seduction and not coercion; after all, cults are the best seducers in the business.

The First Step

So how do you go from casual consumer to brand fanatic? The answer: It's a journey. And like all journeys, it begins with a single step.

The overall pattern of cult activities leads people deeper and deeper into the experience—the very activity at the core of the brand hijack. But the enticement that attracts people to a cult or brand tribe in the first place is probably not what you'd expect: It's a sense of belonging rather than an ideology.

Rodney Stark, a professor of sociology and comparative religion at the University of Washington, found that people who join cults "profess a lack of religious belief prior to joining. They are drawn to new religious movements primarily for social reasons rather than theological ones." He argues

> The main thing you've got to recognize is that success is really about relationships and not about faith. What happens is that people form relationships and only then come to embrace a religion. It doesn't happen the other way around. That's really critical, and it's something that you can only learn by going out and watching people convert to new movements. We would never, ever have figured that out in the library. You can never find that sort of thing out after the fact [either]—because after the fact people *do* think it's about faith. And they're not lying, by the way. They are just projecting backwards.

People join brand tribes in much the same way. Marketing academic Andrew Ehrenberg has built a strong case that consumers change their minds about brands only after they change their behavior.

It's quite a contrary position in the world of consumer behavior theory, but it makes sense for hijacked brands: The larger meaning of the brand is only shaped over time with the market's input.

This may seem contradictory to our earlier discussions concerning the importance of hijacked brands leading with a purpose. But these points still hold true from the brand owners' perspective. What we're talking about is how brand tribes form from the *consumers'* perspective.

In other words, just as recruits don't *initially* join cults because of the ideology, so consumers don't *initially* join tribes because of the brand's value proposition. The brand tribe community—like the warm, welcoming outreach team of the cult—is the bait that lures people in. Only over time do consumers begin to engage in the process of co-creation, building a personal connection to the brand, and eventually helping to shape its cultural meaning.

It's like buying an Apple computer for the first time. You do it partially because you know that when you whip out your laptop at your local coffee shop, other members of the Cult of Mac will give you a nod. Don't kid yourself: Gaining their approval is a big reason to purchase the computer in the first place. Over time, you may buy into the anti-Microsoft, underdog mentality. You may become intrigued by the increasing layers of brand complexity. You may even become a brand fanatic, leading the charge. But that happens slowly, over time. Joining the tribe, like joining a cult, is a gradual process.

The Path to (Brand) Enlightenment

Both cult and brand tribe members take similar steps on their quasi-spiritual journeys: Initially, they get their foot in the door, get a glimpse of the community, and become privy to insider information. They then get initiated into the community. Next, they must prove their dedication and work their way up the organizational hierarchy. Finally, they fully buy into the ideology, which they help to evolve. Let's take a closer look at this journey:

Stage 1: The curious consumer crosses the "members only" firewall.
Stage 2: The handpicked consumer gets brandwashed.

Stage 3: The dedicated brand tribe member helps create a parallel social universe.

Stage 4: The brand fanatic drinks the Kool-Aid.

A Note on Methodology

John Grant and I studied the lifecycle of four religious organizations: the Moonies, Maharishis, Jehovah's Witnesses, and Scientologists. All of these groups encourage isolation from family and friends, demand immense personal sacrifices, dictate a regimented lifestyle, and are guided by a single, strong leader. We relied on eyewitness testimonies from past members and their families, as well as reports by cult watchers and the groups' own materials. The testimony of ex-cult members was the most candid source of information about what cults actually do, although some might say it was also the most suspect. We chose to take their word at face value. Please note: The study was intended to understand patterns of behavior, not religious doctrines.

STAGE 1: CROSSING THE "MEMBERS-ONLY" FIREWALL

IRC Pop-Up:

This site is private and you are not allowed entry without permission. If you are a member or supporter of a law enforcement agency, software company, anti-piracy organization, university, or federal/government investigation teams or you were a member at one point you are not permitted to access this site and may not access any of the material on it, regardless of intentions.

Cults have closed borders. You're either in or you're out. The borders set the members apart, encourage strong group identity, and create the foundation for the groups' psychological architecture: the "us versus them" mentality. This polarization creates passionate solidarity among the members.

Hijacked brands have similar, yet far more benign boundaries. They communicate with outsiders via unusually scarce, deliberate, and targeted advertising, PR, and promotions. This adds to the mystique of the brands and rewards those in the know.

The Moonies and Linux provide great illustrations of how this tactic works in both cults and brand tribes.

The Cult of Linus

In 1991, Linus Torvalds was a twenty-one-year-old computer science major at Helsinki University. Working in a dark room, dressed in a ratty bathrobe, he was trying to improve an existing operating system with a passing resemblance to Unix as a school project. Linus posted his results on a bulletin board for reviews and feedback. Linux was born.

By making his project public and asking users to contribute, Torvalds unintentionally instigated a revolution within the coder community. Coders were furious at the vast commercial computer empires that had been keeping operating system codes under proprietary lock and key and were therefore eager to rebel. Torvalds gave them the opportunity they were looking for. He allowed people to download Linux for free as long as they agreed to make their improvements to the code available online at no charge. Linux became an evolving public document.

As more and more coders got involved, the Open Source movement was launched. Its manifesto was a famous white paper published in 1998 entitled "The Cathedral and the Bazaar" (or CatB in coder lingo). In it, author Eric S. Raymond called for a replacement of the hierarchy and demagogy of companies like Microsoft with a free and uninhibited exchange of information. The Free Software Foundation, IRC, and other Open Source initiatives were Linux's peers, spreading the message even further.

How did a kid in Sweden end up creating a brand that was hijacked by its users to take on Microsoft head-to-head? He competed outside of the realm of capitalism—with no financial interest, yet with moral superiority. Or, as Torvalds himself said: "Software is like sex. It's better when it's free."

No wonder Linux has a cultlike following.

Shying Away from the Limelight

Cults often build a protective barrier to keep themselves out of public view. Only those committed to the cause are fully in the know. Outsiders are kept largely in the dark.

The Moonies are defended by religious status, secrecy, and armies of lawyers and lobbyists with powerful ties to the Washington establishment. Responding to criticism of brainwashing and hard sell tactics, the group renamed itself "The Family Federation of World Peace and Unification." Most outsiders don't even realize this group is the Moonies.	The Linux community for years extended as far as other hackers and no further. It was buried in Internet bulletin boards and on college campuses. The software innovator kept only its tribe members in the loop, relying on stealth communication. It believed and behaved as if it were driving a revolution. Even now that there are more than eighteen million Linux users, they still preserve the mystique, preferring, for the most part, to remain invisible.

David and Goliath

Cults define themselves by what they're not. They identify a powerful enemy in the outside world and foster a sense of being under attack by that enemy. This tactic reinforces members' commitment to their underdog cause.

The Moonies' main enemy is Christianity. The religion proclaims that "Moon's Church will replace Christianity in America." Furthermore, it teaches that "Jesus	Linux's spiritual enemy has always been Microsoft. The establishment did not initially see Linux as a threat: It was like Hannibal coming over the Alps with his elephants. *(cont'd)*

| is not in the kingdom of heaven" because he "did not succeed in his mission," and that the blessed children of the Moonies are better than Jesus. | But Microsoft has since recognized the revolt and launched a counterattack. Yet Jim Allchin, who runs Microsoft's platforms division, only strengthened the Open Source cause when he called the non-capitalist movement un-American: "I am an American. I believe in the American way. I worry if the government encourages open source . . ." |

Internal vs. External Communication

Members have privileged information. Communication within this group is intimate, extensive, and frequent. Outsiders are often fed a completely different story. Furthermore, cults make it clear that only those on the inside know the truth; outsiders should not be listened to.

| The Moonies control internal communication rigorously. No new members, or "first weekers," are allowed to talk to other first weekers, presumably so that they do not discuss their doubts or second thoughts.

Externally, the organization often uses affiliates to distribute information. The group publishes a sex education program for public schools called "Total Abstinence." It owns the newspaper *The Washington Times*. | Communication between Linux tribe members occurs almost exclusively online. Anonymity is crucial, as most of the people moonlighting for the Linux cause work as developers for large, Microsoft-friendly companies during their daylight hours.

There's a fun rumor floating around that FedEx's CTO sent an anonymous note about a secret Linux meeting to his team to ensure that no one was actually working on the code. More than a hundred people turned up, including some of his direct reports. |

Leaks and Stunts

Cults do occasionally provide the public with selective glimpses of their interior universes. In order to capture the interest of potential new recruits, they will stage dramatic and newsworthy events.

The Moonies hold ecstatic public rallies and mass weddings. They court celebrity endorsements through charity award dinners attended by high-level politicians. They parade high-profile converts such as Catholic Archbishop Emmanuel Millingo (in 2001).	When Linux went public, it went *public*. After all, the Open Source movement had its share of Silicon Valley veteran insiders. They knew that the one event that could put Linux on the map was a "coronation" on Wall Street.
	Supported by those veterans, VA Linux Systems, which sells Linux-based software, became the most successful IPO ever, soaring 700 percent on its first day of trading.

STAGE 2: GETTING BRANDWASHED

It's actually not that easy to get into a cult. You can't just walk in the door and say, "Sign me up!" There's no reason for cults to allow someone who is not fully committed to join, or to invest in someone who won't be valuable later.

That's why there's a specific, often meticulously detailed, initiation process. If it does the job, the initiation will simultaneously weed out bad apples and convert new recruits to be fully dedicated members.

Hijacked brands behave the same way. They deliberately sacrifice a larger market for a smaller inner circle that they can take through an elaborate "initiation" process intended to foster solidarity. Getting accepted into the brand tribe is a process we call *brandwashing*.

The Maharishis and IKEA both set the standard in terms of indoctrination.

The Unböring Furniture Store

From the beginning, IKEA's mission was to "make life better for the many" by offering superior aesthetics at the lowest possible price that still allowed for profit. A noble goal, for sure. But taking this socialist approach to business required the company to completely change people's expectations of how a retail store should behave.

The real challenge IKEA faced was convincing consumers that self-service, self-delivery, and self-assembly were not inconveniences, but rather part of a better overall shopping experience.

Shoppers are required to write down complex product codes and then search a giant warehouse to locate items, which are frequently out of stock. Even if they do manage to locate the product they're looking for, many items are quite large and heavy, making it difficult to fit them onto a shopping cart. Finally, getting the product home and assembling it with the cryptic instructions are major feats.

Furthermore, IKEA's store openings cause traffic jams and parking nightmares. People drive an average of two hours to get to a store. Once there, they are forced to walk a long, fixed path through the facility and endure long checkout lines. One New York City shopper lamented, "I've never had to work so hard to spend my money."

Yet despite all these inconveniences, IKEA has become the world's largest furniture retailer. Its popularity continues unabated. Clearly, this has to do with more than just good taste and low prices. IKEA has gotten its brand tribe members to completely buy into its way of shopping.

Selective Targeting

Cult recruiters focus not on "who we can get," but "who is ready."

The Maharishi's followers know that people going through dramatic life changes make excellent recruits: New students and recent divorcees are prime targets.	IKEA also targets people going through life changes: young families with kids, couples starting out on their own, and college students (who get 10 percent off their purchases). In short, people whose tastes exceed their budgets.

Baiting the Hook

No one wakes up one day and says, "You know, I think I'll join a cult today." Cults use bait to invite people in for some other purpose. It's often an activity that encourages frequent visits and provides repeated exposure to the groups' members, style, and space.

The Maharishi's bait is Transcendental Meditation—a meditation practice that blends traditional techniques with Hindu religious ceremonies. TM sessions are often new members' first introduction to the Maharishi community.	IKEA lures people in with the promise of great style, instant gratification, and unbeatable prices. It also makes the shopping experience easier by offering free child care. The restaurant gives people a chance to recuperate so that they can go back for more shopping.
	It then forces customers to walk through the entire store from showroom to showroom in a set pattern. It's almost impossible to find a way out. This is a great way to indoctrinate people to the company's aesthetics, educate them about its entire product range, and get them to buy items they had not intended to purchase.

Love Bombings

Cults aim to meet a fundamental human need—belonging. Imagine stumbling across a weird and wonderful community where everyone instantly loves and accepts you.

Only those cult members who have shown an aptitude for attracting and reassuring potential recruits are included in the Maharishi introductory TM sessions. These members build deep relationships with the recruits across a series of convivial social meetings.

Every IKEA has a nursery at the front entrance. Even if it's usually empty, it's the thought that counts. The nursery projects an image of togetherness. "The Great American Furniture Tradeoff" program rewards shoppers who donate to the Salvation Army or Goodwill with store discounts.

Stores also try to please customers with personable touches. For example, one California location gives free coffee to customers waiting in the returns line.

Initiatives like these give customers the feeling that IKEA cares about them and their community.

Cultivating True Believers

Next comes the matriculation phase, a critical process that is carefully managed. Recruits can't just become instant members; they have to experience an initiation. If brainwashing occurs, this is when it happens. This can be an intense, isolating experience designed to break down recruits so that the cults can then build them back up as true believers.

After the introductory TM sessions, an instructor interviews recruits to decide if they are prepared for a private session. The aim then is to get the recruits to declare themselves

IKEA is famous for breaking people down. Ask anyone and they'll tell you that shopping there is a miserable experience: horrible traffic in the parking lots, labyrinthine corridors "ready for the knowledge" and to accept the Maharishi as the only source of "inner truth." If they pass, recruits are finally shown the sacred techniques.

One former member described the Maharishi initiation process this way: "It's like one of those large, funnel shaped nets that's dragged along by a trawler. The farther down the funnel you go, the more intense it gets. Finally, at the end, is the cult initiation ceremony, called a 'knowledge session,' designed to flop you out the other end, on a cold table, where the master stands with his fish knife, ready to liberate you."

between endless showrooms, items too big to fit into the shopping carts, out-of-stock products, lack of staff, and—at the end of it all—long checkout lines.

But the retailer also knows that in order to earn customers' loyalty, it then needs to build them back up again. IKEA constantly tells consumers how smart they are for shopping there—whether by catalog, in the store, or on the Web site. And it's recently introduced a "Linebusters" initiative that has dramatically reduced the time customers must spend waiting in line at the end of their long shopping day.

In the end, IKEA's brandwashing process leaves its members feeling like they had to work to earn their place in the tribe, but that the effort they put in was worthwhile.

STAGE 3: CREATING A PARALLEL SOCIAL UNIVERSE

Cults use a variety of tactics to gain full commitment from their new recruits and to keep all members actively engaged. Their ultimate goal is to separate people from their previous existences by luring them completely into a parallel social universe with its own rituals, relationship structures, and experiences.

Similarly, a brand tribe is bound together by its passion for the brand. The community often has its own rituals, vocabulary, and hierarchy.

Jehovah's Witnesses and eBay both have passionate communities that have developed their own parallel social universes.

Community Justice

In 1997, eBay found itself in a tough spot. News of major fraud scandals threatened its credibility and business model. The online auction company was in danger of going from something that felt like a neighborhood garage sale to a nasty and risky black market.

Two users, Sonny Stemple and Luan Chau, cheated buyers out of more than $100,000. Complex bidding schemes sprung up. One involved a trio of cons who inflated prices under various screen names in more than 600 auctions. The most embarrassing incident was Katie-gate, a snafu involving *The Today Show*. Hosts Katie Couric and Matt Lauer autographed a jacket to auction off for charity. Matt and Katie proudly announced on air that the bids had reached the $200,000 level, only to discover later that the highest bids were all pranks (the highest real bid was only $11,400).

But the company knew that if it introduced draconian regulations in the typical top-down business fashion, it would kill the folksy vibe and ruin eBay even faster than the scandals would. So it turned to its community instead.

In a short time, the brand tribe had established a whole new architecture of trust, ethics, and etiquette involving a rating system, peer reviews, and other vigilante methods. The community rallied to keep the company going. Today, eBay is one of the world's largest economies.

Pyramid Schemes

Cults know that when everyone is treated the same, no one feels special or motivated to go beyond the call of duty. So these tight-knit communities often set up what amounts to emotional pyramid schemes: They require members to climb the organizational ladder, rewarding them with greater power and insider status at every level.

The Jehovah's Witnesses organization is known as the Watchtower. Each Kingdom Hall is led by elders. Members are not allowed to take any	eBay has established "loyalty tiers": The more you trade, the higher you get in the hierarchy, via a rating scheme. If you cheat or defraud, you

initiatives on their own, but in all matters must await orders from their immediate superiors. Anyone who questions an order is kicked out for "dis-fellowship."	get thrown out. Sellers with a higher rating can actually command a premium of up to 30 percent. eBay supports its biggest customers, such as people who make their entire living off of auctioning there, with a top tier of membership called the Power Selling Program.

Active Participation

Cults keep people very busy—too busy to stop and think. Every member has many basic duties: Do homework, recruit, maintain property, etc.

Idleness is a sin. The most common complaint of ex-Jehovah's Witnesses is not about the spiritual content but the time commitment. Members' spare time is often devoted entirely to work, like mending the Kingdom Hall roof and trudging from doorstep to doorstep proselytizing.	The average eBay user spends 3.5 hours on the site, longer than anywhere else in e-commerce. Instead of just getting in and getting out, the bidding process encourages multiple visits, as buyers check the status of their bids. After each sale, users have to take the time to rate the other party. Furthermore, eBay chapters have started sprouting up. eBabes, a national club of eBay sellers, holds regular local meetings to discuss strategies and issues.

Psychological Twists

Cults are fueled by extraordinary commitments of time and money on the part of their members. But, contrary to popular belief, they seldom coerce people into these commitments. You can't, for example, donate money to cults—you have to be asked.

Cults use psychological twists, such as competition and strong peer pressure, to exert control over members' behaviors.

Jehovah's Witnesses live by an exceptionally strict code. They must avoid "bad association"—relationships with non-Witnesses—and cannot lie, cheat, or drink. The psychological twist here is called the Theocratic Strategy, which is a system of exceptions to the rules. Members can, for instance, lie about the cult to everyone who "doesn't have the right to know."	eBay has several psychological quirks, including the fact that its business model turns e-commerce into gambling. People bid frequently and furiously. There's a thrill to winning a bid. Many users experience a high with each victory and a low with each defeat—and people get easily addicted. One self-proclaimed eBay Queen confessed, "I've never had anything that I enjoy as much as doing this. I watch the bidding every day like a little kid." Today, a net addiction Web site offers help to people with unhealthy web habits, namely, "cybersex, problem day trading, and eBay addiction." One woman has taken up a collection to help relieve her husband's eBay debt. She naturally accepts Paypal.

Momentum

Cults stay relevant and vibrant by maintaining their momentum. If there is nothing much happening, cults rely on setting false deadlines, engaging in apparently random acts of insanity, or demanding proof of loyalty to keep things interesting.

The Watchtower, the Witness's magazine, has been saying that Armageddon is "coming soon" since 1884.	In response to the early fraud threats, eBay introduced insurance of up to $200 against fraud, a seller identity verification service, a ban on sellers bidding on their own products, and a ban on buyers who win the auction but do not complete the sale. But rather than launching all these programs at once, it rolled them out one by one, attracting media attention each time.
	Luckily for the company, the eBay tribe now keeps its momentum going largely on its own. The entire disgruntled IT department of a Silicon Valley company recently auctioned itself off to another company. A woman put her hand in marriage up for bids. These stories make the news, keeping loyal fans engaged and earning the company new recruits.

STAGE 4: DRINKING THE KOOL-AID

Cults program what their members think and do. (Think of the many famous cases of cult members refusing medical treatment.) They do this by offering strong leadership, coded communication, a simplified worldview, and a clear value system.

Hijacked brands, also centered on clear ideologies and led by visionaries, are similarly on a mission to change the world.

The Church of Scientology and Adbusters are both undeniably on such missions.

Beating Us at Our Own Game

To many marketers, *Adbusters* is a Canadian magazine that has become an underground hit with the young scions of the advertising industry—freelancers, designers, and writers. But in reality, it is far more than just a monthly rag. It is emerging as the preeminent anti-consumption brand. Its founder, Kalle Lasn, believes in harnessing the power of images and words to shock people out of their habitual complacency and acquiescence.

In addition to publishing the magazine, Adbusters fosters a network of what it calls "culture jammers," citizen activists who use guerrilla tactics to subvert the intended meaning of ads by creating "anti-ads." In addition, they sponsor anti-consumption campaigns such as Buy Nothing Day and Turn Off TV Week. Adbusters' agency, Powershift, also works for other non-profit organizations.

Adbusters' members are allowed to remain anonymous and participate in whatever capacity they want to: by contributing money to buy anti-ads; by planning an anti-consumption event; by putting up posters and stickers, which they can download from the Web site; or even by designing anti-ads themselves.

To celebrate the creativity and chutzpa of its members, Adbusters asks them to submit "reports" after every campaign, which it then posts on its Web site. This serves to create a sense of accountability, give credit where it's due, bolster morale, and spread the word.

The company is small, staffed with just nine people. The magazine's circulation is low, at 100,000. *Adbusters*' interest is decidedly narrow, focusing on the effects of advertising on culture and society. Yet the organization's impact is growing because the company feels that its task is no less than to put a stop to rampant commercialism. And those who hear the message find it appealing.

Charismatic Leaders

Cults tend to be personality-driven. The leaders' story is the story of the cult. The leaders' word is law. The cults use the leaders' demonstrations of love and affection as tools to manipulate community members. Access to the leader is an exclusive reward offered only to the higher-ups.

The Scientologists revere founder L. Ron Hubbard. Everything he says is taken as the literal truth. His writings are even described as "data." Anything he's written or said is referred to as "the tech" (as in, "psychiatry doesn't work because they don't have the tech").	Kalle Lasn is Adbusters. His book, *Culture Jam: How to Reverse America's Suicidal Consumer Binge—and Why We Must,* was the rallying cry for anti-consumption crusaders everywhere. *The Utne Reader* dubbed him "Madison Avenue's Worst Nightmare." His vision has been the driving force behind the magazine and the foundation, which owns it.
	Famous apostles of Lasn include like-minded authors Thomas Frank and Naomi Klein.

Coded Communication

Cult members develop their own vocabulary, their own way of speaking. Cults are also fond of closing debates or awkward discussions with "wise sayings." There is an implicit social pressure to master the language and understand the symbols. The message is: "To speak like us is to belong."

Scientology has developed an extensive proprietary language. L. Ron Hubbard's techniques are "the tech." The hierarchy is "the gradient." Process is across "the bridge." Recruitment is of "stats." Disciplinary action is "ethics."	For an anti-advertising movement, Adbusters is steeped in the jargon of Madison Avenue. Its editors have coined terms such as "anti-ads," "culture jam," "subvertisements," "nega-marketing," and "demarketing loops" to refer to their activities.
The lexicon is designed to convey scientific authority and stifle debate. (Sounds a bit like marketing jargon, doesn't it?)	Adbusters gears its communications at the people who already get it: advertising mavens and cultural academics. It thereby creates a barrier to the outside world.

Simplified Worldviews

Cults are masters of the simple message. Part of their appeal is that they offer a black-and-white view of reality, far from the mess of real relationships and life conflicts. This worldview is often pinned to a broadly defined aim that few could disagree with, like "peace and clarity." They reinforce this aim through constant repetition.

Scientology claims to offer to "set men spiritually free" by teaching them principles set forth by L. Ron Hubbard. These teachings are the driving force behind the Church of Scientology worldview. They are considered to be 100 percent correct. Members learn these teachings in courses, which they take at their own expense. If members don't understand or challenge a teaching, they are told they don't "get it" and "need handling." It's their fault, after all . . .	Adbusters' worldview is that all advertising is evil: It pollutes public space, creates unnecessary desires, and contributes to environmental degradation. Consequently, the organization's goal is to use the tools of advertising against itself by creating "anti-ads." Examples include Joe Chemo, a mockery of Joe Camel, and a take-off of the Calvin Klein Obsession ad that shows a woman throwing up in the toilet.

Shared Value Systems

Seemingly arbitrary restrictions, complicated codes, and rules only serve to reinforce the group's way of life. They provide the community with a value system to live by.

Scientologists value secrecy and obedience. The only way to become a "clear" is to go through the church's "auditing" process, which requires the members to be hypnotized while	Adbusters values competition, action, and creativity. To its members, culture is a war of ideas, and in order to win, they need to engage in guerilla tactics.

church leaders help them to reach advanced levels of human functioning. The process takes years and involves "fixed donations" that total up to tens of thousands of dollars.

Those who publicly question the cult, from ex-members to large corporations, are sued. In 1995, the Church of Scientology sued *Time* magazine for an unfavorable cover article. Even though the case was thrown out, the cult got its message across.

For Buy Nothing Day, the group encourages members to spread the message through direct action in whatever way they can. Some protests have included hanging a giant "Buy Nothing Day" banner in the Mall of America, shopping for nothing at Wal-Mart, and offering credit card cutting services to mall shoppers.

The clearest expression of its values, however, is in its manifesto:

> We propose a reversal of priorities in favor of more useful, lasting, and democratic forms of communication—a mindshift away from product marketing and toward the exploration and production of a new kind of meaning.

THE CONFESSION BOOTH

There you have it: a step-by-step guide to becoming more intimate with your brand tribe based largely on the tactics used by religious sects.

I am prepared to hear criticisms of the cult study. Even while conducting the investigation, John Grant and I often wondered, "Do we really have to go here? Do we really want to encourage marketers to behave more like religious cults—groups that often bring emotional strife, and occasionally physically danger, to their members?" At a time when righteous authors like Naomi Klein and Thomas Frank are attacking marketing for being a form of stealth manipulation, is this what our profession needs? Haven't Enron and WorldCom done enough to tarnish corporate America's reputation?

Our intention, however, is not to encourage unethical behavior. On the contrary, it is to reset the marketing industry's ethical bearings.

Like sociologists who study cults for insights into human nature, we studied cults to uncover elements of group behavior and community building. We could just as easily have investigated Alcoholic Anonymous, Weight Watchers, or Amnesty International. And yet none of these groups yielded as clear a comparison to brand tribes as did cults. When we lined up brand tribe behavior next to cult practices, our results came out in Technicolor. I hope the ethical implications have, too.

Our investigation should demonstrate, above all, that creating a brand community is *not* about mass coercion; it's about subtle seduction. Cults are so successful because they understand this. They fine-tune their recruitment processes to play into the nuances of human nature, and they provide meaning to those who are seeking enlightenment.

Hijacked brands must do the same. They must seduce, and not coerce.

THE DEMOCRATIZATION OF BRANDS

Brands that are hijacked by tribes have a powerful new positioning: *non-elite exclusivity*. In several important ways, membership in the club is democratic. In large part, it isn't based on demographic criteria such as age, education, or income level. It's not about snob appeal. Instead, these communities are united by a common worldview and shared set of values, and anyone who meets those criteria is welcome to join.

Anthropologist Mary Douglas calls these modern tribes, which reject both the trappings of traditional society and the hyper-competition of individualism, "egalitarian sects." They value equal opportunity for all regardless of race, class, or creed. Harley democratized motorcycles. Starbucks democratized coffee. Apple democratized computers. These brands were hijacked in part because they are brands for "the rest of us."

In this way, brand tribes deconstruct old barriers. But at the same time, they build up new ones. Membership still has its privileges. We human beings are inherently hierarchical, and gaining access to the upper echelons of any social group isn't easy. It's just that rather than being based on some fixed, external attributes, status within these brand communities is based on one equalizing factor: commitment to the cause.

Hijacked brands' meaning need not be revolutionary, religious, or entirely righteous. But in order for it to take hold, it must be authentic.

CHAPTER 12

The Funny Business of Earning Consumer Devotion

I want to put a ding into the universe.

—Steve Jobs

Does marketing need to become a religious experience? Will we have to start defining a higher purpose for every brand? Will meaning become meaningless through sheer overuse?

Let's be clear: Not every brand needs to act like a cult. Please, let's not all find religion and turn marketing into an evangelical trade. Admiring the preachy leadership of superstar CEOs like Steve Jobs may prove dangerous. It may mislead us into believing that we must open ourselves—professionally speaking—to finding the equivalent of God or going on a quest for some kind of Holy Grail. And that's certainly not what we wanted to express with our cult study.

No, brands with a religious following are not the only ones capable of enchanting tribes of fanatical believers and inspiring lasting devotion.

In fact, there are basically three ways to make consumer groups feel passionate about—and hijack—your brand:

THE DISCOVERY	THE COMMENTARY	THE MISSION
e.g., Palm, *Blair Witch*	e.g., PBR, Dr. Martens	e.g., Apple, Linux
• Engages by either *delighting* or by *being let in on a secret*	• Allows the brand to become either a political or social statement	• Declares a worldview oppositional to a "Big Brother" enemy
• Generally driven by a brand owner's vision for market innovation	• Generally appropriated by the market	• Generally driven by a charismatic, evangelic leader

CREATING A DISCOVERY

People often fall in love with brands that they stumble across at random. Nobody wants something forced upon them, and everybody loves a pleasant surprise. When people believe they have discovered a brand on their own, they feel ownership of it and want to share it with their friends. It's like uncovering a great restaurant, an obscure author, or a new band.

"Discovery" brands are typically created by market innovators. As such, they are not product-driven, nor are they consumer-driven. Rather, they are driven by counterintuition—their ability to see things differently and change the rules of the game. These types of brands often either redefine a category or establish a new one.

Both Palm and *The Crying Game* serve as examples of brands that were initially discovered and propagated by their early markets, but for two very different reasons.

Under-Promise and Over-Deliver

Silicon Valley had given up on the under-performing pen-based computing category. It had witnessed the high profile failures of both the Apple Newton and GO—a startup funded by Kleiner Perkins—and wasted a billion dollars in the process.

But Jeff Hawkins, who was a vendor to the industry, saw things differently. He was frustrated by the big guys' approach in that they'd tried to make the devices into PC substitutes. Hawkins wanted to define handhelds as adjuncts to the PC rather than as replacements. As he put it "I realized that my competition was paper, not computers."

So in 1996, he and a few other folks started their own company—Palm Computing, Inc. Within eighteen months of its release, Palm had shipped over one million devices, at the time making it the fastest-selling computer product in history. It brought mainstream acceptance to handheld computers. And it did all this while spending just a tiny fraction of what the large companies had invested.

The triumph of Palm, a "discovery" brand, was based on this winning principle: under-promise and over-deliver.

Hawkins realized that in order to capture a broad user base, the Palm needed to be as "easy to use as pen and paper." And so Palm's rallying cry became *simplicity;* not just in product development, but throughout all aspects of the company. For instance, Palm made a huge splash at the trade show where it was first introduced when the mothers of the three founders walked onstage to demonstrate the product's ease of use. Now there's a dramatization of simplicity.

Hawkins intuitively understood that since PDAs wouldn't be used like PCs, they needed to break with the PC paradigm. First and foremost, the Palm did not offer all the capabilities of a PC. It just provided a calendar, address book, notepad, and to-do list, with a few extras like a calculator thrown in. This made it an obvious replacement for the traditional paper day-planners that had dominated the business world for decades.

Second, the device had to be readily accessible many times a day. Hence, making it "shirt-pocket sized" was an imperative for the engineering department. Hawkins was even known to carve blocks of wood in his garage and carry them in his shirt pocket for days at a time to determine the optimal size and weight for the Palm.

Palm's killer app was its revolutionary sync function. By pressing a single button, users could make a carbon copy of their Palm's contents on their desktops and vice versa. This breakthrough technology made entering data easier and relieved people of the fear of losing all their most important information.

But in spite of its elegant functionality and simplicity, Palm remained humble. This was the real kicker that drew people in. What a stark contrast to Palm's boastful predecessors in the category that had so woefully under-delivered. Consumers were skeptical to begin with as a result of their previous poor product experiences, but as soon as they picked up a Palm, they were sold. Silicon Valley guru Geoffrey Moore explained what happened:

> People loved this thing. The technology industry management teams took the lead on it, but pretty quickly it was getting passed around to "the rest of us," and the passion did not abate . . .
>
> Success through subtraction is the key lesson here. By contrast, the companies who failed had over-designed for the target market because they were hedging their bets. Ironically, in the act of trying to reduce their market risk, they actually increased it.

Palm made an internal commitment to "delight the user," and it more than delivered.

Let Consumers in on a Secret

Another "discovery" tactic besides the approach taken by Palm is to let consumers in on a secret, to make them the ultimate insiders. We already covered this tactic in detail with *Blair Witch,* but the Miramax feature *The Crying Game* deserves honorable mention. The film was marketed on just one thing: the plot twist. This tactic made *The Crying Game* a $62 million winner at the box office.

A decade later, ABC's *Bachelorette* picked up this familiar tactic, dressed it up, and took it for a spin, making a tremendous splash. A Diageo marketing manager explained in an e-mail what happened:

> Currently getting over my outrage from the season finale of the *Bachelorette* from last night. That was my first and only time seeing it and I watched with a bunch of girls and we all got played by the media!
>
> The media was very clever, because they leaked stories all through New York for the past two weeks (hairstylists,

trendsetters, *NY Post* writers, etc.) that said she picked Charlie. So, we all heard these rumors from "credible sources." One of my friends heard the outcome directly from the show's stylist. Even though I consider us smart New York women, we got cocky and assumed we were "in the know" about Charlie, the financial analyst, and at the end, she picked Ryan, the firefighter.

We called our "credible sources" and found out it was all part of the show's plan to leak it.

GETTING APPROPRIATED FOR SOCIAL/ POLITICAL COMMENTARY

Another way to earn consumer devotion is to allow your brand to become a statement. Once a brand achieves iconic status, it obtains a deeper meaning among its users. The commentary can be either political or social in nature. Sometimes the brand owner leads the vision behind this deeper type of brand. But often it is the market that fully appropriates the brand for its own statement—making it a serendipitous hijack.

In the case of PBR, the commentary was political. The beer became the anti-badge, a protest against material consumption and marketing imagery. In contrast, while Dr. Martens were appropriated by political movements at both extremes of the spectrum, the brand was primarily adopted by youth countercultures making a social statement about defiance.

BEING ON A MISSION

Nevertheless, the strongest way to inspire consumer devotion is to develop a brand religion. Brands with clearly defined purposes can develop a cultlike following. And these brand tribes will truly act as if they were on a mission to change the world. There's no denying the power of this approach.

If there is one master of cult marketing, it's Apple. The company has ticked off every box on the cult scorecard. And it hasn't hidden its intentions, either. When Steve Jobs recruited John Sculley away from Pepsi, he asked, "Do you want to sell sugared water or change the world?"

Umberto Eco put it this way in an article for the Italian news magazine *Espresso:*

> The Mac is like the Catholic Church. It is cheerful, friendly, conciliatory. It tells the faithful how they must proceed step by step to reach—if not the Kingdom of Heaven—the moment in which their document is printed.

The musician Barry Adamson once told *The Guardian:*

> Apple is like a strange drug that you just can't quite get enough of. They shouldn't call it Mac. They should call it crack.

And former Apple CEO Gil Amelio summed it all up in an interview with *Computerworld:*

> It's the cult. It's what kept the damn thing afloat during some of the most incredibly bad business decisions I've ever seen anywhere.

KEEPING IT REAL

There is a good chance that Glad trash bags will never change the world. But even "necessary evils" can get hijacked.

While exploring the "new American luxury," BCG consultants Michael Silverstein and Neil Fiske discovered consumer passion for brands in such unlikely categories as home appliances. In their book, *Trading Up,* they recount reactions to the Duet washer/dryer combo, Whirlpool's seemingly naïve but successful attempt to turn the laundry room into a family hub. Comments like "The Duet is the Ferrari of washing machines," or the bubbly "I would rather leave my husband than my Duet," may make us question humankind, but deep inside, such consumer bliss is every marketer's dream.

The Duet's success demonstrates that it's not always necessary for brands to define a new category, get lassoed to a political ideology, or espouse a higher purpose in order to provoke consumer devotion. There must be another way . . .

Perhaps the common denominator of all hijacked brands is not an ideology, but a sense that the company is true to its values and the product is true to its function. A sense, in other words, that the brand is *authentic*.

Hijacked brands take on a human quality. One Duet user confessed to Silverman's research team, "It is part of my family." The brands' actions are driven by an organic instinct rather than a marketing campaign's series of calculated pretenses. This natural, uninhibited, and spontaneous relationship between manufacturer and market is read by consumers as *authenticity,* that precious attribute missing from the heart of modern politics, media, corporations, and, above all, marketing.

Hijacked brands are differentiated primarily by intrinsic values— like simplicity or a particular aesthetic sensibility—not single-minded functional benefits. (Napster's was transparency. We wanted to take this value to the next level by installing a 24/7 web cam in the board room. The camera would telecast management team decision processes, industry meetings, and everything else that happened in the most important place in the building. Milt Olin, Napster's former COO, liked the idea so much that he wanted to conduct all job interviews in front of the camera and use the room as a post-work confession booth for employees. But we never got to try it because Napster was shut down first.) The brand's authenticity allows the market to intuitively grasp what these values are without having to be told, or without the companies even having to express the values precisely.

This attribute of genuine naturalness in hijacked brands quickly outs poseurs. Take Sirius, the satellite radio provider. In a desperate competitive move against market leader XM-Radio, the company aggressively marketed a lengthy manifesto geared toward idealistic music lovers. "Music shouldn't be brought to you by a double espresso in a can, or jeans that ride amazingly low," opened the rant against commercial radio. Sirius then positioned itself as the platform for "struggling artists yearning to break through." What nobility. The problem was that the campaign lacked even a touch of credibility. Who were they trying to kid? Sirius was a satellite operator that happened to dabble in music because they needed content. Consumers quickly saw through the shallow veneer. Authenticity won, and Sirius stopped its marketing campaign relatively quickly.

Bottom line: Consumer devotion must be earned. It cannot be faked.

PART V

THE BRAND HIJACK ROADMAP

CHAPTER 13

The Kick-Off: Hijack Ideation

If you want to make a difference, make it different.

—Steve Henry

It all starts with an idea. An idea that you seed, nurture, and grow over time into a new cultural norm. An idea that is driven by a major social truth. Napster was appropriated by its community as a tool to rebel against the manipulative record industry. Southwest Airlines gave everyday people the opportunity to go places only the rich had been able to afford. Red Bull became "speed-in-a-can" for today's demanding lifestyle.

eBay was built on a simple social insight: People like to trade with each other but are often put off by the intrusion of dubious middlemen. Hence Pierre Omidyar initially developed eBay as an impartial trading forum (according to the brand mythology, it was exclusively for Pez dispenser collectors at first).

In her influential book *Hitting the Sweet Spot*, Lisa Fortini Campbell argues that great brands find the perfect balance between product performance and consumer insight. That may be the magic sauce for conventional brands, but it's not enough to get people to hijack your brand.

Hijack-able brands help change people's basic habits, or at least their mental maps of a particular brand category. And so their ideation has to be bigger than a consumer insight. It needs to hit the sweet spot between product performance and *social* insight. For it is the social truth that engages consumers at a higher level and motivates them to get deeper into the brand experience.

Uncovering social truths does not lead to mere product innovation. It leads to market innovation. In other words, brands based on social insights make a major leap that dismantles the status quo and changes the rules of the marketplace. As such, market innovation is not generated through a process, but through a fresh way of looking at things, through a visionary way of thinking.

GOOD OLD INTUITION

While on a business trip to Milan, Italy, Howard Schultz, a former technology salesman, had an epiphany: The Italian espresso bar experience should be available in the United States. He started Il Giornale, the coffee shop he eventually merged into Starbucks, because he recognized and fell in love with Italians' intense relationship with coffee, and with coffee bars in general.

It was not an idea born out of a deep analysis of the U.S. coffee market data or projections. It was not an idea born out of a bunch of focus groups claiming dissatisfaction with their current corner coffee shop, either. It was an idea born out of a visionary's personal conviction and drive.

Companies recently have focused a lot of their attention on being consumer-centric, giving the market what it asks for. But this does not work for ideating hijack-able brands because consumers do not tend to make innovative leaps. It's difficult for them to imagine what they don't know. Psychologists call this phenomenon "functional fixedness." By fixating on the way they normally use things, consumers prevent themselves from thinking creatively. They can provide guidance on what they expect, but rarely do they ask for something completely new or different.

As Henry Ford said, "If I had asked the public what they wanted, they would have asked for a faster horse." Adds another visionary, Steve Jobs: "You can't just ask customers what they want and then try to give that to them. By the time you get it built, they'll want something new."

Market innovators don't put into the market what consumers tell them to. They put into the market what they see consumers want—consumers just don't know it yet. These visionaries initially ignore consumers and industry critics and act on their personal conviction.

When Schultz started Il Giornale, he was rather meticulous about translating each element of his personal experience from Italy: bow ties for the wait staff, no low seating—only bar-height tables, Italian opera blasting from the speakers, not even a lowfat milk option.

Consumers loved the concept, but they rejected some of the more esoteric details. Careful not to compromise on the overall vision, Schultz evolved his Italian coffee bar concept into what today is Starbucks.

Market innovators let consumers fine-tune products, not create them. They start by envisioning a step-change in the market and throwing it out there to see if the market adopts their view.

Innovative brands are driven by visionary people or small teams following their intuition. These people have invested tremendous energy, thought, and devotion in their passionate interest in the brand. Business planning often comes second to making a dream come true or realizing a cultural opportunity.

I'm a huge believer in intuition. It is the creative force behind marketing success. But does intuition have to be so unpredictable and limited to the very few natural visionaries in the business? Does it have to rely on a chance business trip to Milan for the lightbulb to go on? Is there a way to discipline intuition and make it accessible to the rest of us without losing its edge? A fresh way to structure market research to better identify these social truths driving market innovation and brand hijacks?

IS IT TIME TO HIJACK MARKET RESEARCH?

Let's face it. Market research is in a state of metamorphosis. Thought leaders such as Jerry Zaltman, David Lewis, Douglas Atkin, Andrew Ehrenberg, Stephen Walker, and Wendy Gordon are challenging our dependence on segmentation studies, focus groups, and consumer insights, as well as our tendency to ask fixed-response questions to guide our marketing research.

Zaltman argues that most moderated research "addresses at a surface level what consumers think about what managers think consumers are thinking about." Go back. Read that last sentence again. It makes a lot of sense.

He says that we need to gather true insights from the unconscious mind of the market rather than the more superficial conscious level. He maintains that we cannot study brand appeal and consumer choice outside of their social context:

> Consumers don't make decisions deliberately. As it turns out, the selection process stems from unconscious forces, and is greatly influenced by the consumer's social and physical context. Consumers cannot readily explain their thinking and behavior.

Lewis argues that "mass markets" no longer exist. He cautions us against segmentation studies:

> The top-down approach of segmentation inevitably ignores or fails to identify developing niche markets and leads companies to reject innovative niche products and services that have potential wider appeal.

Headmint's Stephen Walker predicts that our comfort zone with research will soon be over.

> Anyone attending a focus group today sees how research has itself been "hijacked" by professional respondents, puppet moderators, and a "cover your ass" mentality. We need new ways to harness the input of consumers in the co-creation and evaluation of marketing. Winning marketers will now create new, proprietary ways of learning and creating with, not from, specific versus random consumers of the brand.

Zaltman, Ehrenberg, and Gordon argue that our accepted commandments of consumer behavior are utterly wrong. They claim that effective advertising isn't based on rational consumer behavior that can be easily articulated in a research environment. They assert that competitive brand profiles hardly differ, and that our definition of the consumer "is stuck in a 20th century model of thinking."

> We have spent the last 50 years learning how to be alchemists—how to turn the base metal of product and service into gold. We have developed a whole language to talk about brands. A brand can be constructed, its essence and personality understood. It can then be designed, positioned, repositioned, developed and communicated in such a way that the consumer must be drawn to it. Or so we believe.

In *How Customers Think*, Zaltman references HBS professor Rohit Deshpande, whose study found that "over eighty percent of all market research serves mainly to reinforce existing conclusions, not to test or develop new possibilities."

Douglas Atkin, one of the most outspoken and forward-thinking account planners in the business, claims that "an effective planner is his own worst enemy." He argues that planning currently is about rigging our research to back-sell creative solutions.

> Planners don't make brands. Planners make brands make sense. Reality is never linear . . . until afterwards.

If you don't know Atkin, you could mistake him for a bitter, cynical relic. But he is quite the contrary. A provocateur at heart, he is one of the leaders taking strategic research and planning into the twenty-first century.

THE DAWN OF CULTURAL RESEARCH

The old methods seem to be failing us. So what next?

What's needed is a new approach. And what's emerging is a research discipline that uses in-depth cultural analysis to uncover social insights.

Cultural research goes beyond individual behavior. It studies social trends, emerging values, or simply how consumers live and act within their tribal groups. If this sounds a lot like cultural anthropology, well, it is.

Just in case I haven't been perfectly clear before: I am not talking about hiring cool hunters. Nor will focus groups and ethnographic studies serve to unearth the necessary social insights that drive breakthrough brands. Surface-level descriptive information provided by focus group moderators inevitably lacks the subtlety and depth required to gather the necessary insights that ignite passion for an initiative.

This is not about jumping onto the next fad. Trend reports typically focus on fleeting whims and ephemeral taste profiles. Brand hijackings occur when seeded ideas tap into sustainable cultural insights—insights that will remain stable over time.

Trend reports are further weakened by the way they attempt to interpret current events. Such analysis is often left to the scout as an afterthought. It lacks a thorough and deep exploration into the consumers' own interpretation of their attitudes and behaviors.

No, this is something entirely new, something that marketers are just starting to do. It's about diving deep into the cultural context of your early market to identify stable social trends.

The discipline of cultural research is about projects such as analyzing how cults work in order to apply that knowledge to brand tribes; researching what values and principles today's consumers share in order to understand why PBR was chosen as the "anti-brand" badge; creating a personal image of what your target community looks like by reading the magazines and books they read and watching the TV shows they watch; and delving deep into the socio-historical context of what "defiance" stands for in the twenty-first century to rebuild Dr. Martens.

The job function of the market researcher is changing. It's a position that needs to leave its back-seat status and start driving marketing strategy. It needs to evolve from a quantitative and qualitative discipline into an anthropological one. Researchers must take on the mind-set of a journalist, investigating cultural details and crafting compelling narratives from those nuances. They must identify the triggers and hooks that help lead the market to adopt new—and most likely oppositional—social norms. Researchers must become thought-leaders, not mere imitators of pop culture.

They must read and think about the patterns of social interaction: Who influences whom? What codes of conduct and social cues do we use in everyday life? It will be the researchers' responsibility to study how consumers live and act within their tribes.

It will inevitably pay off for research managers to remain ever watchful of how their products are used in the real world. When London bartenders were discovered flavoring their vodkas with fruit, for example, it led to the launch of Absolut Citron and other flavor flankers that kept the category fresh.

Ultimately, it will become the researchers' job to define the seed idea within the social truth they've unearthed and position it at the sweet spot between product and culture. Or, in the words of Harvard's cultural marketing authority Doug Holt:

> Managers must learn to anticipate new [cultural] contradictions and to select the one that best aligns with the brand's authority. And, if that weren't enough, they must then choose to align with the appropriate subculture and understand their ethos deeply enough to construct a credible and evocative [seed idea].
>
> Such knowledge doesn't come from focus groups or ethnography or trend reports—the marketer's usual means for "getting close to the customer." Rather, it comes from a cultural historian's understanding of ideology as it waxes and wanes, a sociologist's charting of the topography of contradictions the ideology produces, and a literary critic's expedition into the culture that engages these contradictions.
>
> To create powerful [seed ideas], managers must get close to culture—and that means looking far beyond consumers as they are known today.

Barbie Gets a Makeover After All

Let's give Mattel another chance. The "Pink Anger" years are behind us now, and Barbie is a prime example of a brand ready for another hijack. Let's take a look at how cultural research could help bring this aging icon into the twenty-first century.

When Barbie debuted in 1959, she was an accurate representation of the adult female ideal of the period: She epitomized the coquettish, submissive blonde beauty. She was a stewardess in the days before there were "flight attendants"; a secretary in the days before there were "personal assistants"; a housewife in the days before there were "stay-at-home dads." But as times changed, Barbie stayed the same while women's roles changed radically. And so she lost her social relevance. Girls, particularly those in their tweens, couldn't relate to Barbie any longer. They needed a more accurate role model.

In order to determine what kind of world is appropriate for Barbie as a "modern woman," cultural marketers could turn to *Sex and the City* for all the answers. Why not simply analyze the social truths behind the TV show to update Barbie? Without diving in too deep, here are some truths that a cultural researcher might come up with:

Women want it all.

Sex and the City broke the taboos that needed to be broken (e.g., women can't talk frankly about sex) and reclaimed the clichés that were too fun to let go (e.g., buying a new pair of Manolo Blahniks solves any problems). It avoided the pitfall of stereotyping women by embracing one extreme and then the other, all while retaining a charming, quirky familiarity.

Modern women want to hang on to the best parts of the traditional female persona as well as the best parts of the feminist revolutionary model. They want to be perceived as being smart and capable as well as sexy. It's not about being sassy, which carries the emotional, trendy value of a classic brand; it's about being savvy, which carries the social value of a hijacked brand. Being savvy means having staying power.

It would be wrong to compare Barbie just to Carrie Bradshaw. Barbie is not the fashionable, capable, yet oftentimes-neurotic main character. She is the combination of all four women: professionally successful and playful, serious and fun-loving, bold and vulnerable, crazy and a little bit conventional.

Girlfriends are more than just friends.

Another truth that cultural researchers could derive from watching the show concerns the role that girlfriends play in the modern woman's life. *Sex and the City* claimed the buddy system for adult women. The level of intensity and intimacy enjoyed by the four main characters was formerly associated only with young men and women who were in college—it was not available to grown-up professionals. The show demonstrated that women could have their ultimate emotional and social bonds with their girlfriends and get anything else they might need from men.

Final episode notwithstanding, *Sex and the City* thereby eliminates the cliché of becoming the bride being the ultimate Barbie fantasy. Instead, it is clear that Barbie needs to live in a world in which real, honest conversations among friends can take place. (The Barbie of the 1960s could never have had a real conversation, and certainly not one about sex.)

THE BRAND HIJACK ROADMAP

Now that you have an idea, what's next? How do you create buzz and get the market involved? How do you cultivate a passionate user base that's eager to act on behalf of your brand? How do you conquer the mainstream?

Market participation arises when a brand hands over an innovation to consumers and allows potential converts to help shape the message. A brand hijack relies on the power of the idea, the chosen early peer-to-peer networks, and the tactics used to expose the idea to a larger audience.

In the early stages of a launch, the key difference between the brand hijack approach and conventional marketing is how the brand initiative catches on. Ideally, a brand hijack involves an early market that is likely to realize the potential of the brand idea, and eventually will help lower the barriers of adoption for the main market. It is crucial to hook this early market with subconscious techniques—rather than through a traditional top-down proposition—before bringing scale to the initiative. This discovery process enables the early market to establish its passion and ownership for the brand.

Only once a brand idea has hit Next Big Thing status will a main market be ready to digest and adopt it. That's the stage when the brand owner needs to take back control of the message and switch to conventional above-the-radar marketing methods.

———————

The following chapters will lead you through the brand hijack roadmap. It demystifies the seeding process and delivers a plan for *how to get hijacked* in an actionable and practical way.

CHAPTER 14

Phase I: Tribal Marketing

You can't mass-produce authenticity.
—David Lewis, *The Soul of the New Consumer*

Once you've nailed the idea, it's time to nurture your early market.
These innovators and early adopters will be the first to realize the potential of the brand and help lower the barriers of adoption for the main market. They will define the brand by incorporating it into the very fabric of their tribe. The brand will become 50 percent "them."

The early market is often a subculture made up primarily of unconventional thinkers or opinion leaders. They are motivated primarily by one of two drivers: a quest for authentic products or a desire to display their social knowledge.

As early as the 1930s, Hungarian philosopher Karl Mannheim had elaborated on how important it is to integrate these early market trendsetters, or as he called them, the "cultural elite":

> Even in mass-democracy, cultural sublimation, as for example in art and fashion, can take place only if small groups of connoisseurs, who create and mold taste, already exist, and slowly diffuse the content and the technique of sublimation over the rest of society. In all spheres of cultural life, the function of such elites is to express cultural and psychological forces in a primary form and to guide collective extraversion and introversion.
>
> If these small groups are destroyed or thwarted in their

selection, the social conditions for the emergence and persistence of culture disappear.

THE ROLE OF THE EARLY MARKET

All this talk about "engaging the marketplace" is well and good, but what does it mean in practice? What specific roles will consumers and other stakeholders play in shaping brands?

Here are just a few possibilities:

Product Developer

You have a virtual army of passionate users ready and waiting to help you optimize your product or service. And you don't even have to pay for their services. Why not harness their creative energy? Linux, eBay, and Palm provide examples of just a few brands that have allowed the market to participate in developing and refining their products.

Satjiv Chahil, Palm's former Chief Marketing Officer, calls his company's collaboration with the market "the Palm Economy." He says:

> Much innovation and development comes from people outside our company, from developers, service providers, consultants, even communities. We encourage people to share our vision and join in the opportunity.

Brand Folklore Creator

Early markets are your best storytellers. They will add meaning to your brand and help translate its message to a larger, more conservative market by creating rituals and myths around it. Brands often "tip," as Gladwell would say, to mainstream acceptance as soon as the market has put its own spin on the meaning.

Authenticator

A recent Roper Report study found that—by a large margin—people prefer to get information from other people. Using peer-to-peer networks to diffuse ideas and brands into the marketplace is extremely powerful because it's organic, authentic, and sustainable.

Roper Report: Best Source of Ideas and Information		
PEOPLE	ADVERTISING	POINT DIFFERENCE
Which brands are best 60%	33%	27

REALITIES OF THE EARLY MARKET

There is a common misconception that early markets must be part of a cool subculture. This is, after all, how a lot of guerrilla marketers make their living—by being gatekeepers to the young, the tragically hip, and the beautiful. They make it easy for themselves by accumulating preselected lists of whom they deem to be cool, and then selling marketers generic access to these tastemakers.

It's one of the great ironies of our industry that just about every brand seems to be in a constant process of "rejuvenating" itself. We all create the same target consumer profiles, pursue the same subcultures, and use the same marketing tools (sponsor music, anyone?).

The typical subculture target? In most marketing plans, it is either a preselected and proprietary list of tastemakers (heavy on the DJs, musicians, and filmsters), the "gay" market, the "urban" market, or the "youth" market. These generic, overused sectors are not bound by values, but rather by superficial factors such as age, sexual orientation, or skin color.

But marketing isn't that easy. It takes a lot of hard work to come up with fresh yet relevant and effective plans.

There are many examples of hijacked brands with seeding initiatives that did not appeal to the coolest of the cool. Less-than-hip librarians drove the success of Michael Moore's book *Stupid White Men*. When HarperCollins asked Moore to tone down the book after the September 11th attacks, he refused. Frustrated, he went to his local library and conducted readings from the book. Librarians quickly took up his cause and inundated Harper with e-mails and phone calls. Eventually, the publisher relented and released the book without the "politically appropriate" edits. It remained on *The New York Times* bestseller list for over a year.

Red Bull offers another example. Although it does have initiatives—such as the DJ school and the can art competition—aimed at "cool" subcultures, the company also values everyday people. It targets truck drivers and Silicon Valley programmers—people in need of a quick energy boost after a long day at work. Hardly what most marketers would consider a sexy proposition.

Let's take a closer look at the potential comeback of Dr. Martens. A guerrilla marketing agency actually proposed sending an "influencer" mailing; sampling existing DJ and publicist lists, existing college lists, and up-and-coming bands as well as A-/B-band lists; and staging product placements at high society events.

But what relevance did this proposal have to the brand? Docs are not part of the beautiful people lifestyle. In its essence, Docs are a practical shoe for hardworking, blue-collar folks. Rather than sampling DJ Premier and the Yeah, Yeah, Yeah's for $2,500 a pop (or the Foo Fighters and Flaming Lips for much more), Docs should position itself as the brand of shoes for the workers behind pop culture, not the stars themselves.

Dr. Martens could focus its marketing efforts on the roadies, the bouncers—the people behind the scenes. It should get back to its working class roots. The skinheads wore Docs because they thought of themselves as working class heroes. It's time to ditch the stars and the ravers, the cool set. To regain credibility, Docs must feed the core and define a new working class. Docs versus trendy sneakers could be like Ken Loach (the filmmaker whose documentaries tackle such subjects as Mexican cleaners on strike in L.A.) versus Hollywood.

Today's social tribes are not generic. In fact, they are becoming more and more narrowly defined. This complexity makes precise targeting—the product of deep understanding of your consumers—critical. Anthropologist Grant McCracken describes the multiple identities and true diversity of the modern consumer:

> There has been a quickening "speciation" among social groups. Teens, for example, were once understood in terms of those who were cool and those who weren't. But in a guided tour of mall life a few years ago, I had 15 types of teen lifestyle pointed out to me, including heavy-metal rockers, surfer-skaters, b-girls, Goths, and punks. Each of these groups sported their own fashion and listened to their own music. The day of the universally known Top 40 list is gone.
>
> Gender types are proliferating. Whole new categories of powerful, forthright femaleness have emerged, while "maleness" is undergoing its own florescence. Gayness, which used to mean adhering to a limited number of public behavioral models, has rapidly subdivided into numerous subgroups. Many of these groups have developed their own literature, music, and even retail communities. They have become social worlds.
>
> New species of social life can form everywhere: around rock groups (Deadheads); football teams (Raider fans); TV series (Trekkies); leisure activities (line dancers); means of transport (Hell's Angels); sports (Ultimate Frisbee); movies *(The Rocky Horror Picture Show)*; technology (Geeks).

The optimal early market for your brand isn't necessarily the heavily pierced, tattooed fringe. The early market is the network of innovators and opinion leaders that are most likely to resonate with your product. Period.

SELECTING THE RIGHT EARLY MARKET

For an idea to really take off, you must choose an early market that has the skills, time, and tools to appreciate your brand. Seth Godin explained why Napster was the ideal initiative to plant with college students: "They combined the three things necessary for the virus to catch on: fast connection, spare time, and an obsession with new music." So it was that Napster came to dominate college dorm rooms (where it also originated).

When evaluating whether a subculture is the suitable early market for your brand, there are four basic criteria to consider:

Credibility with the Main Market

Is the audience you've selected a credible innovator of this brand initiative? Does the main market look to them for innovations?

When Absolut launched in the United States in 1981, it was one of the first mainstream companies to target the gay market. It ran print ads in gay publications such as *The Advocate* and focused distribution in gay nightspots such as San Francisco's Castro district.

Why did the Swedish company take what was at the time such a novel approach? Because it knew that the culturally creative part of the gay community it targeted was associated with urban sophistication and style. As demographer Gary Gates says, gay men are the "canaries" of creative communities. This imprimatur was essential to the success of an unknown spirits brand like Absolut, which had to build its legitimacy on qualities other than provenance and heritage.

Once the taste-making, highbrow gay market had adopted the brand, other urban sophisticates like artists and socialites quickly joined the bandwagon. Eventually, they influenced the main market for whom the brand was originally intended: married, middle-aged, suburban males.

And, of course, this early market paved the way for Absolut's now iconic advertising, which established it as a fashion brand rather than a conventional spirits brand.

AFFINITY TO THE SEED IDEA

Will the seed idea resonate with your subculture?

There is no need to pursue an audience if you cannot convince them of the value of your idea. 3M did not see any potential in the commercial use of Post-Its when they were created. It referred to the product as the "failed adhesive experiment." But the inventor, Art Fry, wouldn't stop pestering his bosses with possible uses. Eventually, they agreed to research the market potential of the product.

At first, results were unpromising. Most people laughed when told about the adhesive notes. They thought the idea was silly and superfluous.

Then someone handed out samples to executive assistants. This early market discovered multiple uses for the product, from sending notes to book-marking documents to labeling files. They thought Post-Its were irresistible. Said one customer: "It's fun to use, it's addictive, it's just so neat." Based on these results, when 3M launched the product, it sent generous samples to the secretaries of high-level executives in large corporations.

Now it's hard to imagine life without Post-It notes.

Willingness and Persuasiveness

Are they willing to participate? Are they able to sway the main market? Are they socially connected, knowledgeable, and articulate?

Right after Pfizer broke the silence about impotence, and before they targeted consumers directly with a TV campaign, they ran a print campaign directed at urologists. Because Viagra is a prescription drug, it was critical to get the attention and involvement of these doctors.

As specialists, urologists played a key role in the promotion of Viagra as a safe and effective cure for impotence. Some, like Dr. Harin Padma-Nathan, promoted Viagra through the media, pronouncing it "very safe" in magazines and newspapers. Others recruited patients to try the drug. For example, Dr. John Stripling of Atlanta wrote three hundred prescriptions the first day Viagra became available. A few even dispensed the drug via the internet after a shady "virtual" consultation.

Within the first six months, these gatekeepers wrote six million prescriptions for more than fifty million of the happy blue pills.

Ability of the Brand to Dominate

Can the brand gain critical mass—either in user base or cultural influence—to tip? Is the context right for the initiative to succeed within this target? You should only target an early market in which you can make an impact.

Instead of thinking big when launching the Macintosh, Apple thought small—five hundred to be exact. Its goal was simply to be the computer of choice within the graphics department of Fortune 500 companies. It was a market that obviously was inspired by Apple's belief that "People with passion can change the world for the better. And we believe that creativity is the force that pushes the human race forward."

Even though this target market was tiny in terms of numbers, Apple knew that it was big in terms of influence. After all, these were the people responsible for a high-profile process—providing presentations for executives and marketing professionals.

It was a market that was easy to penetrate and dominate quickly. From this beachhead, Apple gained credibility within the corporation. Shrugging off the directive of the technology department, senior executives and the marketing and sales departments applauded the technology and raved about the "magic" behind the Mac. Furthermore, this group's influence extended outside the company to vendors such as creative agencies and publishers. Apple set a new standard . . . through the backdoor.

ENTERING THE EARLY MARKET

A breakthrough idea needs both innovators and opinion leaders to create critical mass, and varying numbers of each. Within early markets, the fringe facilitates innovation and the opinion leaders encourage mass adoption. Critical mass is achieved once the rate of adoption is self-sustaining. Making contact with these groups is the most delicate and critical stage of the hijack operation.

The Ripple Effect

Approaching early markets with social initiatives.

Social initiatives are highly visible. Their purpose is to lend social status to the early market. To these trendsetters, having discovered the brand and being the one recommending it works as a sort of social currency. This is particularly true of initiatives for films, music, or fashion. In fact, it applies to any shared entertainment product or badge, where the risk of embarrassing oneself with a bad recommendation or the wrong fashion item is high, but the rewards for being seen as a trusted source of trend information are even higher.

Trendsetters are generally influenced by social outliers—people who exist even further on the outskirts of the mainstream. Let's call these innovators the *influencers of the influencers*. Getting them on board sets in motion a linear pattern of influence from the extreme fringe all the way to the mass public. In their book *The Deviant's Advantage,* Ryan Mathews and Watts Wacker describe this pattern as "the movement from the Fringe, to the Edge, to the Realm of the Cool, to the Next Big Thing, and, finally, to social convention."

We call it the *ripple effect*.

Blair Witch did this well. It first targeted Internet junkies and hardcore film buffs through postings at film sites on the Web. Then it seduced elite art house fans with publicity stunts during the Sundance Film Festival. Next, it enticed more mainstream art house fans through a screening tour at colleges and universities. It wasn't until the initiative created buzz among these communities and the film was released that Artisan advertised *Blair Witch* to the mass market.

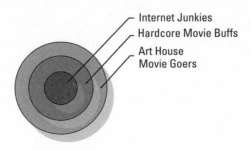

Internet Junkies
Hardcore Movie Buffs
Art House
Movie Goers

Bowling for Users

Approaching early markets with personal initiatives.

Personal initiatives are not as risky as social initiatives. They are less visible, offering a more personal, functional impact rather than status. Fringe innovators are less crucial in this type of diffusion; early adopters are more critical.

Rather than creating a linear ripple effect, the right way to approach early markets for personal initiatives is to create scale by dominating one vertical niche at a time. Tech marketing pioneer Geoffrey Moore gave this entry strategy the name "bowling alley" marketing.

> The goal of bowling alley marketing is to keep moving from niche to niche, developing momentum. Each niche is like a bowling pin, something that can be knocked over in itself but also can help knock over one or more additional pins.

The folks at Palm used this strategy to great effect. When they launched, the initial effort was to target people like themselves: C-level managers in Silicon Valley. This was during the technology boom when C-level executives were the stars of the new economy. These high-profile players were the perfect early market for the Palm: As soon as they adopted it, it became the personal organizer of choice for any professional associated with the New Economy.

However, the company realized that penetration in other professions was lagging. So it created content and add-ons that would appeal to additional vertical markets such as textbook downloads for college students, drug databases for doctors, and grading software for teachers.

Focusing on vertical markets has helped Palm maintain market share leadership despite increased competition.

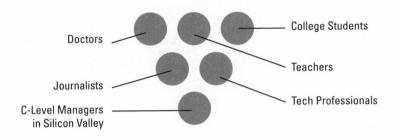

Doctors

College Students

Journalists

Teachers

C-Level Managers
in Silicon Valley

Tech Professionals

THE ART OF SEEDING

The idea behind seeding is to find an emotional hook that will pull the early market deep into the brand experience. The idea should make consumers feel ownership for the brand and encourage them to become shepherds for the initiative.

Hijacked brands incubate on the irrational fringe. Seeding is not about mass coercion. It's about things barely glimpsed from the corner of your eye. It is about giving the early market ownership through subconscious techniques. The art of seeding is the art of playing into the nuances of human nature.

Let's take a look at four of the major seeding techniques.

Declare a New Worldview

Give your initiative greater meaning and authenticity by fostering a belief system, perhaps even visible leadership.

IKEA is not just a furniture retailer; it is an ambassador of Swedish values—equality, simplicity, and community. The company consistently educates consumers about its beliefs in everything it does, from in-store POP to catalogue copy to Web site manifestos.

For founder Ingvar Kamprad, "togetherness" is at the core of the philosophy. He adopts a long-term communitarian attitude toward employees, suppliers, and customers. In addition, the company strengthens ties with its customers through its babysitting service and donations to charities like Habitat for Humanity.

It is this larger worldview that helps to keep consumers loyal, so they will put up with all the inconveniences of shopping there. Kamprad has humanized his company. In an era marked by increasing backlash to corporate globalization, IKEA manages to continue expanding its global empire with minimal public criticism and resistance.

Play Hard to Get

Place only the early market "in-the-know" with an unusually scarce, deliberate, and seductive soft sell. Persuade, don't sell at this phase.

Dickies Workwear has been the Next Big Thing for more than a decade. When grunge devotees started to favor its utilitarian clothes in the 1990s, the eighty-year-old company was heralded as an emerging brand. Flushed by the attention, it entered the youth market with a street-wear line.

A decade later, the company is still the "new" hip brand. Madonna wore a pair of customized Dickies pants for one of her Academy Award performances. Its work clothes are sold in chic boutiques alongside Armani and are favored by stars such as Puff Daddy and Kate Moss. The company has managed an annual growth rate of 10 percent for much of the past decade.

How has Dickies managed to keep up with the chic set? Reverse psychology.

In 2000, the company decided to stop chasing cool. It eliminated the street-wear line and focused on its working class heritage. Said Dickies' in-house creative director, Mark Krauter:

> The decision was made to get back to our roots and eliminate products from our line that didn't fit with work-wear. Of course people wear our clothes for all kinds of reasons. But our decision is to market it as work-wear. People can buy us for their own reasons.

At the same time, it has bolstered the blue-collar message by increasing placements in paint and hardware stores and sponsoring an annual "Worker of the Year" Award. This decision has been pivotal in keeping Dickies authentic.

Even though they no longer directly target hipsters, Dickies does practice indirect targeting. The company outfits staff members at trendy SoHo restaurants. And while advertising is targeted at the working class market, the company selects music and graphics that young people can relate to.

Dickies' refusal to openly chase the youth market is based on an old seduction principle: Play hard to get. Robert Greene writes in *The Art of Seduction:*

> If your targets become too used to you as the aggressor, they will give less of their own energy, and the tension will slacken. You need to waken them up, turn the tables. . . . Begin with a touch of aloofness, an unexpected nonappearance, a hint that you are growing bored. Stir the plot by seeming interested in someone else. Make none of this explicit; let them only sense it and their imagination will do the rest, creating the doubt you desire. Soon they will want to possess you . . .

Create Brand Folklore

Develop specific customs, rituals, vocabulary, relationships, and experiences to build a passionate community.

Starbucks created coffee culture; it introduced a new morning routine. Before Starbucks was around, most Americans were content to boil water, pour it into a cup of flavored crystals, and call it coffee. Things weren't much better at the office, where you could get a cup of joe for fifty cents from a vending machine. Starbucks changed all this. Coffee became civilized, imbued with the complexity and nuances of ritual. Americans learned to buy beans, grind them, and brew real coffee at home. Or, just as likely, they queued up before going to work, learning the differences between machiatto and espresso, Kona and Colombian.

In addition to coffee rituals, Starbucks introduced a new vocabulary; an entirely different language was used to communicate with the barista. Your command of the lingo reveals if you are a regular customer or not. Simply asking for a "large" coffee instead of a "venti" can be an embarrassing faux pas.

The company now has over 6,300 stores. Much of Starbucks' growth can be attributed to what's called "social proof." The long lines, the smell of the beans, the ubiquitous white cups emblazoned with the green logo—all these cues, co-created by Starbucks customers, have helped to attract new customers.

Simply put, people learn new behaviors by observing their peers, and the more they see others engaging in that behavior, the more likely they are to copy it. Research psychologist Robert O'Connor confirmed this principle with his study of timid children. He showed the children a video with eleven scenes, each of a solitary child watching a group and then successfully joining the group. Afterward, the shy children interacted with their peers at a normal level. After six weeks, they were the most socially active kids in their schools.

Through a similar process, Starbucks customers learned their new coffee habit by modeling their behavior after that of their peers. Social proof is a key factor in the exponential growth of the stores.

Reward Insiders

The social currency of the early market is being part of the Next Big Thing. Keep it exclusive. Don't make it too easy for people to "get in."

Palm was a master seducer when it came to seeding early markets. It used the power of exclusivity and scarcity to get C-level managers at industry events to buy the Palm Pilot at a special price. (Please note: It did not give the devices away for free. The early market passion and ownership was a lot more authentic because the managers still had to pay for the Palm.)

Studies such as Stephen Worchel's cookie experiment show that when something is scarce, people desire and value it more. In this study, consumers were given cookies in a jar. One group had a jar with ten cookies in it; the other had a jar with two. Each group was asked to rate the taste and quality of the cookies. The group with the scarce supply rated the cookies "as more desirable to eat in the future, more attractive as a consumer item, and more costly than the identical cookie in abundant supply." In other words, we automatically assume that something that is limited in supply is more desirable and valuable. Introducing the

Palm Pilot to C-level managers in exclusive environments automatically made the gadget seem more reliable and made those managers who had a Palm feel special.

Palm also introduced initiatives to reward its loyal insiders. In New York City, it installed one hundred beaming stations that gave users access to downloads ranging from restaurant reviews to haiku. These tactics created a sense of privilege and community for its users. Only they could use the stations. At the same time, since Palm owners used the stations in public, they served as a means of educating non-users about the device.

In other words, Palm effectively used two seduction techniques. First, in offering free perks from beaming stations, it harnessed the law of reciprocation, which states that we try to repay in kind what another person has provided us. Studies have shown the power of this rule. In one experiment, a college professor sent Christmas cards to a sample of strangers. The majority returned the gesture without even asking who he was. The stations operated on this deeper social level, making it more likely that customers would spread positive buzz about Palm.

Secondly, by encouraging people to use their Palms in public, the company tapped into the social proof principle. In situations of ambiguity, people invariably look toward others to decide what behavior is appropriate. In this case, the ambiguous situation was the use of a new technology: "Should I adopt an electronic organizer or not?" Seeing others use the Palm increased the likelihood that the answer would be "yes."

Creating a Logical Context

Now that we've looked at some seeding techniques, let's complicate things further. Let's talk pre-seeding the social context before a brand can be seeded.

Pre-seeding is not necessary for every brand. It should only be done in the rare cases when you need to establish a logic so that the idea driving your brand makes sense.

It's sometimes the case that the context behind the brand—the social insight—needs to be disseminated into the market before the brand can be successfully launched. If this is the case, companies will need to conduct a

(cont'd)

marketing campaign not for the brand itself, but for the insight that primes the market for the brand. Gap did this when it pre-seeded the idea that khakis were classic—and not work-wear—before introducing khakis as the business casual brand.

Viagra also pre-seeded the market. The pharmaceutical was initially developed to treat angina. I'll spare you any cheap puns, but throughout tests, Pfizer concluded that Viagra had some pretty interesting side effects among male study participants.

The problem was that Viagra was a cure for something nobody wanted to talk about. Sufferers were embarrassed by their condition and often wouldn't readily admit to it, even to their doctors.

So in the months leading up to the drug's release, Pfizer conducted a publicity campaign to educate the public about the pervasiveness of impotence. To defuse the stigma of the condition, the company cleverly introduced the market to the euphemism "erectile dysfunction," which they further simplified into the acronym "ED."

Once the condition was disguised in this new language, the taboo surrounding it diminished and the media pounced on the story. ED became a staple of late night jokes throughout the summer of 1998, even before the launch of Viagra was announced. By the time the drug was announced, people felt comfortable enough to talk with their doctors about their problems and ask for a prescription, something most never would have dared do prior to Pfizer's pre-seeding campaign.

GOOD THINGS COME IN SMALL INITIATIVES

To gain momentum, hijacked brands execute a number of small initiatives instead of focusing their efforts on one big advertising idea, as conventional brands do.

They do this because they want to stimulate market involvement rather than stifle it. If the company's message to the market starts out too loud, is too widely broadcast or is too narrowly focused, consumers won't feel like a partner in the brand's evolution. Developing too precise a message early on also puts you at risk for missing the mark—the marketer's own interpretations of the brand's subtlety may be off base.

In a brand hijack, the market must significantly influence the true meaning of the brand.

John Grant calls this the "sperm" strategy. Put several marketing programs into the market, he says, and then wait to see which catch on and develop a life of their own.

Hubertus Bigend, William Gibson's imaginary ad man in *Pattern Recognition* puts the following spin on it:

> I want to make the public aware of something they don't quite yet know that they know—or have them feel that way. Because they'll move on that. They'll think they've thought of it first. It's about transferring information, but at the same time about a certain lack of specificity.

THE RISK OF NOT SEEDING PROPERLY

Yes, seeding is tough. It's intuitive and subtle. It goes against most doctrines of conventional marketing. But it is a tactic that needs to be used for breakthrough brand initiatives. And used right. Let's look at some brands that ignored the needs of their subcultures or went about seeding in entirely the wrong way.

Blowing It by Going Directly Mainstream

One way to blow it is by ignoring seeding altogether.

Nike thought it could own action sports by going directly mainstream. Although its 1998 television campaign attempted to capture the skater mentality, it was soundly rejected. (The spots showed runners and tennis players being chased by police and posed the question, "What if all athletes were treated like skateboarders?")

Nike failed to understand the culture of its early market. It failed to enter the scene with low-key, incremental initiatives. It failed to focus marketing efforts on specialty boarder shops. In so doing, it utterly failed to demonstrate a real commitment to the tribe.

The negative response from the action sports community was unanimous: "Screw Nike. Support those who support the sport."

Cultural critic Thomas Frank described how Nike tried to remedy the situation:

> One day, Nike had decided to sell special shoes to skateboarders. But there was a problem. Not the obvious problem of whether or not skateboarders actually required special shoes but the problem of skater resistance.
>
> As Kelly Evans-Pfeifer of Goodby, Silverstein [Nike's agency] spun the tale, the problem when Nike "decided to get into the skateboarding market" was that "skateboarders did not want them there."
>
> Skateboarding, it turned out, was "an alternative culture" populated with difficult people who "don't really like this attention they're getting from mainstream companies." The cultural task the Planners faced was not to decide whether this hostility was deserved or warranted but to liquidate it.
>
> The objective for the advertising was not to reach a certain sales goal, but rather it had a more basic, grassroots task, which was that it needed to begin to start a relationship between Nike and skateboarders, and make skateboarders think that it wasn't such a bad thing that Nike was going to get involved.
>
> The key to bringing skaters into the brand's fold, then, was to transform Nike from an enemy into a sympathizer, "to acknowledge and harness all those feelings of persecution."

But the damage was done. Nike had blown it, and for several years it was locked out of the market.

Recently, as a new, less anti-corporate generation of skaters has emerged on the scene, Nike has made some headway. In trying to get it right with the early market this time around, the company has hired an editor from the skateboarding magazine *Transworld*, acquired the surf and skate company Hurley, and dramatically improved the quality of its shoes.

Blowing It by Providing the Wrong Product

Another way to blow it is by ignoring the specific needs of one's early market.

Let's take digital radio. Great idea, right? It's radio on steroids. It puts the listener back in the driver's seat, giving them the control to listen to the audio they like or the freedom to discover new music. And it's available everywhere, in top quality sound, with no interruptions. Surely, music and other audio lovers, as well as folks who always want to have the latest gadgets, would pay a premium for this service. Or so you'd think . . .

And yet more than a year after its release, XM-Radio had a mere 300,000 subscribers. Its rival Sirius had just a tenth of that.

Digital radio is a disruptive idea, a prime candidate for a brand hijack. It asks consumers to change their mindset: People aren't accustomed to investing in and paying for radio. As such, we would have expected digital radio's marketing to be more collaborative with early markets and the channels to be more directly targeted at innovators and early adopters.

Instead, digital radio is making the mistake of trying to provide a mass-market product for its early market. It's offering generic channels geared toward a mainstream listener rather than innovative channels for music freaks. For instance, there is a general hip-hop station on air. But for the early market of music fanatics, that genre is too broad. Old-school rap is unlike down-tempo, is unlike dancehall, is unlike afrobeat, etc.

Could alternative music classifications make sense to get digital radio off the ground? A genealogy channel (i.e., family tree of influence), a BPM channel (i.e., consistent beats per minute), tastemaker channel (i.e., opinion leader DJs), rare jazz recording channel—this is the sort of micro-appeal that will endear the service with niche markets.

Whatever the solution, it has to be built on an understanding of how to best serve your early market's need rather than how to hit mainstream as quickly as possible.

Blowing It by Underselling the Idea

You can also blow it through an underwhelming articulation of your seed idea.

TiVo is the next killer app in entertainment, a category killer. In a sense the brand has already made it: It has a small but passionate user base, and to "TiVo" has become a commonly used verb. But the company is on the brink of bankruptcy. As of early 2004, its stock was down to four dollars from a high of eighty. Between the time of its inception in 1997 and the winter of 2003, it had spent more than $300 million on advertising and had not yet signed up even half a million users. That's a customer acquisition cost upward of $600 per user. Cynics could comment that it would have been much cheaper for the company to give the product away.

Passionate TiVo users know that the device completely changes their viewing habits. And that's precisely where TiVo blew it. It marketed itself merely as a glorified VCR. But it is so much more than that. It reverses the leverage of control between TV, its channels, and the viewer. The marketing of TiVo lacks the articulation of the TiVo worldview: "You control your TV, it does not control you." That's the big idea. That's something that early adopters can rally around and passionately support. It has the David vs. Goliath aura, and it has a vision for the future of television. It is suddenly an easy-to-communicate concept, rather than a confusing, multi-benefit campaign that Goodby had put on air.

Blowing It by Focusing on the Wrong Networks

Are you sure that you have identified the right set of early adopters?

Remember Betamax? It was a far superior technology to VHS. But VHS became the standard in video recording because—as legend has it—it understood who its early market was: the porn industry.

JVC understood that the early adopters would not be the general population. Instead, they recognized a historical trend: Pornography is typically the first content created with any new media. Sony missed this insight and refused to give licensing rights to the industry. This decision sealed the fate of Betamax.

It was the adult film industry that created the first videos for VCRs. In fact, porn videos came out a full year before Hollywood movie releases. During the late '70s and early '80s, over 50 percent of all video rentals were X-rated. By refusing to give rights to this industry, Sony shot itself in the foot. It forced the early adopters to buy VHS instead.

Blowing It by Being Inauthentic

Consumers can tell the difference between genuine passion and hype.

I will never forget a seminar that I attended in London on cause-related marketing. Ben Cohen from Ben & Jerry's was the first speaker. He passionately talked about the company's sustainable mission. Even when he overdid it at times (e.g., his PowerPoint charts and spreadsheets looked handwritten, though they were clearly done on a computer—anything to appear "folksy"), he was genuine and credible.

After Ben Cohen's speech, Coca-Cola's U.K. General Manager went to the podium dressed in gray pinstripes to lecture us on the karmic and psychedelic free spirit of Fruitopia, a drink that would make the world a better place . . .

Everyone in the audience knew right then that Fruitopia would fail. Its pseudo '60s hippie persona was simply too much of a stretch for the buttoned-up executives from the American South. Fruitopia was exposed as a corporate poseur before it even launched, despite the valiant effort by Chiat/Day's Marty Cooke and his creative team.

Consumers never bought into the "feeling good and having fun" proposition of Coke's latest product. As one blogger ranted:

> As a general rule I hate advertising. Nonetheless that doesn't explain my intense aversion to the latest campaign for Coca-Cola's Fruitopia. (Did you know Fruitopia was a Coca-Cola product? Probably not. Part of the campaign is a deliberate effort to make you think that Fruitopia is made by a small, friendly company like Snapple instead of a big, mean, union-busting, corporate terrorist like Coca-Cola. Of course Snapple is now owned

by Quaker Oats; but as usual in advertising only image counts, not reality.)

The problem isn't the "feeling good and having fun." It's the idea that this is all there is; that it's all we should do. And the fact is, a nation in which all anyone does is feel good and have fun would be as sickeningly sweet, boring, uninteresting, and unfulfilling as Fruitopia itself.

It's important to note here that the point isn't that major corporations can't support brand hijacks. If that were the case, then IBM's support of the Linux operating system would have faced a similar premature death. Big Blue backing an anticapitalist movement? Come on. Of course, IBM's motive was economically driven. It believed that Linux was a great operating system and so became the brand's most committed major partner. Nevertheless, IBM made a genuine effort to maintain the support and involvement of the Linux community, and these efforts seem to be paying off.

IBM sends representatives to speak at open source conferences. It builds deep websites for developers and provides them with tools. It develops new apps. It stays in an open dialogue with the market. (And the one billion dollars that IBM committed to support Linux did not hurt either.)

The most visible, and likely most effective, tactic that Big Blue used was appointing a passionate evangelist to lead IBM's Linux efforts. Irving Wladawsky-Berger, an IBM-lifer, declared IBM's authentic support for the brand in *Linux Magazine:* "We are members of an industry that's out to change the world." IBM has backed up this lip service with action and attitude.

What, then, is the secret to being perceived by the market as authentic? "Confidence contrived does not work," states HBS prof Jerry Zaltman. You must truly believe in what you're doing in order to be effective. He cites a study about dental patients who received a placebo painkiller during a typically painful dental procedure:

The patients experienced a lack of discomfort *only if* the dentists also believed that the treatment they administered was an authentic painkiller. Unconscious behaviors emanating from these dentists reinforced their patients' belief in the placebo. However, when the dentists knew that the treatment was not authentic and merely pretended it was, patients experienced considerable discomfort.

Selecting and nurturing the most suitable early market for your brand is damn hard work. But the rewards in terms of diffusion of the message to the mainstream market are immeasurable.

CHAPTER 15

Phase II: Co-creation

I want to give the audience a hint of a scene. No more than that. Give them too much and they won't contribute anything themselves. Give them just a suggestion and you get them working with you.

—Orson Welles

Once the early market is hooked, it takes ownership of the brand's message. We generally call that *buzz*. Malcolm Gladwell calls it *the tipping point*. Yet, in spite of all the buzz about buzz, the concept remains one of the most misunderstood phenomena in marketing. Most marketers see buzz as another tool, another tactic. But buzz is actually an end, not a means. It's the byproduct of the skillful seeding of an early market.

Buzz can be both the message and the medium in the early and middle stages of a brand hijack. Dynamic peer-to-peer communication can "tip" a new idea to the main market. Buzz allows the trendsetting 20 percent to act as ad agency, dictating what the other 80 percent think is cool. It is the bridge that connects the two.

Furthermore, buzz transmits the brand message through interpersonal media. It gets the idea behind the brand—and not just the product or service itself—into the culture. As such, buzz is not just noise. More than just awareness, buzz delivers conviction. Buzz is a powerful medium that allows the market to discover, engage with, and ultimately help shape brand meaning. It occurs when brand owners let the market participate as co-creators voluntarily and enthusiastically, hence persuasively.

WHY BUZZ WORKS

Buzz communicates a new convention to the main market in a way that no other medium can because it travels with a few qualities that traditional media left behind long ago:

Attention

Buzz doesn't look, sound, or feel like any of the hundreds or thousands of conventional ads that bombard us daily. We take notice of buzz because it's fresh and hence stands out.

Learning

Buzz works mostly on a subconscious level. Psychologist Daniel Wegner once said that "most of what we know we don't know we know." Experts agree that about 95 percent of our learning occurs in the subconscious mind, and that's where buzz is most effective. In this sense, buzz goes way beyond awareness: We widely adopt the new norms that we learn from buzz without even being conscious of what we're doing.

Credibility

Consumers perceive personal recommendations as more than three times more credible than messages from traditional media, as is demonstrated by studies like this one from Britain's Henley Centre.

WHICH SOURCES OF INFORMATION ARE TRUSTED?

Husband/wife/partner	90%	And the credibility stakes are even higher when you go beyond information to imitation, etc.
Friends	82%	
Work Colleagues	69%	
TV News	50%	
Retailers	27%	
Manufacturers	27%	
Government	14%	
Adverts	14%	

Source: Henley Centre, UK

Likeability

Buzz benefits from the "halo" effect. When the messenger is a friend—not a manufacturer—the message is more likely to be received with respect.

Authenticity

Achieving buzz for your brand is the ultimate marketing reward and nearly impossible to reconstruct or benchmark. It will make your competitors envious because it is an undeniable indication that the market perceives your brand as authentic.

THE MANY FACES OF BUZZ

Buzz is a kind of "peer-to-peer storytelling," an easily misinterpreted term. It goes way beyond word-of-mouth. It is, in fact, predominantly non-verbal. Net, buzz is the sum of all *interpersonal interaction* related to a brand.

Linguists such as Harlan Lane, James Wertsch, and Jeffrey Pittman have found that about three-quarters of human communication is transmitted through nonverbal means. Anthropologist Edward Hall takes it a step further. He's identified ten "primary message systems," only one of which is verbal. Buzz is clearly more than literal "word-of-mouth"—peers actually communicate with one another mostly through nonverbal channels.

Buzz can spread through various verbal and nonverbal contagious forms, all of which tap into deep human social processes of learning and adaptation.

Verbal Buzz

The best-known form of buzz is verbal. It is buzz developed by seeding news. Word-of-mouth is what made *Cold Mountain* by Charles Frazier sell 1.6 million copies in just nine months in 1998. Not bad for a first novel about something as pastoral as a Southern soldier's journey home after the Civil War. The book enjoyed brisk sales from the get-go, especially in Southern independent bookstores where word-of-mouth was strong. Southerners connected with the story because it gave them a glimpse of what life might have been like for their ancestors after the war, and so they recommended the book to others.

The press often amplifies word-of-mouth, and one of the most influential "big mouths" is Oprah Winfrey. TiVo credits Winfrey with record sales when the talk show host did a seven-minute how-to segment on the product. TiVo's Brody Keast confirms: "We reached a peak in sales that we'd never seen before over the next two weeks. Oprah owns a TiVo, and she acted like a pitchwoman for the product."

Urban myths are also a form of verbal buzz. Just think what the alleged hallucinogenic properties of the worm in Mescal did to Tequila sales.

Finally, memes are a form of verbal buzz. Jay Conrad Levinson defines memes as a "self-explanatory message that communicates an entire idea . . . that is easily understandable in a matter of seconds." The TV show *The Apprentice* provides an example of a meme. Donald Trump's catchphrase, "You're fired!" amplified the program's impact on pop culture.

Advertisers obviously have caught on. Budweiser's "Whassup" commercials may have paved the way, but other advertisers soon followed. Verizon's "Can you hear me now?" tagline was quickly imitated by Jay Leno and SNL, a sure sign that the meme had become part of our everyday language.

Visual Buzz

Despite the fact that most people think of buzz as being verbal, other forms of buzz can prove more effective. They are more intuitive, and therefore have stronger learning and adaptation potential.

Buzz can catch on by being exceedingly visible. Visual buzz can be either behavioral or symbolic.

In the case of Palm, the behavioral buzz was demonstrative. Every time someone used a Palm handheld in a meeting or airport lounge, it acted as a product demonstration to an attentive audience. Palm caught on and used that technique to seed other niches. For instance, it supplied journalists with Palm Pilots at the Cannes Film Festival.

Imitation is another important behavioral amplifier. Fashion badges, like Gucci's baguette bag or Hilfiger clothing, catch buzz when the mainstream begins imitating tastemakers. That is why retailer Abercrombie & Fitch hires popular fraternity members to work in its stores. They will wear A&F clothes around college campuses and attract clientele to the store.

The cognitive scientist Albert Bandura is one of the fathers of the school of observational learning. He demonstrated very powerfully that you can learn a behavior by observing others. In an extreme clinical research study, he had herpephobics (people with a neurotic fear of snakes) watch a man go through a slow approach toward a snake, open the snake cage, sit down on a chair, and drape the snake over his neck, all the while giving himself calming instructions. Most of the project participants—lifelong phobics—were able to imitate this routine their first time around, after only one observational viewing. This is the power of observation and imitation.

However, visual buzz can also be symbolic in nature, spread by an increased awareness of the meaning behind a social initiative. Emblems can be used as an amplifier, for example. The AIDS ribbon was used to unite the gay community behind AIDS prevention and education. The cause "Against Animal Testing" was a buzz amplifier that established The Body Shop in the minds of socially conscious consumers worldwide.

Viral Buzz

Lastly, buzz can catch on virally. In these situations, the contagions are inherent in the brand initiatives, which blow away their early adopters by exceeding expectations.

Viral buzz is mostly cited in the context of digital amplification. Much has been made of Hotmail's "Get your free email at Hotmail.com" tagline, which accompanied each email message the service transmitted. But viral marketing does not have to be digital. FedEx was a market innovator in its time, using the package itself as a key marketing tool. Whenever a package was sent, it served as its own best advertising, introducing the recipient to the service.

One important aspect of viral buzz is that its effect is immediate and short-term. Only verbal and visual buzz can be sustained over long periods of time.

The Many Faces of Buzz

FORM	EXAMPLE	AMPLIFIER	TACTIC
Verbal	*Blair Witch*, Viagra, *The Apprentice*	Word-of-mouth, urban myth, press, meme	Seed news
Visual	Behavioral: Palm, Abercrombie & Fitch	Demonstration, imitation	Increase visibility
	Symbolic: AIDS awareness, The Body Shop	Emblem, causes	Increase awareness
Viral	Hotmail, FedEx	Inherent in product	Over-deliver

WHY BUZZ OUTLASTS HYPE

Buzz is not an outrageous stunt, a cool promotion, or a roach-bait trick. In other words, buzz is not hype.

Buzz is authentic opinion from consumers. According to David Lewis, "It is the infectious chatter that spreads from consumer to consumer about something of genuine interest to them." Because it is genuine, buzz is trusted.

Hype, on the other hand, is usually paid for by the brand owner through media and advertising. It is "targeted at consumers" and, as such, rightfully invites skepticism and distrust.

Perhaps the most important difference between the two is that buzz starts with a big social idea, whereas hype starts with a big media blitz. With hype, the message is primarily about the product or a "borrowed interest," not the product's meaning.

Sometimes, in creating hype, arrogance can lead companies to make overoptimistic claims and promises. BT Cellnet was accused of misleading advertising for its "Surf the Mobile Net" campaign of 2002. Cell phone users found themselves crawling the mobile net rather than surfing it.

It's most helpful to look at hype as a bad habit. This is particularly true in industries with products that don't have an objective standard of performance, such as the entertainment industry.

In Hollywood, hype is costing the studios dearly by making media effectiveness dwindle. Ten years ago, the average movie cost $12 million to market; now it costs $31 million. Why such a meteoric rise? The Hollywood machine has created a sort of advertising "arms race" as studios load up on ads and promotions, afraid of being out-shouted by the competition. The result is a tremendous amount of clutter. A recent Warner Brothers study revealed that an average of thirty movies are advertised on TV each week. In addition to clutter, hyper-spending has shortened the life cycle of movies in the theaters. "If you don't hit it within twenty-four to seventy-two hours, you're out of the game," said Universal Studio's Vice Chairman Marc Shmuger.

These two factors have contributed to making Hollywood advertising synonymous with hype and bluster . . . and left even some executives wishing it could rein things in. As New Line's Marketing President Russell Schwartz says, "If there was some kind of spending cap to keep us from our bad habits, it would be greatly welcomed."

Sometimes hype arises from an authentic "moment of insanity." Brandi Chastain and a Nike sports bra both got more than their respective fifteen minutes of fame when Chastain took off her shirt after scoring the winning kick in the 1999 Women's World Cup. Nike capitalized on the spurt of attention by releasing a parody ad in which Chastain battled the NBA's Kevin Garnett in a foosball game.

More often, however, hype-hungry stunts are the product of marketing campaigns. Guerrilla media tactics set out to catch people off guard, create awareness and talk value, and maybe provoke a smile. But all too often those tactics have nothing to do with the product itself. While funny or head turning, they don't carry a brand message. Puma used the Atlanta Olympics for one of its high-profile stunts when it paid track star Linford Christie to wear Puma contact lenses.

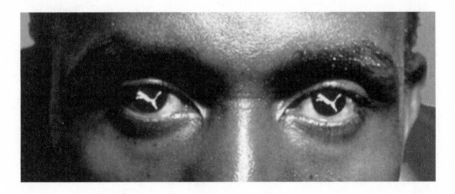

Guerrilla media stunts require balls. They are not about being illegal, but they are most effective when conducted in the gray zone, deliberately confronting the risk of conflict with authority. Of course, mischief marketing can backfire, sometimes in unexpected ways. For his movie *The Big One*, Michael Moore tried to use Nike's own style against itself—he challenged CEO Phil Knight to a footrace. If Moore were to win, Knight would have to build a shoe factory in Flint, Michigan. If Knight won, Moore would have to wear Nikes in public for life. Needless to say, Knight resisted the bait.

Marketers don't need to abandon hype tactics altogether. They can be effective media tools. But they have major limitations. By definition, hype tactics are loud, aggressive, and short-term in nature.

Buzz, on the other hand, has nothing to do with noise; it's about seduction. It involves the marketplace in the dissemination of a big idea. It helps consumers learn about a new norm and can be sustained long term. It is, put simply, a marketing and media tool of a higher order.

The Difference Between Buzz and Hype

BUZZ	HYPE
Is genuine	Is fabricated
Is co-created with the market	Is autocratic, leaked by the brand owner; the market is an audience, not a participant
Travels through grassroots, peer-to-peer communication	Uses mass media and staged events
Carries an authentic social message; it's *news*	Carries a biased product message; it's *publicity*
Is seductive and spreads exponentially	Is loud and aggressive
Is trustworthy	Can easily be distrusted
Is a long-term learning model	**Creates short-term awareness**

"THE CONSUMER AS ART DIRECTOR"

Anthropologist Ted Polhemus coined this phrase in the context of fringe fashion. But it rings true for all hijacked brands: The market becomes the co-creator, or more symbolically, the ad agency, for the brand it passionately endorses.

Buzz is at its most powerful when the early market enhances the original brand idea by creating new uses or rituals for the product, and then translates that message to the mainstream. In these situations, buzz can cause the brand to finally "tip."

Palm truly became mainstream when Silicon Valley managers

introduced a whole new ritual around exchanging virtual business cards. They started beaming their personal data from one PDA to another at the end of meetings. Palm itself could not have dictated this behavior to the market. Consumers had to create it themselves. All Palm could do was facilitate it (by introducing wireless technology with its Palm V), and let the market take over from there.

Red Bull tipped as soon as bartenders introduced the Stoli Bully across Europe. The legendary cocktail, comprised of Red Bull and Stolichnaya vodka, was rumored to have the power of Ecstasy. Again, Red Bull's sales force never could have dictated a signature drink like this to bartenders. But by targeting on-premise distribution at the right nightspots, it was able to facilitate the evolution of the product's usage.

Lambesis' former head of research, DeeDee Gordon, explains how early market involvement can move a trend from the fringe to the mainstream in the context of fashion:

> Those kids make things more palatable for mainstream people. They see what the really wired kids are doing and they tweak it. They start doing it themselves, but they change it a bit. They make it more usable.
>
> Maybe there's a kid who rolls up his jeans and puts duct tape around the bottom because he's the one bike messenger in school. Well, the translators like that look. But they won't use tape. They'll buy something with Velcro.
>
> Or then there was the whole baby-doll T-shirt thing. One girl starts wearing a shrunken down T-shirt. She goes to Toys 'Я Us and buys the Barbie T-shirt. And the others say, that's so cool. But they might not get it so small, and they might not get it with Barbie on. But there's a way I can change it and make it okay. Then it takes off.

These are all examples of the influence early markets can have on the adoption of new ideas. These consumers alter brand initiatives to make sense in their lives, thereby turning the brands into something the main market can understand. As a result, the brand initiatives themselves are imbued with greater cultural significance.

CHAPTER 16

Phase III: Mass Marketing

Companies will become story owners rather than product owners.

—Rolf Jensen, *The Dream Society*

Once an initiative has hit Next Big Thing status, the main market is ready to adopt it. Hijack marketing is not just about being stealth. It does not favor person-to-person interaction over mass media. Rather, it views media sequentially—recognizing the need to use different tactics throughout the phased go-to-market approach.

During the seeding phase, a hijack relies on interpersonal media to seduce the early market and make the brand digestible for the mass market. But as soon as the early market's buzz has reached the mainstream, it is crucial to switch back to conventional, above-the-radar marketing methods in order to build momentum and broaden awareness. In other words, it is time for the brand owner to take back control.

THE MAIN MARKET IS A PASSIVE FOLLOWER

Unlike the early market, the mainstream is not motivated by self-discovery and being in-the-know. It does not love breakthrough brand initiatives for the sake of the excitement of discovery. It needs cultural editors to recognize the truly cool stories, brands, communities, and behaviors. It emulates these early adopters and then establishes their deviance as convention.

The mass market is conservative. Rather than being revolutionary, it is evolutionary at best and pessimistic at worst. It is skeptical that the Next Big Thing really is the new standard. While the early market is excited to be the first to use a brand, the main market is content to follow the tastemakers.

The early market is mostly interested in cultural ideas that have the ability to evolve. Trendsetters and early adopters are not easily influenced by group consensus. They are way up in the old Maslow hierarchy, seeking self-actualization. And yet, while they will follow their own convictions, they also share a philosophical grounding, such as a belief in the expression of cultural creativity or a loathing for commercialization.

The main market, on the other hand, is mostly outer-directed. According to David Riesman, the sociologist who came up with this classification in 1950, outer-directed people tap into aspiration. They are largely influenced by what others think of them, and so they readily adopt status symbols.

The differences in mindset between these markets makes it clear why marketers must employ different media tactics throughout the adoption life cycle of a brand.

MAINTAINING MOMENTUM

If buzz is the driver of the early market, then momentum is the driver of the mass market. When momentum is maintained, it sends a signal to the mainstream that the initiative is legitimate and sustainable. The meaning of the brand has been established and the initiative has been translated into terms the main market can digest.

BMW's MINI Cooper Division has been breaking with automotive marketing convention (e.g., launch with TV, never show a dirty car, always show a silver car) from the start. And its novel approach has certainly generated buzz: Austin Powers, Madonna, and Sting all own one. But the brand has a major challenge ahead to keep momentum going in a category that has recently seen two "hot cars of the year"—the

VW Beetle and the PT Cruiser—fall from overexposure to obscurity in no time.

Alex Bogusky, cofounder of Crispin Porter, an agency with a track record of (co-) creating and maintaining hot brands in the business, nails the challenge:

> You try to talk about the car in ways that aren't about "hotness." You want to find a place in popular culture that doesn't go away. You can get fifteen minutes. The idea is to get more.

The agency is, for the most part, keeping with the spirit of the original campaign, though some elements have been retooled to look fresh. It has articulated the MINI manifesto, titled "Manual of Motoring," as a supplement in thought-leading magazines so that consumers clearly understand what the quirky British car stands for. In addition, the agency is making a push for more interaction on the MINI Cooper Web site, which allows enthusiasts to customize their cars in the "Trick out Your Own MINI" section. This initiative ties in with the campaign's overall marketing message:

> The message will be that if you go into a Mini dealership, you'll come out with something that's totally yours. Everyone has a scheme for his or her Mini: "I'm going to get this and that." We're saying: "Scheme away. We're all for that. Do something wild."

But perhaps the most innovative tactic the agency has employed stems from cultural research. It has decided to maintain momentum by treating the MINI like an icon. As head of Planning Tom Birk explained:

> We didn't want to become a fad. In fact, being a fad was exactly what kept us up at night. So we analyzed icons (the opposite of fads) within and outside the automotive category. We identified half a dozen characteristics common to iconic brands and then tried to bring these characteristics to life for the new MINI.
>
> One characteristic of icons is a signature look (think Absolut bottle), so we showcased MINI's size and contrasting roof and

mirror colors. Another characteristic was that icons hang out with other icons, so we created an Evel Knievel car, Dukes of Hazzard car, etc. Another characteristic was that icons turn mere loyalty into devotion (think Deadheads or Trekkies), thus the "enthusiast group."

Almost everything we do for MINI goes through this iconic filter.

KEEPING THE LOVE FOR THE EARLY MARKET

The tricky part of the mass market adoption phase is staying true to your early market. Successful brands manage to take back control of the message while still giving their early adopters special treatment by building in exclusivity, for example. After all, opinion leaders are—and remain—the lifeblood of the brand.

Brands like Levi's (in Europe), Red Bull, and Sony Playstation have done this well. They've kept their core while expanding their reach. Their brand initiatives have preserved their credibility.

Netscape, on the other hand, wasn't so considerate. It let down its visionary early adopters when it stopped delivering the cutting-edge product they expected and demanded. And it paid the price: The brand basically only exists as a memory.

The brand's demise is generally attributed to "Big Brother" Microsoft, but in truth it was poor marketing that destroyed Netscape. As a matter of fact, Microsoft wanted to embed the browser in Windows 95. Only when Netscape flamboyantly declined the invitation did Microsoft develop its own browser.

Netscape enthusiasts were tech-savvy people who passionately stood behind the brand's decision not to go to bed with Microsoft. And so it was all the more disappointing when the underdog company let them down. Between 1999 and 2002, Netscape did not produce a single software innovation. What's more, it completely moved away from its counter-Microsoft "thin client" strategy—its file size nearly doubled. Despite being purchased by AOL, Netscape couldn't regain a significant loyal user base.

Airwalk offers another illustration of a brand that betrayed its die-hard consumers. The sneaker company squandered its lead in active casual footwear by going mainstream and neglecting its core, the skateboarder culture. It failed to see the potential in star skaters like Tony Hawk, whom it had sponsored for years but never really promoted.

Meanwhile, Vans saw the void Airwalk was leaving behind and leaped at the opportunity to step in. Vans captured the early market and kept it happy by building skate parks, giving the skate shops exclusive premium footwear, and sponsoring the Warped Tour (a punk music festival). Vans is now the clear market leader, while Airwalk went from a $30 million business to a $330 million business to near bankruptcy in a mere six years. Lee Smith, Airwalk's former President, confessed: "Cool brands treat people well. We didn't."

Sine qua non, as a launch evolves, traditional mainstream tactics are needed to capture the main market. But don't forget your roots.

LETTING GO OF AN IDEA

Remember how we began the entire roadmap with a discussion about how to pick the right idea, and then seed it with the right early markets? Well, the fascinating thing about seed ideas is that they grow. Once you've picked the idea and seeded it, the early market adopts it and turns it into something new, something with a full-blown deeper social purpose.

When Pierre Omidyar launched eBay, he wanted to create a "perfect marketplace" where all buyers and sellers had equal access to information. So over Labor Day weekend in 1995, he wrote the program for AuctionWeb (eBay's original name) and posted it on the internet. Because Omidyar's vision was to have his site be an impartial trading platform, he made it utilitarian, with chunky black and blue text, a gray background, and limited functionality. Visitors could do only one of three things: list, view, or bid on an item.

But over time, Omidyar's platform grew into something much bigger than what he had initially conceived. eBay became a trusted community. It was the world's first virtual flea market, where geographically dispersed collectors could socialize and share their passions for Beanie Babies, pickle jars, and lunch boxes. Friendships were formed. Customs developed. Users took on the habit of trying to post at 10:22:22 P.M. to get the tag 22:22:22. A hierarchy formed as sellers with higher ratings commanded price premiums.

But while the community grew partially thanks to people's shared interests, it really took off because, from the early days on, Omidyar encouraged users to settle their own disputes and resolve their own problems. His attitude gave users a sense of ownership and initiative. Many of them eventually became eBay entrepreneurs.

Seed ideas should be allowed to evolve. If you let the market participate in building your brand, it will add its own meaning and experiences, making the eventual outcome much bigger in scope.

INTRODUCING THE CULTURAL BENEFIT

Market participation introduces a new dimension to brands. Instead of focusing on what the brand *is* (functional benefit) or what the brand *does* (emotional benefit), we turn to the cultural benefit, or what the brand *means*. This spiritual component provides the foundation for the most enduring relationships.

For individual users, a brand with a cultural component holds greater significance than do other types of brands. For society at large, a brand with a cultural component becomes part of the social fabric.

Conventional brands' benefits are personal, determined by the brand owner after unearthing the right product truths (functional) and consumer truths (emotional). A cultural benefit, on the other hand, is public property. It's co-created with the market and based on a social truth.

Red Bull became "the legal rush." eBay unexpectedly developed into both a trusted community and socially acceptable gambling.

Personal Benefits		Public Benefits
· Determined by Brand Owner		· Co-created with the Market
Functional Benefit	**Emotional Benefit**	**Cultural Benefit**
➢ Product Truth	➢ Consumer Truth	➢ Social Truth

This is the next way to differentiate brands. As Linux, Napster, and Starbucks have shown, brands with cultural benefits can change the world.

WARNING: THIS COULD BE HABIT FORMING

The most effective way to accelerate the rate at which consumers adopt a new idea is to encourage them to change their behavior—to form a new habit.

A habit is defined as a recurrent, often unconscious pattern of behavior that is acquired through frequent repetition and is eventually practiced automatically. New habit formation is an immense marketing challenge. It is also consistently undervalued as a marketing tool. Our craft focuses its efforts almost entirely on trial rather than early market adoption in our introductory marketing plans.

Getting consumers to adopt new habits is a fragile process that can break down at any point during its evolution. It is a diffused process that often appears chaotic and random. But there is method to the madness: Habit formation is a powerful approach that can turn the Next Big Thing into the new societal norm.

So, how do new habits form?

The French folklorist Arnold van Gennep coined the phrase "rites of passage" in 1905 to describe the various rituals that human societies perform at critical, transitional moments in people's lives. These rites of passage—such as births, weddings, and funerals—help facilitate the shift from one life phase to the next. They also constitute the collective conscience of a culture.

Linguist Edward Berry further developed the rites of passage concept by breaking it into three key stages:

- An initial *stage of separation*, in which the individual is divorced from his familiar environment.
- A *transitional stage*, in which the old identity is destroyed and a new one created.
- A final *stage of incorporation*, in which the individual is reintegrated into society in a new role.

We can use this cultural rites of passage model to understand how new habits are formed. In the same way that societies use rites of passage to transition individuals from one phase of life to the next, so brand initiatives can use rites of passage to transition consumers from one habit to the next.

In the chart below, I compare an analysis of marriage as a rite of passage (by Gonzaga University's Kip Wheeler) to the brand hijack process, using Starbucks as the example.

RITES OF PASSAGE PROCESS	BRAND HIJACK PROCESS
Stage 1: Rites of Separation	**Phase 1: Hijack Ideation/ Tribal Marketing**
The first stage in a rite of passage is the process of separation from an existing form—a loss of identity, so to speak.	The first stage in a hijack is coming up with a breakthrough brand idea. In order to have a deep and enduring impact on everyday customs and habits, brand initiatives need to take advantage of current trends that are opposed to the contemporary norm.
Marriage in most cultures cannot occur until the individuals in the couple are prepared to move out of their parents' houses, to separate from their former nuclear families, and start a new family of their own.	*Starbucks played right into two major cultural disruptions: the spare time of the emerging subculture of the self- and unemployed; and the rise of "affordable luxuries," which allowed the non-wealthy intelligentsia to cultivate the aura of affluence at an affordable price point.*
Stage 2: Rites of Transition	**Phase 2: Co-creation**
This is the stage of uncertainty and transition. It is the "liminal," in-between time during which the participant has lost his identity but has not yet fully reincorporated into the community with a new identity. It's a period of experimentation.	This is the stage of adjustment and learning. The early markets have discovered the new initiative and now are actively shaping it into something that will be a useful part of theirs and other people's lives.

(cont'd)

RITES OF PASSAGE PROCESS	BRAND HIJACK PROCESS
The fiancé and fiancée often go through an extended period called "engagement" prior to taking their formal vows. This period is often marked by some risky behavior (such as bachelor parties). It also involves preparation for marriage. For example, many religions require the couple to undergo instruction and counseling; communities often shower the couple with gifts to ensure that they have what they need to live on their own.	*In the early days, Starbucks did not advertise, relying instead on its customers. Word-of-mouth, convenient locations, and branded cups provided the salience Starbucks needed. Simply by carrying a fresh-brewed cup into the office, Starbucks customers spread the habit one person at a time.* *Just as important, its customers helped the company change Americans' idea of coffee. Coffee was no longer just a drink. It became a culture, imbued with ritual (the morning wait), a place of worship (a local Starbucks), its own nomenclature (barista, grande), and badges of belonging (the branded cup).*

Stage 3: Rites of Incorporation	Phase 3: Mass Marketing
The final stage of the process moves the participant out of isolation and back into the community with a new identity. He re-enters society at a higher status. The whole community participates.	The final stage moves the initiative out of the fringe and into the mainstream. The brand has now gained wide acceptance among the mass market as the new norm.
The bride traditionally gives up her old name and gains a new one. In many cultures, she wears a disguise (a veil). The actual ceremony involves giving each other gifts (exchange of rings). The participants wear traditional clothes (tuxedo and white dress). Following the couple's ceremony, the community shows approval by offering wedding gifts, eating together, and dancing. Now the couple has experienced "incorporation."	*Now that coffee house culture has been established in America, Starbucks is placing more emphasis on the atmosphere of their shops and sponsoring local events such as coffee tastings and live music. It is recognizing the important social function that the stores serve as a "third place" between home and office in which Americans can interact with one another in a public yet intimate environment. Starbucks advertising is finally filling the pages of magazines as well, demonstrating how mainstream the brand has become.*

LOWERING RESISTANCE

There are several major tactics brand owners can utilize to reduce the barriers to new habit formation. Let's use eBay as our case study—it not only facilitated the formation of a new habit, it even turned online auctioning into an addiction.

Familiarity Breeds Trust

Make the new habit appear less disruptive by linking it to an existing one. That way, consumers will see it as a mere habit replacement rather than a totally new behavior.

eBay provided the necessary link in consumers' minds between the virtual flea market and the real world, a tangible one. Rather than focusing its early marketing efforts online (with click-through banners and such), it went to actual flea markets and collector trade shows, where it sponsored the events and advertised in the show magazines. Also, in 1999, eBay embarked on a highly successful road show promotion called "From Our Homepage to Your Hometown," which starred several branded vans that traveled across the country.

These initiatives made a revolutionary idea—an impartial online trading platform—feel evolutionary, and therefore less threatening.

Lower the Barriers

Reduce barriers by easing people into the experience. Then let the marketplace practice the new habit frequently.

One of the reasons eBay caught on so quickly was because of the pricing structure. Buyers did not (and still do not) have to pay to use the service. Pierre Omidyar decided that only sellers should have to pay, and only when they made a sale—that's when eBay charges a small percentage of the winning bid value. In addition to keeping pricing simple, this setup ensures that interested users can peruse the site and even participate in an auction without incurring any penalties.

What's more, it means that bidders can, and do, practice their new habit often—they must visit the site frequently when competing with others to win an auction.

Provide Social Reinforcement

Reduce social resistance to the formation of the new habit. Foster a community to encourage deeper engagement with the brand.

From the beginning, Pierre Omidyar encouraged users to solve their own problems. His instincts have proven to be right on target. This self-policing policy has built a valuable community, one that competitors such as Auction Universe and Amazon have been unable to match.

In 1996, Omidyar encouraged interaction and dialogue among users through the Feedback Forum—a precursor to the rating system— and the Bulletin Board, which became a sort of meetinghouse for users. Through this bulletin board and other nonofficial sites, new users were able to have their questions answered, friendships were able to form, and ancillary businesses were able to start and thrive.

Since, as a group, collectors tend to be geographically isolated from each other, the site became a natural meeting place for hobbyists of various stripes. People really got to know one another. Trust was so high in the early days that it was not uncommon for buyers to send goods before they received their money. One time, a group even pitched in to buy a computer for a member whose machine had crashed. It was this climate of camaraderie that provided the social reinforcement to make eBay the company that it is today.

Reward and Delight

Positive reinforcement is a key driver in any behavior modification program. It's a great way to get people to try out new things. Even better, to ensure that they turn a single trial into consistent behavior, delight your consumers by exceeding their expectations.

The eBay experience has many built-in rewards, from being able to easily track down hard-to-find items within seconds (imagine the time it would take to find a particular rare stamp, for instance, in a flea market), to winning the bid, to the final reward of receiving the item in the mail.

But the gambling thrill that eBay offers is something no local flea market can provide. This is the quality that surprises and frequently causes users to form a real eBay habit (or even addiction). eBay is not only more convenient and safe, it is also more fun than the real thing.

The Brand Hijack Creative Brief

Planning
- Why should this brand (initiative) catch on?
- What is the relevant seed idea?
- Do we need to prime the market for the launch?

Seeding
- Who will co-develop it?
- How should the early market first meet the seed idea?

Buzz
- What message do we ideally want the market to create?
- How can we facilitate that?

Mainstream
- Who will be the main user of the initiative?
- And how will momentum be maintained:
  - With the early market?
  - With the mainstream?

Cultural Benefit
- What larger meaning would we ideally like to create as a result?

PART VI

THE HIJACKER'S THREATS AND OPPORTUNITIES

CHAPTER 17

The Threat: "A Few Words from Our Sponsor"

The revolution will not go better with Coke.

—Gil Scott Heron

Beware: A brand hijack attempt doesn't provide us with a license to kill. It doesn't give the marketer permission to cross ethical lines, even if we're giving the *illusion* of marketing without marketing. While marketing itself is not evil, those of us in the trade have developed bad habits over time. And the current emphasis on nontraditional media and seduction techniques may tempt us more than ever to cross that fine line . . .

A NEED FOR DIALOGUE

The discussion of the ethics of marketing is an important and a timely one. But it doesn't really seem like a debate. Rather, it seems that there are just two polar opposite opinions being expressed. On the one side, critics indict our craft as the root cause for an ever-widening array of social illnesses, from weakening morals to the corruption of democracy. More content to criticize than facilitate constructive dialog, this school of thought often succeeds only in alienating the other side: the marketing community.

From the marketers' standpoint, reality can be overwhelming: We have a job to do. And so, caught up in our daily routine of delivering campaigns and short-term tangible results, we often forget to pause and reflect on the consequences of our collective activity. Yet few professionals would deny that marketing in America has crossed a line, blurry though that line may be. As individuals, but especially as members of agencies and brand teams, we don't feel a sufficient sense of accountability to a larger community—whether that community is our peers in marketing in particular, or society in general.

It is this issue of insufficient responsibility that has left the marketing community most tongue-tied in the face of critics' charges. We cannot engage in thoughtful conversation on this topic until we accept and address the importance of our role in shaping the social landscape. We must step up to the challenge. Marketing is not inherently evil. Our craft is creative, artistic, and astute. Its potency has brought the world powerful cultural icons and communal experiences that help define who we are today. But, as French philosopher Michel Foucault warned long ago, there is great danger in "power without responsibility."

POWER . . .

Of course, there are some who would challenge just how much "power" brands actually have. Interbrand's Chair Rita Clifton argues:

> It is absurd to say that brands can be too powerful. Brands are the ultimate accountable institution. If people fall out of love with your brand, you go out of business.
>
> I am not going to be an apologist for bad decisions and poor business timing. Rather, I will emphasize that good and real "brand" activity generates real (as opposed to manipulated) value for customers.

Journalists like *The Economist*'s Sameena Ahmad echo the same message: "Brands are not as powerful as their opponents allege, nor is the public as easily manipulated. The reality is more complicated."

Complicated indeed. For at the heart of it all is the very nature of human consciousness, and the inherent immorality in attempting to manipulate it to your advantage.

Some experts, in defending the current state of marketing, downplay the efficacy of such attempts. Jerry Zaltman argues:

> Managers cannot control people's minds, much less brainwash them unconsciously or consciously into making continued unwise decisions or unwanted purchase decisions.

Others say that even if managers could work such magic, it wouldn't be unethical. In his book *The Art of Seduction*, Robert Greene maintains that those who give in to seduction "do so willingly and happily. There is rarely any resentment on their part; they forgive you any kind of manipulation because you have brought them pleasure, a rare commodity in this world."

Clinical psychologist Steve Hassan, who deprograms ex-members of destructive religious cults, agrees. He points to the respective innocence of brand cults.

> There is definitely a cult of Mac out there. I guess I could be called a member of that group. I'm also a member of the cult of bicycles, scuba diving, and a few other things I care about.
>
> There is a vast difference between the Mac cult and a destructive cult. There is a continuum from healthy to destructive. If everyone needed to dress like Steve Jobs, talk like Steve Jobs and think like Steve Jobs, you'd have a [real, destructive] cult. As long as it's not destructive, it's a healthy affiliation.

The Art of Seduction

Many techniques of the marketing world are by no means a modern invention. Explorer Ernest Shackleton proved the power of seduction on December 5, 1914, when he posted the following notice to recruit a crew of officers, scientists, and sailors to embark with him on an expedition to the Antarctic:

> NOTICE.
> Men wanted for hazardous journey.
> Small wages. Bitter cold.
> Long months of complete darkness.
> Constant danger. Safe return doubtful.
> Honour and recognition in case of success.
> —Ernest Shackleton

Hundreds applied, but only twenty-seven were chosen for the near-tragic journey. (They were stranded for two years in the Antarctic before being heroically rescued by their captain.) It was a masterful piece of advertising, working through reverse psychology to ensure that the right candidates would apply and be selected. Indeed, every single member of the crew survived.

. . . WITHOUT RESPONSIBILITY

When weighing the opposing points of view regarding the effects of marketing, I find that I cannot fully buy Interbrand's party line. Marketing may, in fact, be too powerful.

Collectively, our actions as marketers have had an immense effect on society—dramatically affecting culture and not just reflecting it. In doing so, we have created a kind of Prisoner's Dilemma, eroding the usefulness of our tactics and the nerves of our consumers.

The following criticisms have been collected from the opinions of varied and diverse cultural critics. They are not meant to be definitive. They are only meant to start the conversation.

Marketing trivializes authentic culture.

Critics call it "culture vulturing." They claim that our prolific use of cultural icons and codes to sell product results in erosion of meaning and significance in our lives. At its worst, culture vulturing coopts grand issues of social justice and revolutionary struggle just to sell more product.

This was the case when a Canadian beverage manufacturer launched Revolution Soda, a new brand with none other than the likeness of Che Guevara on the label. Adbusters wryly began to speculate on whether the revolution may be carbonated after all.

> If you want to physically taste the sweet nectar of defeat, to enjoy the exact moment at which, for you, the revolution has officially failed, then run—don't walk—to your local convenience store and pick up a bottle of Revolution Soda.
>
> There's Che—stripped of all his context, his AK-47 nowhere in sight, and the dictator Batista all but shaking his hand. But somehow, he's still Che . . . they can't rob him of his meaning, can they?
>
> They can. The same people who turned "Born in the USA" into a patriotic anthem and got Spike Lee to direct Nike commercials. The ones who got Ice Cube to do malt liquor ads. And marketed Volkswagens with "If you sold your soul in the eighties, here's your chance to buy it back." They've won.
>
> As Che crouched bleeding in the bushes of Bolivia, feeling the tightening circle of government troops, awaiting the bullets which would remove all his problems of political logistics and bestow omnipresence and omnipotence to his legend like some secular Obi-Wan Kenobi, he must certainly have guessed that the imperialists would do all they could to smear his good name. But it's safe to say he never imagined his visage being used as a soda pop mascot!

Too often we try to borrow authenticity rather than earn it. Almost every youth brand wants to associate itself with "the urban market" or "hip-hop culture." But only a few have done so genuinely and respectfully. Eckō and Code Red have made themselves a part of youth culture by finding and supporting the right innovators first, before advertising their connections. In effect, they allowed themselves to be hijacked, a strategy that breeds authenticity.

Other companies eager to be associated with black culture have come across as callous or insensitive. In their rush to capitalize on it, they reduce black culture to fashion, buzzwords, and trends—raiding it for "everything but the burden."

Nissan, for example, ran a series of billboard and print ads celebrating the "The Black Experience." They were meant to "speak to perseverance, freedom and hope," but all good intentions aside . . . a Japanese company, telling African Americans what the "black experience" is? After receiving a number of determined complaints, the company pulled the ads and issued a statement apologizing for any offense.

But culture vulturing isn't only targeted at African Americans. Just about every major minority group, stereotyped subculture, and ethnic group can be turned into a marketing symbol. Think of what happened with punk, grunge, and extreme sports, or how "Zen" is used to sell everything these days from furniture to clothes to cars.

Marketing has prioritized consumption over citizenship.

After the tragic September 11th attacks, President Bush told a nation of anxious Americans to continue on with our daily lives. In particular, he told us to continue spending money.

> When they struck, they wanted to create an atmosphere of fear. And one of the great goals of this nation's war is to restore public confidence in the airline industry. It's to tell the traveling public: Get on board. Do your business around the country. Fly and enjoy America's great destination spots. Get down to Disney World in Florida. Take your families and enjoy life, the way we want it to be enjoyed.

These remarks were received without much criticism from the press, and even less from Americans. Afterward, the tourism industry ran commercials that combined clips of the president with shots of talking heads repeating his appeal to patriotism. It was a less than subtle reminder that our greatest responsibility as Americans is not to vote, but to buy.

No longer is history or government or the church at the center of our culture. It is instead the products of our marketing-driven economy that now create the greatest common bond between us. James Twitchell, an English professor at the University of Florida, conducted a little experiment to prove this point. With his undergraduates, he collected a list of words from the book *Cultural Literacy: What Every American Needs to Know*, words like Hoover Dam, National Guard, Neville Chamberlain. He then asked his students to define or explain them, yet was uniformly met with empty stares and yawns. Then he showed them a list of marketing slogans and jingles, and "they were so excited they were shouting entries for me to consider."

It is the school system, in fact, where the tension between citizenship and marketing has become most apparent. As cash-strapped school districts desperately seek more funding, they are turning more and more frequently to corporate subsidizations. It is an uneasy partnership, as educators and marketers seek to define the ethical boundaries.

One company that has repeatedly pushed the envelope of appropriateness is General Mills. It has entered the space with promotions and product samples thinly disguised as educational supplements. When it introduced a new line of candy, the company sent samples accompanied by pamphlets called "Gushers: Wonders of the Earth" that encouraged kids to learn about geysers by biting into the fruit snack. In another promotion, General Mills paid ten Minnesota teachers $250 a month to have their cars shrink-wrapped with the Reese's Puffs cereal logo and then instructed the teachers to park near school buses for maximum visibility.

Marketing is responsible for youth's loss of innocence.

Critics charge that consumerism is responsible for the early sexualization of today's youth, as well as their warped values and damaged self-esteem. According to Alissa Quart in *Branded: The Buying and Selling of Teenagers*, marketing spending targeted at children increased twenty-fold from the 1980s to the 1990s. Studies show that kids spend more time in front of the TV than at school. This is socialization through branding, and it's teaching kids to have attitudes, aspirations, and problems beyond their years.

Isn't it ironic that a major media brand has declared itself the advocate of kids with a battle cry of "Just give us back our freedom"? In a series of focus groups conducted as part of the "Freedom" campaign for Viacom's *Nickelodeon*, kids said they were "terrified about growing up. Our parents have us deprogrammed, we're being hurried, and we don't have a childhood."

It may seem outrageous to hold brands responsible for kids growing up too fast, but it's naive to ignore the following events:

Abercrombie and Fitch started a national debate when it sold thong underwear to preteen girls. A company spokeswoman responded that the underwear, labeled with words like "wink wink" and "eye candy," was meant to be "cute and fun and very tongue-in-cheek."

The beauty industry is now targeting kids with "spa packages" and one New York City salon even has a back-to-school waxing special for teens.

In Brooklyn, a gang called Lo Lifes got their start stealing Polo by Ralph Lauren clothing. For them, the brand was the symbol of the good life. It gave them status within their circle of friends and acquaintances.

For some wealthier children, rites of passage rituals like bar mitzvahs and quinceañeras have lost most of their intended social and religious meanings. They are now simply celebrations of excess and wealth. It is not uncommon in certain communities for bar mitzvahs to cost $40,000 and take a year to plan. Said one concerned parent, "These are out of control celebrations in which you deify the child rather than celebrating their becoming part of the community."

Some children have internalized marketing principles to such an extent that they are even selling themselves. They have become both producers and consumers in today's hyper-commercialized world. One of the most adept is JT Leroy, a teenage writer whose book *Sarah* is a semi-autobiographical piece about a cross-dressing teen prostitute. Leroy has leveraged the notoriety of his past into fame and fortune. Or, as he says, "I'm way into pimping Sarah."

In Japan, schoolgirls have been known to prostitute themselves for expensive accessories, such as Prada bags. In the United States, a virtual version of this phenomenon has emerged with web cam girls. Teen and even preteen girls like "Lana" set up cameras in their bedrooms and allow strangers to peek into their lives. They compete for traffic by showing more skin than others. In return for the voyeuristic thrills, the girls have wish lists of products such as video games, CDs, dolls, and digital cameras that they hope fans will buy for them. "The cuter you are, the more presents you get off your wish lists," says Lana.

Whether or not you fully agree with this list of charges, there is more than enough evidence here to give critics ammunition in their campaign against the evils of marketing.

A SOLUTION?

Unlike most critics, I condemn not the craft at large, but only the bad practices we have adopted over time. The real questions we should be asking ourselves are: How do we break these bad practices? What can I, the *individual* marketer, do better? With our knowledge of how to effectively persuade comes an immense responsibility not to abuse that power.

In 2002, Young & Rubicam launched a buzz campaign code-named "fake tourist" for Sony Ericsson's new T68i, a mobile phone/digital camera. Actors and models pretended to be tourists, faking impartial excitement and "natural" product demos for the new gadget.

A Bloomberg report reviewed the campaign and dubbed it "human spam." In contrast, *Brandweek* awarded the campaign "Guerrilla Marketer of the Year" status. And marketing spokespeople, such as this man from a small Pittsburgh-based promotions agency, appeared utterly clueless as to why this stunt might offend people:

> I can see why people feel manipulated, but I don't see the harm in it. I would say the guerrilla marketing has no rules. The whole world's a stage for you to perform on.

To be fair to Y&R and its "Brand Buzz" division then, it is not alone and should not be singled out. Volvo has used similarly deceitful tactics. So has the entire liquor industry. So does just about any brand that uses celebrity sponsorship. After all, do you really think that Jamie Foxx drinks Coors Light?

I doubt that most marketers are purposely deceitful. We just don't think about the effects of our actions. We don't realize that, like mass media, the effectiveness of buzz marketing—a relatively recent concept—could also decline.

The so-called guerrilla arena is also being polluted. It's filled with cheap stunts rather than well thought-out orchestrations, and by manipulative campaigns rather than ones that let the consumer in on the joke. The result is a double whammy: These campaigns not only ruin things for the rest of us, they simply don't work.

Consumers deserve respect. And respectful marketing works. We need to move back to honest buzz. We ought to aim to surprise and engage an early market without abusing them.

One of the all-time top blunders was from OK Soda, the much-anticipated "Gen-X" drink Coca-Cola launched in the 1980s. Consumers quickly got turned off when the company planted fictitious messages from "disaffected teens" protesting OK slogans and OK advertising on a 1-800 hotline. The launch got pulled within months. Curiously, even today the brand maintains a passionate following of alternative culture geeks and soda freaks. But honest buzz could have made that brand the billion-dollar launch Coke had projected all along.

A Call to Action

How can we effect change for marketing with integrity? As individuals, we need to realize the effect our actions have on society. And as a craft, we need to strive for sustainable behavior.

As a first and easy step, I suggest we ought to evaluate marketing plans differently. Add a criterion to agency submissions. In addition to the standard elements, why not assess the plan's *appropriateness*?

That's just the beginning. We also ought take the time to listen to the cultural critics. Why has the marketing industry not embraced Naomi Klein's and Thomas Frank's advice on how to create more ethical campaigns? Our profession unwisely ignores even the less confrontational thinkers in the field. I spoke at a conference that also featured John Krewson, the publisher of *The Onion*—the source of some of the best cultural satire around. If anyone has a handle on the pulse of our times, it is this man. In his talk, he offered several wry observations, using storylines from his newspaper. After the conference, I spoke with a client about *The Onion*. She told me her company had actually advertised in the paper, used it as a medium, but never considered collaborating with it on developing a more authentic message. What a missed opportunity.

But the most important step we can take is to adopt a voluntary marketing code of conduct. Sound like a wild idea? It's not so uncommon. Both the cigarette and liquor industries have developed voluntary industry codes as acts of self-preservation.

This is not about assigning blame. Every experienced marketer probably has made decisions that made him or her uncomfortable. I have to thank Ricki Seidman, the former head of *Rock the Vote* and my colleague at Napster, for discouraging me from utilizing digital street teams to appear as "independent" fans of the site and spread the Napster gospel in dire times. And there are other skeletons in my marketing closet.

There is, of course, a practical self-sustaining interest. In order to be more effective with our campaigns, and to preserve our craft for the future without the danger of an imminent backlash, we must take the initiative.

As a thought-starter, here are three guidelines that we should strive to act upon:

Don't deceive.

Ensure that people are in on the joke.

Dr. Pepper/Seven Up was taken by surprise when a recent "blogging" initiative backfired. The company recruited five popular bloggers and plied them with freebies such as T-shirts, Amazon gift certificates, and trips to company HQs in Texas. In return, the bloggers were asked to put links on their web pages to the site ragingcow.com, and to pump Raging Cow, a new milk-based drink, to their friends.

The problem was that they specifically asked the bloggers not to reveal their ties with the company. It didn't take long for the blogging community to catch on, and when it did it was outraged:

> This Web site is FAKE. When you are advertising under false
> pretenses and not being up front about what you're doing . . .
> that isn't just wrong, it's immoral and disgusting.

Bloggerheads.com called for a boycott of the brand. It was miffed not by the commercial intrusion, but by the deception. Dr. Pepper had tried to enter into the community without understanding its rules and standards. Commented another blogger:

> The people who make the cash decisions need to know that
> charging into our arena expecting it all for nothing is a very
> bad idea. If people want to reach us, they need to know that
> it's going to be on our terms.

This incident is a classic example of "roach marketing," when marketers disguise advertisement as spontaneous interactions between people. Even though liquor companies have done this for years in clubs and bars, brands need to be respectful of the rules when entering into intimate tribal communities.

But being respectful doesn't mean you have to be boring. The British soft drink Tango carried tricksterism to a whole new level. For the launch of its new line of non-carbonated drinks, it ran ads warning consumers about a "rogue" drink, asking people to report new "Still" Tango by calling a toll free number. The 300,000 people who called the number were informed: "You've been Tangoed."

The British ITC responded angrily, saying that it was unacceptable to trespass on public confidence in this manner. But the ITC missed the point. Tango's deception wasn't malicious. The trick was in the spirit of good clean fun. People were let in on the joke. It was a free call, after all.

No doubt my call for honesty will spark debate over what exactly constitutes "good clean fun." Were Red Bull's reluctant denials of its wild origins and possible side effects actually sins of omission? Was *Blair Witch* engaging in mythmaking or blatantly lying? Did the trickery enrich people's lives or abuse their trust in an attempt to manufacture "authenticity"? Certainly, if, as many critics charge, *Blair Witch's* online "fan reviews" were actually "faux reviews," there are obvious ethical concerns. But most of the time there are no easy answers. All we can do is consider both the short-term consequences and the long-term effects in making our decisions and be wary of any initiative that threatens to further erode consumers' already decimated trust in us.

Don't intrude.
Ensure that your presence is a welcome break rather than a distraction. You don't have to be invited, but when you gatecrash, you better make it worth their while.

Ads are turning up in new spaces like coffee cups, bathroom stalls, inside taxis, on turnstiles, and even on the sides of cows. It seems that marketing spaces are only limited by one's imagination. This makes it difficult for marketers to know where to draw the line. How do we determine whether a space is appropriate or sacred? How do we figure out if the message will be welcomed or repelled?

Fringe groups like Adbusters have led the effort to fight against visual pollution—album ads blanketing abandoned lots, billboards blocking urban skyline—and reclaim public spaces. Part of its solution is to call for creative resistance against these urban eyesores. Adbusters celebrates activist groups like PAINTBAIT, which paints public art over corporate urban wallpaper. Its campaign to "Unbrand" America also calls for us to black out unwanted corporate messages with a simple black spot. With these initiatives, Adbusters is creating a movement, the twenty-first century's new "ism": mental environmentalism. This new movement even comes complete with a manifesto:

> We have lost confidence in what we are seeing, hearing and reading: too much infotainment and not enough news; too many outlets telling the same stories; too much commercialism and too much hype. Every day, this commercial information system distorts our view of the world.

For now, activist groups like these are an exception, but many consumers share the sentiment they espouse. In order to stop the hemorrhaging of the public trust, we must restrain ourselves from invading all public space.

One way to ensure you don't intrude is to offer your product without demanding that it be showered with attention. Guinness masters this approach when it installs kegs in the homes and dressing rooms of Hollywood stars. George Clooney, Ben Affleck, and David Arquette have all been known to have Guinness on tap in their homes. It's a small gesture, but it didn't take long for Guinness to start showing up in films and become the bar call of choice for some A-listers.

Don't co-opt.
Ensure that the cultural equity you attach to your brand will benefit from your involvement.

There are plenty of examples of advertisers who have overstepped their bounds. Coca-Cola was widely criticized as the "Red Rash" during the Atlanta Olympics. It spent $500 million to make sure that consumers were saturated with the Coke message in their hometown. Tactics included a heavy presence during the Torch Relay—where "Coke was even more visible than the torch carrier"—the Coca-Cola Olympic City theme park, and a host of retailer and consumer promotions along with more than seventy commercials.

Coca-Cola clearly approached the Olympics from a self-centered rather than altruistic perspective. Instead of thinking of itself as a gracious host, it viewed the Olympics as a property that it could coopt.

In approaching tribal communities, brands are better served by positioning themselves as members or participants. Absolut Vodka has done a great job of supporting the art community. It's a sponsor, an enabler of self-expression. It never approaches the artist or the event as something it owns. Through initiatives such as Absolut Expressions, the company has been able to stay true to the spirit of the arts.

We, as marketers, have a responsibility to our culture. In order to preserve our craft, we must act with heightened awareness. We must enter into an honest dialogue with our critics, our colleagues, and disillusioned consumers alike. Good practices should not be enforced through marketing regulation. Rather, like any hijacked brand, we should rely on ourselves to self-regulate.

This is not an appeal to make marketing defensive, safe, and boring. The last thing we should do is to gag our creativity or stifle our vision. All I ask is that we stop, think, and apply a bit of common sense as we begin planning our communications efforts. Once we have checked our actions with our internal moral compasses, then we should plunge forward with enthusiasm and daring.

Marketing needs to stay bold, brave, and surprising. It needs to stay effective not by employing deceptive and underhanded tactics, but by genuinely earning consumer devotion.

CHAPTER 18

The Opportunity:
The Ultimate Pay-Off

You know, there's a lot of fine women out there, but not all of them bring you lasagna at work. Most of them just cheat on you.

—Silent Bob, *Clerks*

I will never forget the moment I totally got how special Napster was. We were preparing for a crucial and top-secret meeting with Sony's CEO, Nobuyuki Idei. He was a big—albeit closet—fan of the service, even though his record label had joined the lawsuit against it. Bertelsmann's then-CEO Thomas Middelhoff had arranged a meeting for us to give him a closer look.

While doing prep work, we came across Landor's 2001 "Global ImagePower" study. It was unbelievable: With a marketing budget of under a million dollars and only a year in existence, Napster had achieved a global rank close to that of Sony, a brand with at least a billion dollar lifetime marketing investment. Imagine that. A months-old, garage start-up with equal brand value to one of the global superbrands.

A once in a lifetime example, you might think. But there are plenty of others out there. The "doughnut theater" of Krispy Kreme, for example, inspired a similar degree of consumer passion. It's now considered a badge of honor to wait in line for hours to buy a dozen glazed. The NATO base in Keflavik, Iceland, ships in 350 boxes each week via a C-130 from Virginia Beach. That is brand fanaticism and that is good business: Krispy Kreme grew more than 30 percent in sales during the deep recession of 2002, doubling its profits and butchering rival Dunkin Donuts in every per-store key success measure.

Starbucks also showed impressive double-digit growth in spite of a weak economy. Its profits remain about five times greater than those of the industry average, and no American retailer has a higher frequency of customer visits. *New Yorker* columnist James Surowiecki put the following perspective on it:

> The real measure of Starbucks' success is that it helped turn America into a nation of java junkies again. During the nineties, the number of coffee drinkers rose by almost forty million. More than seven thousand new coffee houses have opened since 1996.
>
> Instead of competing for a share of an existing market, Starbucks invented its own, heeding the advice of the economist Joseph Schumpeter, who wrote, in 1939, "It was not enough to produce satisfactory soap, it was also necessary to induce people to wash."
>
> This is harder than it sounds; it's one thing to foist a fad on people, and another to have a deep and enduring impact on their everyday customs and habits.
>
> Starbucks changed not just what people drank but how they drank it. Instead of gulping down swill on the fly, people learned to desire the experience of leisurely sipping a grande latte, while eavesdropping on job interviews, at one of Starbucks' six thousand convenient locations worldwide.

The Starbucks brand is so powerful that it completely changed people's habits. Only a decade ago, the premium coffee share was at a mere 3 percent of the overall category. Today, it has risen to about 40 percent.

Southwest Airlines, another co-created brand, is the only major airline in the United States that is profitable. The company even received monetary contributions from frequent flyers after 9/11, its customers' attempt to ensure that it would not go under as a result of the tragedy.

Hijacked brands, whether fully appropriated or participatory in nature, inspire devotion. Their users become not mere consumers, but committed advocates, even partners-in-crime.

In fact, dedication to a brand can even outlast corporate blunders. *Wired*'s Leander Kahney explains:

> One of the defining characteristics of the Mac community is its loyalty to Apple. Through thick and thin, Apple's customers stick by the company. This summer [2002], Apple upset the Mac community by suddenly announcing a $100 annual subscription fee for its .mac online services, which were formerly free. On top of this, an upgrade to OSX—the kind of upgrade users usually don't pay for—would cost $130.
>
> The new pricing policies prompted howls of protest. Web sites, online forums, and news stories were full of acrimonious kvetching about "gouging" and "bait and switch." Long-time users launched petitions, fired off angry letters and for the first time in years, there were lots of threats to leave the Mac platform altogether.
>
> But despite the howling, there's been no mass exodus to Windows. The opposite, in fact, seems to be true. Anecdotal evidence points to more and more people switching to the Mac.
>
> Could any other [computer] company get away with this? Probably not.

This passion isn't for entertainment purposes only, either. Businesses profit from it. Most hijacked brands have an extremely healthy bottom line.

LOYALTY VS. RETENTION

Marketers love to talk about "loyalty." Loyalty is their Holy Grail. It is an objective written into every marketing plan. Every major brand tracks it quantitatively by measuring frequency of use and amount of brand switching.

The problem is that what most marketers think of as "loyalty" is nothing of the sort—it is actually "retention." And it's not just a matter of semantics: Retention is about consumer behavior; loyalty is an attitude.

Let's stay with Napster to illustrate the point. In its heyday, the Napster community was so devoted to the service that it became part of a daily routine to sign in and search for tunes. It was an important and welcome break from the daily grind.

These users had positive feelings associated with Napster. They liked the platform and the brand's persona; they appreciated the service; they believed in the movement behind it. This is true loyalty. And it led to activism: When the brand came under legal attack by the music industry, nearly a million users signed up with Napster's Action Network to defend it.

Now compare Napster to AOL. I have been a member of AOL since 1995. And yet I am not passionate about the service. I believe other ISPs outperform AOL; its customer service sucks; it disrespects its user base (Have you ever tried canceling your subscription? Nothing short of actually canceling your credit card seems to work. In fact, the State of Ohio sued AOL in 2003 for unauthorized charges, failure to disconnect after a free trial, and deceptive advertising). But according to traditional definitions, I am a "loyal" user despite my negative attitude. Why? Because I don't want to lose my e-mail address. That's why I pay the five bucks a month.

David Lewis, author of *The Soul of the New Consumer,* calls this "pseudo loyalty." I call it retention. The authors of *Driving Customer Equity,* define the impact of retention as "the customer's perceived cost associated with leaving the relationship." By building high exit barriers, AOL may keep people like me from switching brands as often. But it does not foster loyalty—their users' attitude can be described as neutral at best.

This doesn't mean that retention tools like mileage programs or any of the conventional packaged goods rewards programs have no role. They can spark growth. They just don't build loyalty. Such programs are, for the most part, generic tools, whose benefits can be neutralized by competitors who copy them or even turn them into one-upmanship contests. They bribe rather than enthuse the consumer.

Many of the dot-com pioneers had to learn the hard way that you cannot buy true loyalty. And many a guerrilla marketer has had to learn the same way that you cannot buy word-of-mouth either. With all due respect to Seth Godin, paying consumers so that they willingly pay attention to a branded message, a tactic he calls "permission marketing," is not the solution. Permission, again, is at best neutral. Offering a material incentive to volunteer on behalf of a brand is by definition inauthentic, hence ineffective.

But retention mistaken for "loyalty" isn't a dangerous measure only in the so-called new economy. Brand dinosaurs with "pseudo loyalty" may be lulled into a false sense of security as well.

The English tea market offers a great example of how illusory retention really is. PG Tips had been the almighty brand leader in this very traditional and stable category since the 1950s. It had a "loyal" user base habitually buying it because it had the strongest brand name. That is, until a competitor, Tetley, came along and took the company completely off-guard.

John Grant, who worked on the PG Tips account at the time, recounts what happened in the early '90s:

> Tetley launched a seemingly small innovation—the round tea bag. Every conventional wisdom about marketing would say that this kind of innovation wouldn't work. It would be dismissed as a gimmick by loyal followers of PG Tips, who were hooked to the brand's slightly sharper taste and its consistent place in their (and often their parents') lives. It might even put off some of Tetley's older, more traditional following. Or at best what it would do was restage the brand. To suggest that it was keeping up with the times and also gain a fraction of a share point from disloyal people at the margins who tend to buy whatever is top of their mind.
>
> What actually happened was that Tetley took brand leadership, within a year. Why? To paraphrase Marshall McLuhan: The change was the message. In a market that had become dull, quaint and boring, somebody did something new and dynamic. I don't believe for a minute that round tea bags are preferred for some subtle psychological reason. (Any more than the lime in the neck of the bottle of Sol was part of the foodie movement.) The brand had changed and it thrived.

> In the light of the round tea bag, we could see that people
> had become bored with tea and tea brands. It was there, taken
> for granted, bought out of habit, but very recessive. And ripe
> for innovation.
>
> This is my favorite example to make brand Pharisees stop
> and think. One change was all it took to topple thirty-five years
> of what they would call loyalty or goodwill.

A similar thing happened in the U.S. dental care market to Crest, the perennial market leader. Colgate snatched its number one spot by introducing "Total" toothpaste. I bet the folks on the Crest brand team had strong "loyalty" data in their hands and probably never saw the threat coming.

True loyalty is about something bigger than retention or even the financially driven "lifetime customer value" concept. It is about authenticity. It is about passion. It leads to ambassadorship and activism on behalf of the brand. And—ultimately—it leads to off-the-charts brand value scores.

TRUE LOYALTY	RETENTION ("PSEUDO LOYALTY")
• Is an attitude	• Is a behavior
• Connotes *active passion* for a brand	• Achieves a *neutral, passive* consumer reaction at best
• Is long-term	• Is mostly short-term
• Is the true Holy Grail in marketing	• Can be dangerously misleading, lulling brand owners into a false sense of security

BARRIERS TO LOYALTY

Retention tactics are Machiavellian. They temporarily keep consumers buying the brand, granted, but they do so without developing an up close and personal bond. As soon as a better deal appears, consumers will be gone. Building genuine loyalty is not about conniving gimmicks.

Retention, or "pseudo loyalty," is primarily driven by one of the following factors:

Boring Old Habit

In spite of all our efforts and behind-the-scenes scheming, consumers often choose brands for no reasons other than convenience, laziness, or habit. This is something that market leaders strive for, particularly in mature markets. But it is an indefensible position once a challenger enters the market. PG Tips was a legacy brand that relied on mere retention, and Tetley's round bag was all it took to steal away consumers. Same thing goes for Crest and Colgate.

Bogus Bait

Mileage programs are proven to lock in consumers. But there's no evidence that they inspire true loyalty to the brand. People are not necessarily loyal to United or American Airlines; they are loyal to the free flights, earned perks, and increased status. In essence, most frequent flyers are promiscuous, ready to hop into bed with whichever company offers the best deal.

In contrast, flyers demonstrate real loyalty to visionaries in the airline industry such as Virgin Atlantic, Southwest, and JetBlue. These airlines don't bribe consumers, but rather thrive on delivering a more pleasurable—and less expensive—travel experience. They do constant analysis of every aspect of pre-, in-, and post-flight service to ensure that their flyers thoroughly enjoy their flights. So states Virgin's credo: "We cut fares, not corners."

And they do it with panache. These airlines have won their passengers' loyalty through force of personality. They employ happy, and occasionally even funny, employees. Virgin was the first airline to apply Walkman technology to headphones and to offer a choice of hot meals in economy. It is also the only airline ever to offer live entertainment (from mind-readers to jugglers) and massages on board. JetBlue is toying around with the idea of awarding the best-dressed passenger on each flight with a free ticket. There are Web sites dedicated to SWA anecdotes like the following announcement on a flight:

> Here at Southwest, we flight attendants get up real early and go to the airport so we can sign up for a flight with the most handsome pilots. When you are departing the aircraft, look in the cockpit and you'll see that today we slept late.

High Exit Barriers

Lock-ins are only secure until a competitor can figure out a way to reduce the exit barriers or offer value higher than the consumers' perceived cost of switching. If an ISP were to figure out a way to divert my AOL emails to a new address, I would switch to it in a flash.

The recent implementation of cell phone number portability has eliminated completely the presence of exit barriers in the industry. Cell phone companies, of course, have been moaning about the potential costs of consumers' search for the latest deal. But if they're wise, they'll realize that a real opportunity now exists to make consumers loyal to their service.

COPYCATS

A key question regarding true loyalty is whether competitors can replicate it. Should Netflix be worried about Blockbuster and Wal-Mart? Should Southwest Airlines be concerned about Delta's Song? This question drives at the heart of hijacking principles. The answer: Only originals will foster true loyalty.

Blockbuster's entry into the online movie rental business has not been able to slow down Netflix's continued growth. In fact, Netflix closed its 2003 books with 75 percent more customers than the year before, and a revenue increase of 80 percent. Consumers recognized that Blockbuster was merely a copycat that mistakenly thought overall size could buy devotion. It gained no credibility with its initiative. A Netflix customer expressed the general skepticism of the market: "A corporate model like Blockbuster's relies on people to make mistakes."

SWA is certainly paying attention to JetBlue (whose CEO David Neeleman proudly accepts the compliment that his carrier is Southwest Airlines, new and improved). The airline industry newcomer admittedly took the SWA model as its platform. But it also changed the way that people think about flying by proving that low cost does not have to mean no-frills—a video monitor displaying live satellite TV in every leather seat, extra leg room, and new planes being just some of the perks.

Delta's Song, on the other hand, feels like a consultant's benchmarking exercise gone wrong. Song's "boutique hotel in the sky" concept may sound interesting on paper, but it doesn't fit with a low-fare carrier—the groovy hip neighborhood hotels of the world are expensive and exclusive. More important, its nonconformist personality does not fit under the umbrella of a major corporation.

SWA flight attendants are funny by nature. The company devotes a lot of money and effort to recruiting the right employees and maintaining a loose, enjoyable work culture. Hence the joking tone on the flights is natural. Yet Song actually scripts lines for its staff. But you simply can't regulate humor.

Journalist Jonathan Dee had a spooky Song experience. After his initial flight was filled with blonde jokes, beer drinking songs (did they really mean "boutique hotel" in the sky, or was it "spring break"?), and the repeated mention of the strategic words "bright and cheerful," the return flight was typically Delta. Humor and enjoyment had apparently not yet been rolled out throughout the entire fleet.

Contrast that to the genuine efforts made by JetBlue to humanize the experience and deliver superior customer service. During the 2003 East Coast blackout, most major airlines canceled their flights. But not JetBlue. Headquarters management went to work at JFK to help the ground crew stay on schedule. Even General Counsel Jim Hnat was seen loading luggage.

My editor, Amy Hertz, tells a story about her parents flying to Buffalo from Florida on an early morning JetBlue flight. When the plane stopped for a layover at JFK, her father wanted to step off the plane to buy a copy of *The New York Times*. But there wasn't enough time for passengers to de-board. The flight attendants said, "We'll see what we can do." Ten minutes later, one of them arrived with the $3.50 paper in hand and refused reimbursement.

The difference between Song's pseudo-loyalty style and JetBlue's quest for true loyalty is clear: By September 2003, Song had filled less than half the seats on its flights, whereas JetBlue was posting its eleventh consecutive quarter of profitability.

THE PATH TO TRUE LOYALTY

It all starts with you telling a story, but tailoring that story to exactly the audience you have in mind, and introducing the story to them at a time and a place where they will be able to remember your story.

It is about telling your audience exactly what they want to hear, but don't know it until they hear it. Without giving away any specifics to allow plenty of room for interpretation.

It's about making those who hear the story become your storytellers, and allowing them to make up and add parts to the story as long as they get the title right and the critical elements within the same ballpark.

It's approaching marketing as a journalist, an editor, an anthropologist. It's studying the cultural details and taking everything you can to craft a compelling story; then letting that story find its audience and making the final outcome of that story dependent on the audience's (inter-) personal life and experience.

It's a damn hard job with the ultimate payoff: lasting consumer devotion to your brand.

Dedication and Acknowledgments

This book is dedicated to my parents, Rolf and Käthe Wipperfürth, who have not only tolerated my subversive nature but even encouraged it.

Thanks to all the collaborators on this book: Foremost Amy Hertz, Anh-Chi Pham, Mei Mei Fox, Kat Hennessey, and John Grant. Also Mark Lewman, Rob Walker, Everett Harper, Benno Dorer, Kris Sirchio, Kate Brooks, Steve Douty, Liz Brooking, Ivan Wicksteed, Bernard Cova, Leander Kahney, Flora Skivington, Tom Birk, Reinhards Markenbüro, Gareth Harwood, and John Yates.

Thanks to my mentors: Thomas Paudler, Reini Springer, Laurent Philippe, Chris Start, Rob Malcolm, and Jacqueline Bauernfeind.

Thanks to the gang at—and surrounding—Plan B: Scott Barnum, Bink Green, Neil Cohen, thejohngrant, thepham, Lew, Gareth, Tiff-time Hein, Ken Sacharin, Frank Striefler, Chris Stephenson, John Parkin, Ricki Seidman, Stephen Walker, the Core gang, the Juice girls, Austin McGhie, Joe Kennedy, Marty Cooke and Mark Kaminsky, Lucjam, Nina Lalic, Stefan Mauerer, Ian, Suha and Steve Portigal, Dave Richardson, thedrew Breunig, Rizzo, D-Dog, Jeff Tremaine, Maggie Hallahan, Jessica Abel, Jackie Niebisch, Mark Barden, Jeff Steinhour, Jérémie, John Yost, Scott Leonard, and Jon Cohen.

Thanks to my thought leaders who have turned me into the Milli Vanilli of marketing writers: John Grant, Douglas Atkin, David Lewis, Naomi Klein, Thomas Frank, Adam Morgan, the Cluetrain conductors, Gerald Zaltman, Scott Bedbury, Rob Walker, Malcolm Gladwell, Mark Earls, Doug Holt, Bernard Cova, Mary Douglas, and Joseph Campbell.

Gratitude to the folks in the business for giving me the opportunity to get published and for their guidance and mentorship: Adrian Zackheim and Richard Pine. Thanks to Alan Webber and Douglas Atkin for their support and guidance.

And a shout-out to my friends: Suz, Slurp, E, Mags, Fanny, Rotter, Juice & Gops, Lynn, Obie & Suzie Q, Joey, Laura, the Honorable Art Agnos, Tommie K und Ina, Phil, Bergen, Gianni, Liska O, Michi T, Dirk, Eric, Money Mike & Wendy, Bennooo, Martina, UlliUlliUlli, Kai, Chief, and Murray P.

Notes

Chapter 1. The "No Marketing" Myth

4   **"The perception that these events":** Rob Walker, "The Marketing of Red Bull," *Outside Magazine* (April 2002).

5   **They rejected Coke's omnipresence:** For more on this story see Naomi Klein, *No Logo* (New York: Picador, 2002).

8   **"Leaving things up to the consumers' imagination":** Sergio Zyman with Armin Brott, *The End of Advertising As We Know It* (Indianapolis, IN: Wiley, 2002).

Chapter 2. Public Property: The Serendipitous Hijack

13   **"What were you thinking?!":** A nod to my former colleague at Plan B, Neil Cohen, who asked this question.

14   **"Fast branding doesn't work":** Randall Rothenberg, "Still Hooked on 'Fast Brand'? Ponder the Lessons of Boo.com," *Advertising Age* (May 29, 2000).

14   **We are graciously not counting:** Eric Boehlert, "Napster Will Sponsor Free Summer Tour for Limp Bizkit," Salon.com (April 24, 2000).

16   **"No more Britney Spears crap":** MSNBC message board.

17   **One of the quintessential brands:** Background information on Dr. Martens came from client conversations and *Dr. Martens* (Italy, AirWair Limited, 1999).

17   **"The shoe was the right answer":** Ibid.

19   **"Traditionalists insist these should be flat":** *The Deviant's Dictionary,* http://public.diversity.org.uk/deviant/frames.htm, listed under Boots and Shoes.

20   **"It's a fact!":** *Dr. Martens.*

21   **Sales of Miller High Life:** James B. Andorfer, "Miller Restages High Life Brand with Nod to Past," *Advertising Age* (May 18, 1998).

21   **"We're having fun with Bubba":** Interview with Jeff Kling, October 9, 2002.

22   **When Miller's marketing department halted the campaign:** *Beer Handbook,* "Popular Beer" (2001).

22   **Imagine Bubba as the next Archie Bunker:** Richard Linnett, "High Life Spots to Spawn Sitcom," *Advertising Age* (January 12, 2004).

22   **Sales grew in double digits:** According to internal memos from Pabst Brewing.

23   **"Sis's Place is an illegal bar":** Adam Davies, *The Frog King: A Love Story* (New York: Riverhead Books, 2002).

24   **"It's two bad tastes that taste great together":** "Pabst Blue Ribbon: Beer of the Year," *Men's Journal* (December 2003).

24   **"I have to laugh every time I see PBR":** Posting from Google newsgroup alt.beer.

24   **"You know I blame those damn microbrews":** Ibid.

24   **"The best tasting domestic beer":** Robert Latham et al, *The Hipster's Handbook* (New York: Anchor, 2003).

25   **"We walk a short distance down the street":** Posting from Google newsgroup rec.motorcycles.harley.

26   **By 2001, the total number of messages sent:** David Reed, "Texting 'Bout a Revolution," *Direct* (May 15, 2001).

26   **Worldwide volume for SMS:** "Text Craze: 360B Messages Expected to be Sent in 2002," *Asia Africa Intelligence Wire* (September 10, 2002).

26   **Texting accounts for about 15 percent:** Peter Martin, "Ruup4 multimedia messaging?" *The Financial Times* (March 12, 2002).

28   **"By referring to it as the wireless Web":** Donny Jackson, "Download; Settling the flap surrounding WAP," *Telephony* (January 8, 2001).

29   **"Everyone has grown weary of the excuses":** "SMS.ac Chief Challenges U.S. Wireless Operators to Help End Industry Woes," *PrimeZone Media Network* (March 5, 2002).

29   **"The 166th In-N-Out Burger restaurant opened":** Tom McNichol, "The Secret Behind a Burger Cult," *The New York Times* (August 14, 2002).

30   **"Over the years":** Ibid.

31   **"Its agency, the T&O group, uses camp sixty-second radio commercials":** www.topsecretrecipes.com/sleuth/sleuth2.htm.

Chapter 3. The Marketer's Guide to the Serendipitous Hijack

33   **During the trial:** Jim Gardner, "Barbie Gets a New Outfit in San Francisco: A Legal Suit," *San Francisco Business Times* (November 1997).

33   **Hanson settled and agreed:** Lisa Bannon, "Barrister Barbie: Mattel Plays Rough," *The Wall Street Journal* (January 9, 1998).

33   **In one trademark infringement case:** Mattel vs. MCA Records, no. 10483, Ninth Circuit Court of Appeals, Opinion by Judge Alex Kozinski, July 24, 2002.

34   **"They [Mattel] really cut off their nose":** Interview with Paul David, January 15, 2004.

34 **"It is also a great compliment to the strength of the brand":** Interviews with Flora Skivington, January 2004.

35 **Take Burberry, for example:** Emily Lambert, "Yo, Plaid," *Forbes* (October 14, 2002).

35 **Stars such as Jay-Z:** Ibid.

36 **"I had faith that the viewing public":** Colleen Barrett, "Fasten Your Seat Belt," *Adweek* (January 26, 2004).

36 **The image was ripe for appropriation:** Josh McHugh, "Vox Unpopuli," *Forbes ASAP* (October 7, 2002).

41 **"A brand is the sum":** Scott Bedbury with Stephen Fenichell, *A New Brand World* (New York: Penguin Books, 2003).

42 **"Yeah, I used to wear Dr. Marten's when I went to shows":** Plan B consumer intercept, San Francisco, Summer 2001.

44 **"We walked away from those distribution channels":** Kevin Braddock, "When a Brand Becomes Guilty by Association," *The Financial Times* (July 17, 2003).

Chapter 4. A "No Marketing" Illusion: The Co-created Hijack

48 **"Kids want simultaneously to be acceptable":** Dick Pountain and David Robins, *Cool Rules: Anatomy of an Attitude* (London, Reaktion, 2000).

50 **"Red Bull is willing to invest a lot":** Kate Fitzgerald, "Red Bull Charged Up," *Advertising Age* (August 21, 2000).

51 **"The collection of 60 aspiring deejays from Croatia":** Kenneth Hein, "Red Bull Charges Ahead," *Brandweek* (October 15, 2001).

54 **"Ask someone to define it":** Ibid.

54 **"Outrageous is what we want":** *The Cleveland Plain Dealer* (February 29, 2004).

57 **"It's no wonder that rival beverage companies":** Kenneth Hein, "Red Bull Charges Ahead."

59 **All three companies tried to copy:** As of March 2004, AMP is third, KMX is fourth, and 180 is tenth in drugstore and supermarket sales.

60 **"There were people all dressed in orange":** www.playgroundsmag.com/features/areal.htm.

61 **"KMX is an energy drink made by Coca-Cola":** Posting from Google newsgroup rec.food.drink.beer.

65 **"It's a difficult ticket to get":** Tim Carvell, "How *The Blair Witch Project* Built Up So Much Buzz: Movie Moguldom on a Shoestring," *Fortune* (August 16, 1999).

66 **In the end, *Blair Witch* became:** Richard Corliss, "Blair Witch Craft: Mix Eye of Heather with a Pinch of Horror, Promote Well and Serve the Film Event of '99," *Time* (August 16, 1999).

66 **"From a business point of view":** Jesse McKinley, "A Slump, or the Curse of the Blair Witch?" *New York Times* (January 19, 2004).

67 **"The Web site . . . looks anything but low-budget":** The 11thhour.com,

September 1999. "1999's horror hit *The Blair Witch Project* isn't all that it seems. Just ask the makers of *The Last Broadcast:* The Wild, Wild Web."

67   **"No, we're not going to sue":** Ibid.

68   **"Both Web sites encourage the viewer":** Ibid.

69   **"We had people handing out flyers":** Ibid.

72   **It was, at the time:** www.imdb.com.

Chapter 5. A Dangerous Attitude

73   **An oppositional attitude:** Dick Pountain and David Robins, *Cool Rules: Anatomy of an Attitude* (London, Reaktion, 2000).

74   **"Over a twenty-year period":** Kalle Lasn, *Culture Jam* (New York: Eagle Brook, 1999).

74   **The definition of cool has changed:** Pountain and Robins, *Cool Rules.*

75   **"Cool is indefinable and unable to be chased":** Marcel Knobil, "What Makes a Brand Cool?" *Market Leader: The Journal of the Marketing Society* (Issue 18, Autumn 2002).

76   **Early in his career:** James Kaplan, "Angry Middle-Aged Man," *The New Yorker* (January 19, 2004).

77   **"There is something missing":** Interview with Mark Lewman, April 2004.

78   **Global PR powerhouse Hill & Knowlton:** D. Parvaz, "They're on a Quest for What's Cool," *Seattle Post-Intelligencer* (November 20, 2003).

78   **While discovering:** Both "trends" are taken as excerpts from Euro RSCG's 2003 fads and trends white paper, "The Power of Pop Culture." www.eurorscglife.com.

79   **"If blue is the next black":** As the president of cool hunting shop Youth Intelligence likes to say. Lev Grossman, "The Quest for Cool," *Time* (August 30, 2003).

79   **And it should never involve shelling out:** As predicted in a past issue of the syndicated L-Report.

Chapter 6. The Marketer's Guide to the Co-created Hijack

83   **"I once asked Dave":** Scott Bedbury with Stephen Fenichell, *A New Brand World: 8 Principles for Achieving Brand Leadership in the 21st Century* (New York: Penguin Books, 2003).

85   **"In real life, people wouldn't want to go to a party":** Chuck Klosterman, "On Friendstership," *Esquire* (January 2004).

85   **They posted a profile of him that listed his ambitions:** Interview with Matt Gonzalez, April 17, 2004.

Chapter 7. Brand Hijack Candidates

92   **"Customers learning and teaching each other":** John Grant, *After Image: Mind-Altering Marketing* (London, HarperCollins UK, 2001).

93   **Hotmail had what the Japanese called:** As referenced by David Lewis in

The Soul of the New Consumer (London, U.K.: Nicholas Brealey Publishing, 2001).

94   **Less than 3 percent of users:** Interview with Steve Douty, March 14, 2002.

94   **"In a way, buzz is essentially a pervasive feeling":** Ibid.

95   **Foregoing any branding-type marketing:** Steve Ditlea, "Netflix Effect," *Adweek Magazine's Technology Marketing* (November 2002).

95   **"Seventy percent of our trials come from word-of-mouth":** Ibid.

95   **A whopping 90 percent of trial users:** Ibid.

95   **"For most people":** Ibid.

Chapter 8. The Marketer's Guide to the Corporate Hijack

99   **"P&G went through a state":** E-mail to Alex Wipperfürth.

100   **"One of the reasons we are successful":** Kevin J. O'Brien, "Focusing on Armchair Athletes, Puma Becomes a Leader," *New York Times* (March 12, 2004).

102   **He measured how long it takes:** Gerard Tellis, Stefan Stremersch, and Eden Yin. "The International Take-Off of New Products" (Institute for Operations Research and the Management Sciences, Spring 2003).

102   **"Managers may pull the plug":** "When Will It Fly?", *Economist* (August 9, 2003).

102   **"The key is not to do a John Mayer":** Bob Lefsetz newsletter, "Stealth Marketing" (July 26, 2003).

103   **Getting early backing in Hollywood:** Zogby International Poll data.

106   **"You need to be perfect in every aspect":** Ted Polhemus, *Diesel: World Wide Wear* (London, U.K.: Thames and Hudson Limited, 1998).

108   **"Lomography has an anarchic approach":** Bernard Cova and Véronique Cova, "Tribal Marketing," *European Journal of Marketing* (January 2001).

109   **"I suppose I am what you'd call":** Dan Zevin, *The Day I Turned Uncool: Confessions of a Reluctant Grown-Up* (New York: Villard, 2002).

110   **"There are still a lot of people":** Dale Hrabi, "Macchiato Morons," Salon.com (February 23, 2004).

111   **"Each person takes away his or her own experience":** Rance Crain, "Advertising Must Be True to the Brand Experience," *Advertising Age* (March 8, 2004).

112   **Sales of the product:** "The E-Route to a Whiter Smile: P&G Discovered Huge Benefits When It Launched Whitestrips Online," *Financial Times* (August 26, 2002).

112   **Less than 5 percent of the population:** "P&G's Web Marketing Strategy Shows Its Bite," *Cincinnati Business Courier* (January 22, 2001).

112   **The PR agency estimated:** Jack Neff, "Will PR Kill Advertising? A Look at a Controversial New Book by Al Ries," Adage.com (July 16, 2002).

113   **These enthusiastic early customers:** www.semaphorepartners.com.

113 **"The best salespeople are the users":** "P&G's Web Marketing Strategy Shows Its Bite."

113 **"All four of those targets":** "The E-Route to a Whiter Smile: P&G Discovered Huge Benefits When It Launched Whitestrips Online."

115 **"There's a common perception":** Leander Kahney, "Mac Loyalists: Don't Tread on Us," *Wired News* (December 2, 2002).

Chapter 9. The Dawn of the Next Marketing Era

117 **It didn't matter whether the death:** "Smoke City Looking for Life after Levi's: U.K. Act Hopes Jive Set Will Benefit from Popular Ad," *Billboard* (April 19, 1997).

117 **"We gon' tell that brotha":** Busta Rhymes song, "Pass the Courvoisier."

117 **"You want everyone to like you":** John Leland, "A Chance to Carry on for 130 million," *New York Times* (January 19, 2003).

118 **No wonder San Francisco's cutting edge marketing shop:** www.americanbrandstand.com and the 2003 American *Brandstand* Report.

118 **"American culture is no longer created":** Kalle Lasn, *Culture Jam.*

119 **"to open a movie":** Steve Heyer, "Steve Heyer's Manifesto for a New Advertising Age," Adage.com (February 6, 2003).

119 **"looming threat of personal meaninglessness":** Anthony Giddons, *Modernity and Self-Identity* (Palo Alto, CA: Stanford University Press, 1991).

120 **The London-based "ambient" agency:** Linda Stern, "Using Your Head," *Newsweek* (May 12, 2003).

121 **"how to get attention without contributing":** Ken Sacharin, *Attention!* (Indianapolis, IN: Wiley, 2000).

122 **"One cannot mass-produce authenticity":** David Lewis and Darren Bridger, *The Soul of the New Consumer* (London, Nicholas Brealey Publishing, 2001).

122 **"Certainly there is considerable empirical evidence":** Richard Elliot and Kritsadarat Wattanasawan, "Brands as Symbolic Resources for the Construction of Identity," *International Journal of Advertising* (Vol. 17, No. 2, 1998).

122 **"Thesis # 18":** Rick Levine, Christopher Locke, Doc Searls, and David Weinberger. *The Cluetrain Manifesto: The End of Business as Usual* (New York: Perseus Publishing, 2001).

122 **"Through a story, life invites us to come inside":** Stephen Denning, *The Springboard Story: How Storytelling Ignites Action in Knowledge-Era Organizations* (London, UK: Butterworth-Heineman, 2000).

123 **Supermarkets stock an average:** John De Graaf, David Wann, Thomas H. Naylor, David Horsey, and Scott Simon. *Affluenza: The All-Consuming Epidemic* (San Francisco, CA: Berrett-Koehler, 2001).

123 **Income has doubled:** John Marks Templeton, "A Worldwide Rise in Living Standards," *The Futurist* (January 1999).

123 **"Brand image was usually promising something that wasn't true":** John Grant, *After Image*.

123 **Chart:** Ibid.

124 **"Customers have changed":** Sameena Ahmad, "Who's Wearing the Trousers?" *Economist* (September 8, 2001).

125 **"That's why we're the 'whatever' generation":** Plan B Research, June 2001.

125 **"There was a short window":** "A Campaign to Remember," *Adweek*, Eastern Edition (December 11, 2000).

126 **"A recent JD Power study proclaimed":** As referenced in Mark Earls, *Welcome to the Creative Age* (Indianapolis, IN: Wiley, 2002).

126 **"It is their choice which of the forty-seven":** www.peapod.com.

126 **"Buy Nothing Day":** "Buy Nothing Day," *Dollars and Sense* (January 2002).

126 **"The reality of brands":** Wendy Gordon and Virginia Valentine, "The 21st Century Consumer: An Endlessly Moving Target," *Market Leader: The Journal of the Marketing Society* (Issue 11, 2000).

Chapter 10. The Consumer Collective

129 **Kathy and Jason Curiel of Corpus Christi:** Mark Young, "Baby Named After Network," *Corpus Christi Caller-Times* (April 4, 2001).

130 **They embark on brand pilgrimages:** "Furniture Fans Line Up Early," Palo Alto Online (August 29, 2003).

132 **"People who have finally managed to liberate themselves":** Bernard Cova and Véronique Cova, "Tribal Marketing," European Journal of Marketing (January 2001).

132 **"These groups would escape notice":** Ethan Watters, *Urban Tribes* (London, UK: Bloomsbury, 2003).

132 **Studies show that social groups influence:** Mark Earls, *Welcome to the Creative Age: Bananas, Business and the Death of Marketing* (Indianapolis, IN: Wiley, 2002).

133 **"The individual is no longer viewed":** Per Østergaard and Christian Jantzen in *Interpretive Consumer Research*, edited by D. Beckman and D. C. Elliott (Copenhagen Business School Press, 2000).

133 **"collective I":** Janine Lopiano-Misdom and Joanne De Luca, *Street Trends: How Today's Alternative Youth Cultures are Creating Tomorrow's Mainstream Markets* (New York: HarperCollins, 1998).

133 REACH OUT AND JACK SOMEONE: This headline was lifted from Dennis Lloyd's iPodlounge blog.

133 **"As an individual my iPod allows me to organize my music":** Interview with Ivan Wicksteed, March 30, 2004.

134 **"the next best thing":** Warren St. John, "The World at Ear's Length," *New York Times* (February 15, 2004).

134 **"We listened for about thirty seconds":** Leander Kahney, "Feel Free to Jack into My iPod," *Wired News* (November 21, 2003).

135 **"(iPod sharing] could have fairly":** www.theregister.co.uk.

135   **"Listening to someone else's iPod":** Izzy Grinspan, "Pod People: This Valentine's Day, the Fastest Way to the Heart May be Through the Earbuds," *Village Voice* (February 9, 2004).

135   **"discrimination based not on race":** *The Wesleyan Argus.* See also Leander Kahney, "iTunes Undermines Social Security," *Wired News* (November 12, 2003).

136   **"Product symbolism creates a universe":** Østergaard and Jantzen, *Interpretive Consumer Research.*

137   **"The meaning of tribal symbols":** Bernard Cova and Véronique Cova, *Tribal Marketing.*

137   **"The link is more important than the thing":** As in the leitmotif of postmodernism.

138   **"Have you ever met":** Michael Lewis, *Next: The Future Just Happened* (New York: W. W. Norton and Company, 2001).

Chapter 11. The Inner Workings of the Brand Tribe

140   **John Grant and I decided to explore:** See the white paper "How Cults Seduce and What Marketing Can Learn from Them," www.plan-b.biz.

141   **"profess a lack of religious belief":** Toby Lester, "Oh, gods!" *Atlantic Monthly* (February 2002).

141   **"The main thing you've got to recognize":** Ibid.

143   **IRC Pop-Up:** Michael Lewis, *Next: The Future Just Happened.*

144   **Working in a dark room:** Gary Rivlin, "Linus Torvalds: Leader of the Free World," *Wired* (November 2003).

144   **"Software is like sex":** www.brainyquote.com.

146   **"I am an American":** "Fightin' Words: Open Source Bad for Software and Intellectual Property Says Microsoft's Jim Allchin," *Client Server News* (February 26, 2001).

147   **Supported by those veterans:** "VA Linux IPO Soars Almost 700 Percent," *Info World* (December 13, 1999).

148   **"I've never had to work so hard to spend":** "The Swedes Are on the Beachhead," *HFN: The Weekly Newspaper for the Home Furnishing Network* (February 24, 2003).

151   **"It's like one of those large":** See the white paper "How Cults Seduce and What Marketing Can Learn from Them," www.plan-b.biz.

152   **Today, eBay is one of the world's largest economies:** Robert D. Hof, "The eBay Economy," *Business Week* (August 18, 2003).

153   **eBay supports its biggest customers:** Daniel Roth, "Meg Muscles eBay Uptown," *Fortune* (July 5, 1999).

153   **The average eBay user spends 3.5 hours:** Ibid.

156   *Adbusters'* **interest is decidedly narrow:** Conor Dignam, "Adbusters Are After You," *AdAge Global* (May 2001).

159   **"We propose a reversal of priorities":** "First Things First 2000: A Graphic Designers Manifesto," *Adbusters*, www.adbusters.org.

160   **Like sociologists who study cults:** I'm far from the first to cull lessons from touchy sources. George Lucas studied Leni Riefenstahl's *Triumph of the Will* when creating his crowd scenes in *Star Wars*.

160   **Anthropologist Mary Douglas calls these modern tribes:** Mary Douglas, *The World of Goods: Towards an Anthropology of Consumption* (New York: Routledge, 2001).

Chapter 12. The Funny Business of Earning Consumer Devotion

163   **It had witnessed the high profile failures:** Pat Dillon, "The Next Small Thing," *Fast Company* (June 1998).

164   **"I realized that my competition was paper":** Robert I. Sutton, *Weird Ideas That Work: 11½ Practices for Promoting, Managing and Sustaining Innovation* (New York: Free Press, 2001).

164   **And it did all this while spending just a tiny fraction:** Pat Dillion, "The Next Small Thing."

165   **"People loved this thing":** Geoffrey A. Moore, *Crossing the Chasm: Marketing and Selling High-Tech Products to Mainstream Consumers* (New York: HarperBusiness, 2002).

166   **"Do you want to sell sugared water":** Andrew Leonard, "Do Penguins Eat Apples?" Salon.com (September 28, 1999).

167   **"The Mac is like the Catholic Church":** Leander Kahney, "Worshipping at the Altar of Mac," *Wired News* (December 5, 2002).

167   **"Apple is like a strange drug":** Leander Kahney, "Mac Loyalists: Don't Tread on Us."

167   **"It's the cult":** Ibid.

Chapter 13. The Kick-Off: Hijack Ideation

174   **"If I had asked the public what they wanted":** "Beyond Disruption by Jean-Marie Dru and Business Partners (Interview)," *Sunday Business Post Online* (October 6, 2002).

174   **"You can't just ask customers":** www.brainyquote.com.

175   **"addresses at a surface level":** Gerald Zaltman, *How Customers Think: Essential Insights into the Mind of the Market* (Boston, MA: Harvard Business School Press, 2003).

176   **"Consumers don't make decisions":** Ibid.

176   **"The top-down approach of segmentation":** David Lewis and Darren Bridger, *The Soul of the New Consumer* (London, Nicholas Brealey Publishing, 2001).

176   **"Anyone attending a focus group today":** Interview with Stephen Walker, February 19, 2004.

177   **"Over eighty percent of all market research":** Gerald Zaltman, *How Customers Think*.

177   **"Reality is never linear":** From Doug Atkin's speech at the 2002 APG Conference.

179   **"Managers must learn to anticipate"**: Doug Holt, "What Becomes an Icon Most?" *Harvard Business Review* (March 2003).

Chapter 14. Phase I: Tribal Marketing

183   **"Even in mass-democracy"**: Jay Newman, *Inauthentic Culture* (Montreal, Canada: McGill-Queen's University Press, 1997).

184   **"Much innovation and development comes"**: Shira P. White with G. Patton Wright, *New Ideas About New Ideas* (Cambridge, MA: Perseus Books, 2002).

186   **It remained on the *New York Times* bestseller list:** www.michael moore.com.

187   **"There has been a quickening"**: Grant McCracken, "The Politics of Plenitude," *Reason* (August/September 1998).

187   **"They combined the three things necessary"**: Seth Godin and Malcolm Gladwell, *Unleashing the Ideavirus: Stop Marketing at People! Turn Your Ideas into Epidemics by Helping Your Customers do the Marketing for You* (New York: Hyperion, 2001).

189   **"It's fun to use"**: Cliff Havener and Margaret Thorpe, "Customers Can Tell You What They Want,"*Management Review* (December 1994).

189   **Within the first six months:** "Dying for Sex," *US News & World Report* (January 11, 1999).

190   **"People with passion can change the world"**: From the Apple "Think Different" campaign.

192   **"The goal of bowling alley marketing is to keep moving"**: Geoffrey A. Moore, *Crossing the Chasm.*

194   **The company has managed an annual growth rate of 10 percent:** Kelly Barron, "The Kids Are Crazy About Them," *Forbes* (June 15, 1998).

194   **"The decision was made to get back to our roots"**: J. Dee Hill, "Dickies TV Only Looks Young," *Adweek Southwest* (January 10, 2000).

195   **"If your targets become"**: Robert Greene, *The Art of Seduction* (New York: Penguin Books, 2003).

196   **After six weeks:** Robert B. Cialdini, *Influence: The Psychology of Persuasion* (Perennial Currents, 1998).

196   **"as more desirable to eat in the future"**: Ibid.

197   **First, in offering free parts from beaming stations:** Ibid.

199   **"I want to make the public aware"**: William Gibson, *Pattern Recognition* (New York: Berkeley Publishing Group, 2004).

200   **"One day, Nike had decided to sell special shoes"**: Thomas Frank, "Brand You," *Harper's Magazine* (July 1999).

204   **"As a general rule I hate advertising"**: Online journal entry, June 23, 1997, www.elharo.com/journal.

204   **"Confidence contrived does not work"**: Gerald Zaltman, *How Customers Think.*

204   **"The patients experienced a lack of discomfort"**: Ibid.

Chapter 15. Phase II: Co-creation

207 **"most of what we know":** Daniel M. Wegner, *The Illusion of Conscious Will* (Cambridge, MA: Bradford Books, 2002).

207 **Experts agree that about 95 percent:** As cited in Gerald Zaltman, *How Customers Think.*

208 **He's identified ten:** Edward Hall, *The Silent Language* (Westport, CT: Greenwood Press, 1980).

209 **Jay Conrad Levinson:** Jay Conrad Levinson, *Guerrilla Creativity: Make Your Message Irresistible Through the Power of Memes* (Boston, MA: Mariner Books, 2001).

210 **Most of the project participants:** George C. Boeree, "Albert Bandura," www.ship.edu.

212 **"It is the infectious chatter":** David Lewis and Darren Bridger, *The Soul of the New Consumer.*

212 **Ten years ago:** "Movie Marketing Costs 'Obscene,'" *Onfilm* (November 2002).

212 **"If you don't hit it within twenty-four":** "Advertising Costs Scale the Heights," *Los Angeles Times* (October 20, 2002).

215 **"Those kids make things more palatable":** Malcolm Gladwell, "The Coolhunt," *New Yorker* (March 17, 1997).

Chapter 16. Phase III: Mass Marketing

218 **"The message will be that":** Stuart Elliott, "Maximizing the Mini," *New York Times* (February 4, 2003).

218 **"We didn't want to become a fad":** Interview with Tom Birk, February 17, 2004.

Chapter 17. The Threat: "A Few Words from Our Sponsor"

232 **"It is absurd to say that brands can be too powerful":** Rita Clifton, "Brands and Our Times," Interbrand white paper, www.brandchannel.com.

232 **"Brands are not as powerful as their opponents allege":** Sameena Ahmad, "Who's Wearing the Trousers?" *Economist* (September 6, 2004).

233 **"Managers cannot control people's minds":** Gerald Zaltman, *How Consumers Think.*

233 **"do so willingly and happily":** Robert Greene, *The Art of Seduction.*

233 **"There is definitely a cult of Mac":** Leander Kahney, "Worshipping at the Altar of Mac."

235 **"If you want to physically taste":** Patrick Harrison, "The Revolution Will be Carbonated," *Adbusters* (Autumn 1998).

236 **"everything but the burden":** A nod to Greg Tate's book *Everything But the Burden: What White People Are Taking from Black Culture* (New York: Harlem Moon, 2003).

236 **"When they struck, they wanted to create an atmosphere":** President's Address at O'Hare Airport, September 27, 2001, www.whitehouse.gov/news/releases/2001/09/20010927-1.html.

237 **"they were so excited they were shouting":** James B. Twitchell, *Adcult USA: The Triumph of Advertising in American Culture* (New York: Columbia University Press, 1995).

238 **"terrified about growing up":** Excerpt from Gerry Laybourne's speech at the 1999 APG conference.

239 **"I can see why people feel manipulated":** "Guerrilla Marketing Catches On," *Pittsburgh Post-Gazette* (January 18, 2004).

242 **"This Web site is FAKE":** Jim Heinzl, "Dr. Pepper/Seven Up Cowed by Web Plan," GlobeandMail.com (March 13, 2003).

242 **"The people who make the cash decisions":** Ibid.

243 **"We have lost confidence":** Adbusters, "Media Carta Manifesto," www.adbusters.org.

244 **"Coke was even more visible":** "Cold Fun in the Summertime," *Beverage World* (May 1996).

Chapter 18. The Opportunity: The Ultimate Pay-Off

246 **"Krispy Kreme grew more than 30 percent":** "Krispy Kreme Net Income Up 47% System Sales Jump 28%," *Nation's Restaurant News* (September 1, 2003).

247 **"Starbucks also showed impressive double-digit":** James Surowiecki, "The Tastemakers," *New Yorker* (January 13, 2003).

247 **"The real measure of Starbucks' success":** Ibid.

248 **"One of the defining characteristics of the Mac community":** Leander Kahney, "Mac Loyalists: Don't Tread on Us."

249 **"the customer's perceived cost associated":** Roland T. Rust, Valarie A. Zeithaml, and Katherine N. Lemon. *Driving Customer Equity: How Customer Lifetime Value is Reshaping Corporate Strategy* (New York: Free Press, 2000).

251 **"One change was all it took":** John Grant, *The New Marketing Manifesto: The 12 Rules for Building Successful Brands in the 21st Century* (Texere Publishing, 2001).

253 **"Here at Southwest, we flight attendants":** www.wardell.org/jord/classic/flight_announcements.htm.

254 **"A corporate model like Blockbuster's":** Dina Elboghdady, "Blockbuster Tests Netflix-style Program," *San Francisco Chronicle* (September 3, 2003).

254 **Humor and enjoyment:** Jonathan Dee, "Flying in the Face of Mediocrity," *New York Times Magazine* (November 30, 2003).

254 **Even General Counsel Jim Hnat:** "Better Product, Lower Prices, and They Actually Give a Damn," *Business 2.0* (October 2003).

Index